CAMBRIDGE CONCISE HISTORIES

A Concise History of Greece

Now reissued in a third, updated edition, this book provides a concise, illustrated introduction to the modern history of Greece, from the first stirrings of the national movement in the late eighteenth century to the present day. The current economic crisis has marked a turning point in the country's history. This third edition includes a new final chapter, which analyses contemporary political, economic and social developments. It includes additional illustrations together with updated tables and suggestions for further reading. Designed to provide a basic introduction, the first edition of this hugely successful *Concise History* won the Runciman Award for the best book on an Hellenic topic published in 1992 and has been translated into twelve languages.

RICHARD CLOGG has been Lecturer in Modern Greek History at the School of Slavonic and East European Studies and King's College, University of London; Reader in Modern Greek History at King's College; and Professor of Modern Balkan History in the University of London. From 1990 to 2005 he was a Fellow of St Antony's College, Oxford, and is now an Emeritus Fellow of the College. He has written extensively on Greek history and politics from the eighteenth century to the present.

CAMBRIDGE CONCISE HISTORIES

This is a new series of illustrated 'concise histories' of selected individual countries, intended both as university and college textbooks and as general historical introductions for general readers, travellers and members of the business community.

For a list of titles in the series, see end of book.

A Concise History
of Greece

THIRD EDITION

RICHARD CLOGG

CAMBRIDGE
UNIVERSITY PRESS

CAMBRIDGE
UNIVERSITY PRESS

University Printing House, Cambridge CB2 8BS, United Kingdom

Published in the United States of America by Cambridge University Press,
New York

Cambridge University Press is part of the University of Cambridge.

It furthers the University's mission by disseminating knowledge in the pursuit of
education, learning, and research at the highest international levels of excellence.

www.cambridge.org
Information on this title: www.cambridge.org/9781107612037

First published 1992
Reprinted 5 times
Second edition 2002
10th printing 2012
Third edition 2013

Printed in the United Kingdom by TJ International Ltd. Padstow Cornwall

A catalogue record for this publication is available from the British Library

ISBN 978-1-107-03289-7 Hardback
ISBN 978-1-107-61203-7 Paperback

For Mary Jo

CONTENTS

ILLUSTRATIONS

The author and publishers acknowledge the following sources of copyright material and are grateful for the permissions granted. While every effort has been made, it has not always been possible to identify the sources of all material used, or to trace all copyright holders. If any omissions are brought to our notice, we will be happy to include the appropriate acknowledgements on reprinting.

viii

MAPS

PREFACE

The text has benefited greatly from the critical scrutiny of my friend and colleague Dr Lars Baerentzen and, as always, of Mary Jo Clogg. To both, as to Professor Susannah and Dr Rolandos Katsiaounis, I am much indebted. I am also very grateful to the following for help in connection with the illustrations: Guy Evans, Manos Haritatos, David Howells, Dimitrios Kaloumenos, Paschalis Kitromilidis, John Koliopoulos, Fani Konstantinou, Nikos Linardatos, Ioannis K. Mazarakis-Ainian, Georgios Mountakis, Helen Zeese Papanikolas, Nikos Stavroulakis, Fani-Maria Tsigakou, K. Varfis and Malcolm Wagstaff.

March 1991/2001/2013

I

Introduction

All countries are burdened by their history, but the past weighs particularly heavily on Greece. It is still, regrettably, a commonplace to talk of 'modern Greece' and of 'modern Greek' as though 'Greece' and 'Greek' must necessarily refer to the ancient world. The burden of antiquity has been both a boon and a bane. The degree to which the language and culture of the ancient Greek world was revered throughout Europe (and, indeed, in the United States where some of the founding fathers were nurtured on the classics) during the critical decades of the national revival in the early nineteenth century was a vital factor in stimulating in the Greeks themselves, or at least in the nationalist intelligentsia, a consciousness that they were the heirs to a heritage that was universally admired. Such an awareness had scarcely existed during the centuries of Ottoman rule and this 'sense of the past', imported from western Europe, was a major constituent in the development of the Greek national movement, contributing significantly to its precocity in relation to other Balkan independence movements. The heritage of the past was also important in exciting the interest of liberal, and indeed of conservative, opinion in the fate of the insurgent Greeks. In the 1820s, even such an unreconstructed pillar of the traditional order as Viscount Castlereagh, the British foreign secretary, was moved to ask whether 'those, in admiration of whom we have been educated, be doomed . . . to drag out, for all time to come, the miserable existence to which circumstances have reduced them'. Indeed such attitudes have persisted to the present. During the debate in the British parliament in 1980 over ratification of Greek membership of the European Community, a foreign office minister intoned that Greece's entry would be seen as a 'fitting repayment by the Europe of today of the cultural and political debt that we all owe to a Greek heritage almost three thousand years old'.

That an obsession with past glories should have developed is, in the circumstances, scarcely surprising. *Progonoplexia*, or 'ancestoritis', has been characteristic of so much of the country's cultural life and has given rise to the 'language question', the interminable, and at times violent, controversy over the degree to which the spoken language of the people should be 'purified' to render it more akin to the supposed ideal of ancient Greek. Generations of schoolchildren have been forced to wrestle with the complexities of the *katharevousa*, or 'purifying' form of the language. Only as recently as 1976 was the demotic, or spoken language, formally declared to be the official language of the state and of education. One result of this change, however, is that the new generation of Greeks does not find it easy to read books written in *katharevousa*, which comprise perhaps 80 per cent of the total non-fiction book production of the independent state.

Early Greek nationalists looked for inspiration exclusively to the classical past. When, in the 1830s, the Austrian historian J. P. Fallmerayer cast doubt on one of the founding precepts of modern Greek nationalism, namely that the modern Greeks are the lineal descendants of the ancient, he aroused outrage among the intelligentsia of the fledgeling state. The first American minister to the independent state, Charles Tuckerman, an acute observer of mid-nineteenth-century Greek society, observed that the quickest way to reduce an Athenian professor to apoplexy was to mention the name of Fallmerayer. Such attitudes were accompanied by a corresponding contempt for Greece's medieval, Byzantine past. Adamantios Korais, for instance, the most influential figure of the pre-independence intellectual revival, despised what he dismissed as the priest-ridden obscurantism of Byzantium. Indeed, he once said that to read as much as a single page of a particular Byzantine author was enough to bring on an attack of gout.

It was only towards the middle of the nineteenth century that Konstantinos Paparrigopoulos, a professor of history in the University of Athens, formulated an interpretation of Greek history which linked the ancient, medieval and modern periods in a single continuum. Subsequently, mainstream Greek historiography has laid great emphasis on such continuity. By the end of the century the rediscovery and rehabilitation of the Byzantine past was complete as intellectuals looked more to the glories of the Byzantine Empire than to classical antiquity in justifying the irredentist project of the 'Great Idea'. This vision, which aspired to the unification of all areas of Greek settlement in the Near East within the bounds of a single state with its capital in Constantinople, dominated the independent state during the first century of its existence.

If the nascent intelligentsia of the independence period looked upon the classical past with a reverence that matched their contempt for Byzantium, they had no time at all for the heritage of 400 years of Ottoman rule. Korais, indeed, declared in his autobiography that in his vocabulary 'Turk' and 'wild beast' were synonymous. Yet the period of the *Tourkokratia*, or Turkish rule, had a profound influence in shaping the evolution of Greek society. Ottoman rule had the effect of isolating the Greek world from the great historical movements such as the Renaissance, the Reformation, the seventeenth-century scientific revolution, the Enlightenment and the French and Industrial Revolutions that so influenced the historical evolution of western Europe. For much of the period the boundaries of the Ottoman Empire in Europe broadly coincided with those between Orthodoxy and Catholicism. The conservatism of the hierarchy of the Orthodox Church reinforced this isolation. As late as the 1790s, for instance, Greek clerics continued to denounce the ideas of Copernicus and to argue that the sun revolved around the earth. This conservatism was reinforced by an anti-westernism that had its roots in a profound bitterness at the way in which Catholic Europe had sought to impose papal supremacy as the price of military help as the Byzantine Empire confronted the threat of the Ottoman Turks.

The capriciousness of Ottoman rule and the weakness of the idea of the rule of law helped to shape the underlying values of Greek society and to determine attitudes to the state and to authority that have persisted into the present. One form of self-defence against such arbitrariness was to secure the protection of highly placed patrons who could mediate with those in positions of power and privilege. This was coupled with a distrustful attitude towards those outside the circle of the extended family. The need for patrons continued into the new state and, once constitutional government had been established, parliamentary deputies became the natural focus for clientelist relations, which pervaded the whole of society. In return for their support at the hustings, voters expected those for whom they had voted to help them and their families to find jobs, preferably in the inflated state sector, the only secure source of employment in an underdeveloped economy, and to intercede with a generally obstructive bureaucracy. *Rouspheti*, the reciprocal dispensation of favours that has traditionally oiled the wheels of society, and *mesa*, the connections that are useful, indeed indispensable, in many aspects of daily life, were both reinforced during the period of Turkish rule.

The Greeks are a people of the diaspora. It was during the period of Ottoman rule that patterns of emigration developed that have continued into modern times. Even before the emergence of a Greek state Greek merchants established during the late eighteenth century a mercantile empire in the eastern Mediterranean, in the Balkans and as far afield as India. In the nineteenth century migration developed apace to Egypt, to southern Russia and at the end of the century to the United States. Initially, these migrants to the New World were almost exclusively male. They were driven by poor economic prospects at home and, for the most part, intended to spend only a few years abroad before returning permanently to their motherland. Most, however, stayed in their country of immigration. The emigrant flow was limited by restrictive US legislation during the inter-war period, when Greece herself welcomed within her borders over a million refugees from Asia Minor, Bulgaria and Russia. Emigration once again got under way on a large scale after the Second World War. Prior to the ending of US quota restrictions in the mid-1960s much of this new wave of emigration was to Australia, where Melbourne, with a Greek community of over 200,000, had by the 1980s emerged as one of the principal centres of Greek population in the world. The postwar period also saw large-scale movement of Greeks to western Europe, and in particular to West Germany, as 'guest-workers'. In the course of time many of these returned, using their hard-won capital for the most part to set up small-scale enterprises in the service sector. For a considerable number, however, the status of *Gastarbeiter* took on a more or less permanent nature.

Xeniteia, or sojourning in foreign parts, on either a permanent or temporary basis has thus been central to the historical experience of the Greeks in modern times. As a consequence the relationship of the communities overseas with the homeland has been of critical importance throughout the independence period. The prospect of the election of Michael Dukakis, a second-generation Greek-American, as president of the United States in 1988 naturally aroused great excitement in Greece and, inevitably perhaps, unrealistic expectations. His emergence as the Democratic presidential candidate focused attention on the rapid acculturation of Greek communities abroad to the norms of the host society and highlighted the contrast between the effectiveness of Greeks outside Greece and the problems they experienced at home in developing the efficient and responsive infrastructure of a modern state. The existence of such large populations of Greek origin outside the boundaries of the state raises in an acute form the question of what constitutes 'Greekness' – presumably not language, for many in the second and third generation know little or no Greek. Religion is clearly a factor, but again there is a high incidence of marriage outside the Orthodox Church among Greeks of the emigration. In 119 of the 163 weddings performed at the Greek church of Portland, Oregon, between 1965 and 1977 one of the partners was not of Greek descent. It seems that 'Greekness' is something that a person is born with and can no more easily be lost than it can be acquired by those not of Greek ancestry.

In the United States, in particular, the existence of a substantial, prosperous, articulate and well-educated community of Americans of Greek descent is seen as a resource of increasing importance by politicians in the homeland, even if the political clout attributed to the 'Greek lobby' is sometimes exaggerated, particularly by its opponents. Despite some successes Greek-Americans have had relatively little effect in generating pressure on Turkey to withdraw from northern Cyprus and in negating the tendency of successive US administrations to 'tilt' in favour of Turkey in the continuing Greek-Turkish imbroglio.

Outsiders are inclined to dismiss Greek fears of perceived Turkish expansionism as exaggerated. But those who argue that the facts of geography condemn the two countries, which in the 1970s, 1980s and 1990s more than once came to the brink of war, to friendship, fail to take account of the historical roots of present-day antagonisms and of the extreme sensitivity to perceived threats to national sovereignty that can arise in countries whose frontiers have only relatively recently been established. Whereas the heartland of 'Old' Greece has enjoyed at least a notional independence since the 1830s, large areas of the present Greek state have only been incorporated within living memory. The Dodecanese islands became sovereign Greek territory as recently as 1947, while many of the other Aegean islands, together with Macedonia, Epirus and Thrace, were absorbed only on the eve of the First World War. Konstantinos Karamanlis, elected president for the second time in 1990, was born in 1907 an Ottoman subject.

Geographically, Greece is at once a Balkan and a Mediterranean country. Its access to the sea has given rise to greater contacts with the West than its land-locked Balkan neighbours. It was, indeed, in the eighteenth century that the foundations were laid of a mercantile marine that in the second half of the twentieth century had emerged as the largest in the world, even if a sizeable proportion of it sailed under flags of convenience. Greece's Orthodox and Ottoman heritage had, however, for many centuries cut it off from the mainstream of European history. The country's identity as a European country was uncertain. Indeed, from the earliest days of independence Greeks had talked of travelling to Europe as though their country was not in fact European. Such uncertainty gave Greece's accession to the European Community as its tenth member in 1981 a particular significance, for, aside from the perceived economic and political benefits of accession, it seemed to set the seal in an unambiguous way on her 'Europeanness'. The Greek national movement had been remarkable in that it was the first to develop in a non-Christian environment, that of the Ottoman Empire. One hundred and fifty years later, Greece's full membership of the European Community was significant in that she was the first country with a heritage of Orthodox Christianity and Ottoman rule and with a pattern of historical development that marked her out from the existing members to enter the Community. The process of the reintegration of Greece into 'the common European home' forms a major theme of this book.

2

Ottoman rule and the emergence of the Greek state 1770–1831

Constantinople, the 'City' as it was known in the Greek world, fell to the Ottoman Turks after a lengthy siege on 29 May 1453. This was a Tuesday, a day of the week that continues to be regarded as of ill omen by Greeks. The capture of this great bastion of Christian civilisation against Islam sent shock waves throughout Christendom, but the reaction of the inhabitants of the pitiful remnant of the once mighty empire was ambiguous. The great bulk of the Orthodox Christian populations of the eastern Mediterranean had long previously fallen under Ottoman rule. Moreover, in the dying days of the Byzantine Empire, the Grand Duke Loukas Notaras had declared that he would rather that the turban of the Turk prevailed in the 'City' than the mitre of the Catholic prelate. In this he reflected the feelings of many of his Orthodox co-religionists who resented the way in which western Christendom had sought to browbeat the Orthodox into accepting papal supremacy as the price of military assistance in confronting the Turkish threat. There were bitter memories, too, of the sack of Constantinople in 1204 as a result of the diversion of the Fourth Crusade. At least the Orthodox Christian *pliroma*, or flock, could now expect, as 'People of the Book', to enjoy under the Ottoman Turks the untrammelled exercise of their faith with no pressure to bow before the hated Latins. The fall of the Byzantine Empire, indeed, was widely perceived as forming part of God's dispensation, as a punishment for the manifold sins of the Orthodox. In any case the Ottoman yoke was not expected to last for long. It was widely believed that the end of the world would come

Map 1 *I kath'imas Anatoli*: the Greek East. Greek communities have been widely scattered throughout the Near and Middle East in modern times.

about at the end of the seventh millennium since Creation, which was calculated as the year 1492.

After 1453 the Ottomans gradually consolidated their hold over the few areas of the Greek world that were not already within their grasp. The pocket empire of Trebizond, on the south-eastern shores of the Black Sea, which had been established as a consequence of the Fourth Crusade, was overrun in 1461. Rhodes was captured in 1522, Chios and Naxos in 1566, Cyprus in 1571, and Crete, known as the 'Great Island', fell after a twenty-year siege in 1669. The Ionian islands (with the exception of Levkas) largely escaped Ottoman rule. Corfu, the largest, never fell to the Turks. The islands remained as Venetian dependencies until 1797, when they passed under French, Russian and British rule, constituting a British protectorate between 1815 and 1864.

The Ottoman Turks, nomadic warriors by origin, were confronted with the task of ruling a vast agglomeration of peoples and faiths that embraced much of the Balkan peninsula, north Africa and the Middle East. This they accomplished by grouping populations into *millets* (literally 'nations') which were constituted on the basis of religious confession rather than ethnic origin. Beside the ruling Muslim *millet*, there was the Jewish *millet*, the Gregorian Armenian *millet*, the Catholic *millet* (even, in the nineteenth century, a Protestant *millet*) and finally the Orthodox *millet*, the largest after the Muslim. The *millets* enjoyed a wide degree of administrative autonomy and were ruled over by their respective religious authorities. The Ottoman Turks called the Orthodox the *millet-i Rum*, or 'Greek' *millet*. This was something of a misnomer for, besides the Greeks, it embraced all the Orthodox Christians of the Empire, whether they were Bulgarian, Romanian, Serb, Vlach (a nomadic people scattered throughout the Balkans and speaking a form of Romanian), Albanian or Arab. But the ecumenical patriarch of Constantinople, who was the senior patriarch of the Orthodox Church and the *millet bashi* (head of the *millet*), together with the higher reaches of the Church hierarchy, through which he administered it, were invariably Greek. With the growth of nationalism in the nineteenth century, this Greek dominance of the Orthodox *millet* increasingly came to be resented by its non-Greek members and the hitherto seamless robe of Orthodoxy was rent by the establishment of national Churches.

The *millet* system in its classical form did not develop until quite late and the precise nature of the privileges granted by Sultan Mehmet the Conqueror to the Orthodox Church immediately after the conquest are not clear. The original *firman*, the document in which these were vouchsafed, was lost and Mehmet's concessions to the Church had to be reconstructed in 1520 on the basis of the testimony of three aged members of the sultan's janissary guard who had been present nearly seventy years before when Mehmet had allowed the Greeks to keep their churches. Mehmet chose Georgios Gennadios Scholarios as the first patriarch under the Ottoman dispensation. This choice was welcome to many for Gennadios had been a staunch opponent of the union of the Orthodox and Catholic Churches and it was clearly in Mehmet's interest to perpetuate this traditional hostility. The power and privileges of the Orthodox Church were more extensive under the Ottoman sultans than they had been under the Byzantine emperors. Moreover, the patriarch's authority over the Orthodox faithful extended beyond strictly religious affairs to the regulation of many aspects of everyday life. So much so, indeed, that Orthodox Christians would for the most part have had many more dealings with their own religious authorities than with Ottoman officialdom.

The quid pro quo for the granting of such a high degree of communal autonomy was that the patriarch and the hierarchy were expected to act as guarantors of the loyalty of the Orthodox faithful to the Ottoman state. When the sultan's authority was challenged, then, the hierarchs of the Church, in their role as both religious and civil leaders, were the prime targets for reprisals. Thus it was that, on the outbreak of the war of independence in 1821, the ecumenical patriarch, Grigorios V, together with a number of other religious and civil leaders, was executed in circumstances of particular brutality. His hanging outraged opinion in Christian Europe, and indeed helped to mobilise sympathy for the insurgent Greeks. But to the Ottomans, Grigorios had manifestly failed in his primary duty, that of ensuring the loyalty of the faithful to the sultan. When the Russian ambassador protested about the execution, the *reis efendi*, the Ottoman foreign minister, tartly observed that a Russian *tsar*, Peter the Great, had actually abolished the office of patriarch in his country.

1 The fall of Constantinople, as depicted by Panayiotis Zographos in a series of paintings of scenes from the war of independence, commissioned in the mid-1830s by General Makriyannis, a veteran of the war. Against the background of the city of Constantinople, the victorious sultan, anachronistically smoking a hookah, declines the gifts proffered by the clergy and prominent citizens, and orders that they be placed under the yoke. In the distance, those who have refused to submit have taken to the hills, pursued by Ottoman troops. In the bottom left corner the embodiment of enslaved Greece, in chains, points a reproachful finger at the tyrant. Immediately above, Rigas Velestinlis, the proto-martyr of the independence movement executed by the Turks in 1798, sows the seeds of Greece's eventual freedom. He is flanked by one of the *klefts*, the bandits who, in the popular imagination, symbolised a form of primitive national resistance during the period of the *Tourkokratia*, the centuries of Turkish rule. Makriyannis commissioned the series of twenty-five pictures, whose robust vigour matches that of his own prose, to correct what he considered to be the lies and distortions of certain historians. They are accompanied by detailed captions giving his version of events surrounding many of the major battles of the war. Panayiotis Zographos, the artist, had himself taken part in the war and his two sons helped make the copies. Four sets were made, and in 1839 these were presented by Makriyannis at a great banquet in Athens to King Otto and to the ministers of

The concentration of power, civil as well as religious, in the hands of the Church led to furious rivalries for high office. These were encouraged by the Ottoman authorities, for the grand vezir, the sultan's chief minister, became the recipient of a vast *peshkesh*, or bribe, each time that the office of patriarch changed hands. To recoup the payment the patriarch himself was obliged to accept bribes and the Church thus became enmeshed in the institutionalised rapacity and corruption that was endemic to the Ottoman system of government. In theory a patriarch enjoyed life tenure of his throne but it was not unknown for the same individual to hold office on more than one occasion. Indeed, during the later seventeenth century Dionysios IV Mouselimis was elected patriarch no less than five times, while the 'national martyr', Grigorios V, was executed during his third patriarchate. Small wonder that the gibe of an eighteenth-century Armenian banker that 'you Greeks change your patriarch more often than your shirt' struck home uncomfortably. Nor was it surprising that over the centuries a strong current of popular anti-clericalism, prompted by the exactions of the Church and the greed of many of the clergy, came into existence. In the decades before 1821 this coalesced with the resentment of the nascent nationalist intelligentsia at the extent to which the higher reaches of the Church hierarchy had identified their interests with those of the Ottoman state. The argument advanced by the Patriarch Anthimos of Jerusalem in 1798 that Christians should not challenge the established order because the Ottoman Empire had been raised up by God to protect Orthodoxy from the taint of the heretical, Catholic West was by no means untypical of the views of the hierarchy at large.

Our Lord . . . raised out of nothing this powerful Empire of the Ottomans in the place of our Roman [Byzantine] Empire which had begun, in certain ways, to deviate from the beliefs of the Orthodox faith, and He raised up the Empire of the Ottomans higher than any other Kingdom so as to show without doubt that it came about by Divine Will . . .
Anthimos, Patriarch of Jerusalem, *Didaskalia Patriki* [Paternal Exhortation]
(1798)

Caption for Plate 1 (*cont.*).

the 'Protecting Powers' of the newly independent Greek state, Britain, France and Russia. The British set is still preserved in Windsor Castle.

Notwithstanding the fact that, in keeping with Islamic tradition, the Greek *raya* (literally flock) enjoyed under Ottoman rule a considerable degree of religious freedom, they were nonetheless subject to a number of disabilities which emphasised their inferior status in the Ottoman order of things. The word of a Christian was not accepted in court against that of a Muslim, nor could a Christian marry a Muslim. A Christian might not bear arms and in lieu of military service was required to pay a special tax, the *haradj* (in practice this was a privilege, if an unintended one). Until the demise of the institution towards the end of the seventeenth century, the most feared disability was the *paidomazoma* (literally child gathering) or janissary levy. This was the obligation, imposed at irregular intervals, on Christian families in the Balkans to surrender their bestlooking and most intelligent children for service to the Ottoman state as elite soldiers or bureaucrats. The requirement on those conscripted to convert to Islam, apostasy from which invariably resulted in death, was particularly feared. But because the levy did afford the opportunity for children from poor backgrounds to rise to the very highest echelons of the Ottoman state structure there were instances of Muslim parents trying to pass their children off as Christians so as to be eligible for the levy. Moreover, highly placed janissaries were sometimes able to show favours to relatives or to their native villages.

The various forms of discrimination to which Christians were subject, when coupled with particularly harsh treatment by local Ottoman authorities, could lead to conversion, individual or mass, to Islam. In such instances, which were particularly common in the seventeenth century in the remoter regions of the Empire, it was not unknown for Christians outwardly to subscribe to the tenets of Islam, while secretly adhering to the precepts and practices of Orthodox Christianity. When, in the mid-nineteenth century, the Ottoman Porte (as the central government was known), under pressure from the Christian Powers, formally espoused the notion of the equality of Muslims and Christians, many of these 'crypto-Christians' revealed their true religious allegiance, to the consternation of their erstwhile Muslim co-religionists.

The effect of these various forms of discrimination was mitigated in practice by the fact that, particularly in remote mountainous regions, the control exercised by the Ottoman central government was sketchy. The *Agrapha* villages in the Pindos mountains, for instance, were so called because they were 'unwritten' in the imperial tax registers. Other Greek-inhabited regions of the Empire, such as the prosperous mastic-growing island of Chios, enjoyed particular privileges and immunities.

The sixteenth and seventeenth centuries were something of a 'dark age' in the history of the Greek people. Armenians (regarded by the Turks as the 'faithful' *millet*) and Jews had not been compromised by resistance to Ottoman conquest and at this time enjoyed more favour than the Greeks. From time to time, however, Greeks emerged into prominence. One such was Sheytanoglou (the 'Son of the Devil'), a descendant of the great Byzantine family of the Kantakouzenoi. His control of the fur trade and of the imperial salt monopoly resulted in the amassing of a fortune large enough for him to equip sixty galleys for the sultan's navy. This over-mighty subject was, however, to be executed in 1578.

Even during this darkest period in the fortunes of the Greeks there were sporadic revolts against Ottoman rule. Uprisings on the mainland and in the islands of the Archipelago were prompted by the crushing defeat inflicted on the Ottoman navy by a fleet under the command of Don John of Austria at the Battle of Lepanto in 1571. In 1611 a short-lived revolt was launched in Epirus by Dionysios Skylosophos. Although the prolonged war of 1645–69 between Venice and the Ottoman Empire had resulted in the fall of Crete, nonetheless the Venetian occupation of the Peloponnese between 1684 and 1715 demonstrated that Ottoman power was not invincible.

Moreover, throughout the period of the *Tourkokratia*, the *klefts* afforded a visible and suggestive example of pre-nationalist armed resistance to the Turks. The *klefts* were essentially bandits whose depredations were directed against Greeks and Turks alike. But their attacks on such visible symbols of Ottoman power as tax collectors led to their being seen in the popular imagination as the defenders of the oppressed Greek *raya* against their Muslim overlords and to their being credited with almost superhuman powers of bravery and endurance. In an effort to control brigandage, and to ensure the safety of the mountain passes that were essential for the maintenance of trade and imperial communications, the Ottomans established Christian militia forces known as *armatoloi*. The existence of

Veduta di S. Giorgio della nazione Greca con il suo Colleggio de study

2 A seventeenth-century engraving of the Greek church of
Aghios Georgios (St George) and of the *Phlanginion Phrontiste-
rion*, or College, in Venice. With its large Greek community,
Venice was an important centre of Greek commercial,
religious and cultural activity during the *Tourkokratia*. In 1514
the Greeks were granted permission to build their own church
and the Greek Bishop in the city enjoyed the title of Metropolitan
of Philadelphia in Asia Minor. In 1665 the *Phlanginion Phron-
tisterion*, founded with a lavish benefaction from Thomas
Phlanginis, a former president of the community, opened its
doors to prepare young Greeks for study at the University of
Padua. Catholic Venice's relative tolerance of Orthodox 'schis-
matics' led to the city becoming for a long period the main centre
of printing for the Orthodox world. Almost all the service
books used in churches throughout the Ottoman Empire were
printed in the city, while a lively commercial trade developed in
secular literature. The *Serenissima Repubblica* of Venice ruled
over the one area of the Greek world free of Ottoman rule, the
Ionian islands. These comprised Corfu (Kerkyra), Cephalonia,
Zakynthos (Zante), Cythera, Levkas (Lefkada), Ithaca and
Paxos. Corfu never fell to the Ottomans. The other islands had
only a very brief experience of Ottoman rule, with the exception
of Levkas, which for some 200 years formed part of the sultan's
domains. After the fall of the Venetian republic in 1797 the
islands came under various forms of French, Russian and

such armed formations of Greeks, the one outside the law and the other within it (although boundaries between the two were never rigid), meant that by the time of the outbreak of the struggle for independence in the 1820s the Greeks were beneficiaries of a long, if erratic, tradition of irregular warfare.

During the sixteenth and seventeenth centuries the prospect of throwing off the Ottoman yoke appeared remote indeed. Such aspirations as existed among the Greeks for an eventual restoration of 'their race of princes to the throne and possession of Constantinople' were enshrined in a body of prophetic and apocalyptic beliefs which held out the hope of an eventual deliverance not through human agency but through divine intervention. These reflected the persistence of Byzantine modes of thought which saw all human endeavour as constituting part of the divine dispensation. Particular credence was attached to the legend of the *xanthon genos*, a fair-haired race of liberators from the north, who were widely identified with the Russians, the only Orthodox people not in thrall to the Ottomans. But there was little feeling that the Greek people could hope to bring about their emancipation by virtue of their own efforts.

> We hope for the fair-haired races to deliver us,
> To come from Moscow, to save us.
> We trust in the oracles, in false prophecies,
> And we waste our time on such vanities.
> We place our hope in the north wind
> To take the snare of the Turk from upon us.
> Matthaios, Metropolitan of Myra (seventeenth century)

During the course of the eighteenth century, however, there were a number of highly significant changes in the nature of Greek society.

Caption for Plate 2 (*cont.*).

British rule before being united with the kingdom of Greece in 1864. Between 1204 and 1669 Crete also formed part of the Venetian Empire and witnessed a great flowering of Greek literature which was much influenced by Italian models. It was also the birthplace of the painter Domenikos Theotokopoulos, better known as El Greco. After the fall of the 'Great Island' of Crete to the Turks in 1669, following a twenty-year siege, the Ionian islands remained a window onto the West for the Greeks.

3 Constantine XI Palaiologos, the last emperor of Byzantium, depicted as the 'Emperor turned into Marble' in a sixteenth-century manuscript of the Oracles attributed to Emperor Leo the Wise. Constantine fell fighting alongside his troops in defence of Constantinople on 29 May 1453. This was a Tuesday, a day of the week that remains of ill omen in the Greek world. During the long centuries of the *Tourkokratia* the prospects of the Greeks securing their freedom either through the intervention of the Christian powers or through a successful

These encouraged some bold spirits among the Greeks to plan for a war of liberation against the Turks. But they faced enormous difficulties in persuading their fellow countrymen, who were either fatalistically resigned to their lot or too comfortably wedded to the existing status quo to contemplate resistance, that their schemes were other than fantastic. It was towards the end of the eighteenth century that the first stirrings of the national movement began to manifest themselves. This was ultimately to result in the emergence of an, albeit severely truncated, independent state in the 1830s. The development of this movement has a particular interest as it was not only the first national movement to develop in eastern Europe but the first to emerge in a non-Christian context, that of the Ottoman Empire. The reasons for this relative precocity are several.

There could have been no prospect of successfully sustaining a revolt if the Ottoman Empire had not been weakened militarily, territorially and economically during the course of the eighteenth century. The decline in the Empire's military capacities was symbolised by the descent of the janissary corps from an elite fighting force to an hereditary caste, concerned only with maintaining its power

---

Caption for Plate 3 (*cont.*).

revolt were very distant, but hopes were sustained by a corpus of prophetic beliefs which enjoyed widespread currency throughout the Orthodox world. These promised eventual liberation from the yoke of the Ottomans through divine providence rather than human action. One such, the legend of the *Marmaromenos Vasilias* (the 'Emperor turned into Marble'), held that Constantine Palaiologos, as he was about to be struck down by a Turk, had been seized by an angel and taken to a cave near the *Khrysoporta* (the 'Golden Gate'), one of the gates of Constantinople, and turned into marble. There he awaited the day when the angel would return to arouse him, whereupon he would expel the Turks to their reputed birthplace, the *Kokkini Milia* ('Red Apple Tree'), in central Asia. Such beliefs gained particular credence at the time of the Russo-Turkish war of 1768–74, for the Oracles attributed to Leo the Wise were held to foretell the liberation of Constantinople from the Turks 320 years after its fall, i.e. in 1773. Although the war did not bring about the hoped-for emancipation, belief in the prophecies continued to be widespread into modern times.

and privileges and, until its savage suppression by Sultan Mahmud II in 1826, a permanent thorn in the side of the authority of the central government. Military decline and the failure to adapt to changes in military technology rendered the Ottoman state increasingly open to external challenge, from Austria, from Persia and from Russia. From the late seventeenth century the Empire's territorial, and hence its economic, base began to shrink.

Pressure from the Russians, the 'fair-haired race' of the prophecies and the sole Orthodox power in the world, had a special resonance in the Greek lands. The great war of 1768–74 between Russia and the Ottoman Empire aroused particular excitement, for a prophecy attributed to the Byzantine emperor Leo the Wise foretold the driving out of the Turks from the 'City' of Constantinople 320 years after its capture, i.e. in 1773. Although the Russians were henceforth to claim a protectorate over all the Orthodox Christians of the Empire, the war in fact brought little improvement in the lot of the *raya*. Despite this, many continued to set store by prophecies foretelling their eventual emancipation from the yoke of the Turks.

Retreat on the periphery was accompanied by serious threats to the integrity of the Empire as a unitary state. Anarchy, occasioned by janissary indiscipline, in a number of provincial cities was paralleled by the emergence of provincial war lords, nominal subjects of the sultan who acted in many ways as independent rulers and who held sway over large swathes of imperial territory. One of these in particular, the Muslim Albanian Ali Pasha, numbered many Greek inhabitants in the huge territories which he ruled from his capital in Ioannina in Epirus. The virtual independence of these satraps was an encouraging indication to the Greeks of the degree to which the power of the Ottoman central government had declined by the eighteenth century.

Paradoxically, the process of Ottoman decline was to precipitate a small but influential group of Greeks into positions of power in the highest reaches of the Ottoman state. These were the Phanariots (so named after the Phanar or Lighthouse quarter of Constantinople in which the Ecumenical Patriarchate is situated), who were drawn from a handful of families of Greek or Hellenised Romanian and Albanian origin. The mounting external pressures on the Empire meant that the Ottomans could no longer, as they had at the zenith of their power, dictate peace terms to defeated enemies. They now needed skilled diplomats to salvage what they could from defeat. This role was filled by Phanariots who between 1699, when the Peace of Carlowitz marked the first major retreat of Ottoman power in Europe, and the outbreak of the war for independence in 1821 monopolised the office of principal interpreter to the Porte, a more influential position in the conduct of Ottoman foreign policy than it sounded. Phanariots also acted as interpreters to the *kapudan pasha*, or admiral of the Ottoman fleet, and in this capacity came to act as the *de facto* governors of the islands of the Archipelago, from whose Greek population many of the sailors in the Ottoman fleet were drawn.

The most important offices controlled by Phanariots during the eighteenth and early nineteenth centuries were those of *hospodar*, or prince, of the Danubian principalities of Wallachia and Moldavia. Over these, from their luxurious courts in Bucharest and Jassy, they ruled as the viceroys of the Ottoman sultans. As was the case with high office in the Church there was fierce and corrupt competition for these much-coveted posts, the average tenure of which was less than three years. Phanariot rule was much resented by the Romanian inhabitants of the Principalities but their reputation for capricious rapacity was not wholly deserved. A number of the *hospodars* proved to be enlightened patrons of Greek culture and their courts became channels through which western ideas penetrated the far-flung Orthodox commonwealth that existed, and to a degree flourished, under Ottoman rule. Their courts, which were microcosms of the sultan's court in Constantinople, provided a useful grounding in the art of politics, albeit of the convoluted kind practised in the Ottoman Empire. As the nearest approximation to a Greek aristocracy, however, the Phanariots largely identified their interests with the preservation of the integrity of the Empire and few took an active part in the struggle for independence.

Of greater significance in the development of the national movement was the emergence in the course of the eighteenth century of an entrepreneurial, widely dispersed and prosperous mercantile class, whose activities were as much based outside as within the Ottoman domains. Merchants of Greek origin or culture came to dominate imperial trade, exporting raw materials and importing western

4 A paper 'icon', printed in Vienna in 1798, depicting the
monastery of Aghiou Pavlou (Saint Paul) on Mount Athos.
The inscription at the foot of the engraving is printed in both
Greek and Slavonic, for although most of the twenty monasteries are Greek, the monastic republic of Athos includes
Russian, Serbian, Bulgarian and Romanian foundations and,
under Ottoman rule, attracted pilgrims from throughout the
Orthodox commonwealth. Huge quantities of such engravings
of religious scenes or of great centres of Orthodox pilgrimage
such as Athos, Kykko monastery in Cyprus, the monastery of

manufactures and colonial wares. Greek became the *lingua franca* of Balkan commerce. Greek mercantile *paroikies*, or communities, were established throughout the Mediterranean, the Balkans, central Europe and southern Russia and as far afield as India. At the same time Greek sea captains, based principally on the three 'nautical' islands of Hydra, Spetsai and Psara, were busy laying the foundations of what, in the twentieth century, was to become the largest merchant fleet in the world. The continental blockade imposed by the British during the French revolutionary and Napoleonic wars afforded highly profitable opportunities to those prepared to risk running it. There was little in the way of manufacturing. The hill-town of Ambelakia in Thessaly, which in the last decades of the eighteenth and the first of the nineteenth centuries enjoyed a considerable prosperity through the manufacture of spun red cotton, much of which was exported to central Europe, was an isolated and short-lived example.

The wealthier of the merchants, some with huge fortunes, chafed at the arbitrariness and uncertainty of life in the Ottoman Empire, for this militated against the security of property and the accumulation of capital. Their experience of the ordered commerce of western Europe, where governments gave positive encouragement

---

Caption for Plate 4 (*cont.*).

Soumela near Trebizond on the Black Sea and the Church of the Holy Sepulchre in Jerusalem circulated between the seventeenth and nineteenth centuries. Much cheaper to produce than painted icons, they were sold to raise funds for the maintenance of the monastic foundations which constituted bastions of the Orthodox faith during the centuries of Ottoman rule. Although the Church contributed powerfully to the maintenance of a sense of Greek identity (and of the Greek language) during the *Tourkokratia*, in the decades before the outbreak of the war of independence Greek nationalists, while careful not to attack religion as such, were increasingly critical of the ignorance and corruption that characterised monastic foundations and the hierarchy of the Church. In particular, they came to regard the advocacy of *ethelodouleia*, or willing submission to the Ottoman powers that be, by many clerics as a major obstacle to their attempts to instil a sense of national consciousness in the unlettered masses of the Greeks.

5 Mikhail Soutsos, the Phanariot Grand Dragoman (chief interpreter) to the Ottoman Porte 1817–18, and *hospodar* of Moldavia 1819–21, depicted in characteristically sumptuous attire. During the eighteenth century, as the Ottoman Empire came under increasing external threat, a small group of families known as the Phanariots rose to positions of great power within the Ottoman state. Most were Greek by birth, all were Greek by culture. Until the outbreak of the war of independence in 1821 they monopolised four key positions. As chief interpreters to the Porte they shared with the *reis efendi*, the Ottoman foreign minister, responsibility for the conduct of foreign policy. As

to mercantile enterprise, induced some of them to lend their support to the nascent national movement. But others were not prepared to risk their newly acquired prosperity in such a seemingly hazardous enterprise. If the commitment of the great majority of the merchants to the nationalist cause was to prove lukewarm, their indirect contribution to the development of the movement for independence was nonetheless to prove of the greatest significance.

The merchants were responsible for sustaining the material base of the intellectual revival of the last three decades of the eighteenth and the first two of the nineteenth centuries that was such a vital factor in the development of a national consciousness, an awareness of a specifically Greek rather than merely Orthodox Christian identity. They endowed schools and libraries, and subsidised the publication, principally outside the boundaries of the Empire, of a growing, and increasingly secular, body of literature aimed at a specifically Greek audience. During the last quarter of the eighteenth century seven times as many books were being published as during the first. In the twenty years before 1821 some 1,300 titles were published. Perhaps most important of all, the subventions of merchants enabled young Greeks to study in the universities of western Europe and, in

---

Caption for Plate 5 *(cont.)*.

interpreters to the *kapudan pasha*, or commander of the Ottoman fleet, they acted in effect as governors of the islands of the Aegean Archipelago, whose inhabitants were overwhelmingly Greek. As *hospodars*, or princes, of the Danubian principalities of Moldavia and Wallachia, they acted as viceroys of the sultan, recreating in their courts in Jassy and Bucharest luxurious imitations of the imperial court. The bribery and intrigue provoked by the intense rivalry for office has given the Phanariots a bad reputation, although a number showed a genuine interest in legal and land reform and in promoting Greek education and culture. Most of the Phanariots identified their interests too closely with those of their Ottoman masters to give much encouragement to the national movement. Mikhail Soutsos was an exception. Initiated into the *Philiki Etairia*, he rallied to Alexandros Ypsilantis during his ill-fated invasion of the principalities in 1821 and was active in the politics of the independent kingdom.

6 A lithograph depicting a Greek sea captain on the eve of the war
of independence. During the last decades of the eighteenth century
and the first of the nineteenth the foundations were laid of Greece's
present pre-eminence as a seafaring nation. The embryonic mercantile marine grew rapidly. Huge fortunes were amassed, as the
arkhontika, or mansions, that to this day encircle the harbour of
Hydra, one of the three 'nautical' islands, testify. Raw materials
were exported from the Ottoman Empire to western Europe and
manufactured goods and colonial produce were imported in
return. The crews of the ships of the Ottoman navy were largely
made up of Greeks from the islands of the Archipelago. This
maritime heritage, reinforced by a long tradition of piracy and
privateering, was to be of inestimable advantage in establishing
control of the seas during the war of independence. The growth of
a flourishing mercantile marine was paralleled by the emergence
during the eighteenth century of a commercial bourgeoisie which
dominated the trade of the Balkans. Greek became the language of
Balkan commerce, and Greek merchant communities were established not only in the Balkans but in central Europe, southern
Russia and throughout the Mediterranean. Few members of this
emergent commercial middle class demonstrated much interest in
the nationalist enthusiasms of the nascent intelligentsia. But many
of the newly enriched merchants endowed schools and libraries,
subsidised the publication of books reflecting western ideas and
paid for young Greeks to study in the universities of western
Europe, where they came into contact with Enlightenment philos-
ophies and with the radical notions emanating from the French
Revolution.

particular, those of the German states. Here they came into contact not only with the heady ideas of the Enlightenment, of the French Revolution and of romantic nationalism but they were made aware of the extraordinary hold which the language and civilisation of ancient Greece had over the minds of their educated European contemporaries.

During the centuries of the *Tourkokratia* knowledge of the ancient Greek world had all but died out, but, under the stimulus of western classical scholarship, the budding intelligentsia developed an awareness that they were the heirs to an heritage that was universally revered throughout the civilised world. By the eve of the war of independence this *progonoplexia* (ancestor obsession) and *arkhaiolatreia* (worship of antiquity), to use the expressive Greek terms, had reached almost obsessive proportions. It was precisely during the first decade of the nineteenth century that nationalists, much to the consternation of the Church authorities, began to baptise their children with the names of (and to call their ships after) the worthies of ancient Greece rather than the Christian saints. Some enthusiasts even changed their own names in a similar spirit. It was at this time, too, that the furious, and at times violent, debate that has continued up to the present got under way as to the form of the language appropriate to a regenerated Greece. Some advocated a return to the supposed purity of Attic Greek of the fifth century BC, others that the contemporary spoken language (remarkably little changed from classical times given the enormous time span involved) form the basis of educated discourse. Still others advocated a middle way that entailed the purging of the spoken language of foreign words and usages. In the end the advocates of *katharevousa*, literally 'purifying', Greek prevailed and their influence had a baleful effect on the country's subsequent cultural and educational development.

We have said many times, dear friends, that the worst misfortune that can befall a once renowned race is to forget its ancestral virtues, to be oblivious of its own wretchedness, to neglect and be contemptuous of education. These things, it seems, prevailed after the lamentable downfall of Greece into enslavement. But already, through Divine Providence, the Greeks of their own accord have begun to awake from the deepest lethargy of ignorance, to care for enlightenment and for their re-birth, and to take gigantic steps on the path to the acquisition of their ancestral virtue and religion.

Grigorios Paliouritis, *Arkhaiologia Elliniki* [Greek Archaeology] (1815)

An advocate of a linguistic middle way, who played a key role in inculcating a 'sense of the past' in his fellow countrymen, was Adamantios Korais. He was born in Smyrna (Izmir) in 1748 but spent much of his life in Paris, where he died in 1833. There he established a formidable reputation as a classical scholar and prepared editions of the ancient Greek authors for a specifically Greek readership. In the prefaces to these he sought to encourage awareness of the incomparable intellectual heritage to which his fellow countrymen were heirs and urged them to cast off the mantle of Byzantine ignorance in which they had been enveloped. He had a passionate belief in education as the key to emancipation from what he considered to be the double yoke of the Ottomans ('Turk and wild beast were to my thinking synonyms') and the monkish obscurantism of the hierarchs of the Orthodox Church.

During the first decades of the nineteenth century Greek society was becoming increasingly differentiated and was undergoing rapid change. A small but growing number of Greeks were articulating an ever more explicit national consciousness and were becoming increasingly resentful of the continuance of Ottoman rule. But their efforts faced formidable obstacles. Not least of these was the fact that the elites of pre-independence Greek society – the Phanariots, the higher clergy, the wealthy merchants and the provincial notables (the *kodjabashis*) – were for the most part too comfortably locked into the Ottoman status quo to identify with the national movement. Moreover, the nationalist enthusiasms of the intelligentsia, centred as it was in the communities of the diaspora, were not shared by the unlettered mass of the people. Some catalyst was needed to organise and channel the mounting discontent with Ottoman rule.

One of the first to develop plans for a co-ordinated revolt was Rigas Velestinlis, a Hellenised Vlach from Thessaly. After acquiring his early political experience in the service of the Phanariot *hospodars* of the Danubian principalities, he had been powerfully influenced by the French Revolution during a sojourn in Vienna in the 1790s. The political tracts, and in particular his *Declaration of the Rights of Man*, which he had printed in Vienna and with which he aspired to revolutionise the Balkans, are redolent of the French example. Potentially the most significant was the *New Political Constitution of the Inhabitants of Rumeli, Asia Minor, the Archipelago, Moldavia and Wallachia*. This envisaged the establishment of a revived Byzantine Empire but with the substitution of republican institutions on the French model for the autocracy of Byzantium. Although it was intended to embrace all the inhabitants of the Ottoman Empire, Greeks, whether by birth or by culture, were to predominate. Rigas' carefully articulated schemes were without result for he was betrayed (by a fellow Greek) in Trieste as he was about to leave Habsburg territory to preach the gospel of revolution in the Balkans. With a handful of fellow conspirators he was put to death by the Ottomans in Belgrade in May 1798.

> For how long, o brave young men, shall we live in fastnesses,
> Alone, like lions, on the ridges, in the mountains?
> Shall we dwell in caves, looking out on branches,
> Fleeing from the world on account of bitter serfdom?
> Abandoning brothers, sisters, parents, homeland,
> Friends, children and all our kin?
>
> Better one hour of free life,
> Than forty years of slavery and prison!
>
> Rigas Velestinlis, *Thourios* [War Song] (1797)

Rigas' endeavours may have had no practical outcome but nonetheless they thoroughly alarmed both the Ottoman authorities and the hierarchy of the Orthodox Church, coinciding as they did with the occupation by the French, with all the panoply of 'revolutionary liberation', of the Ionian islands in 1797. This, combined with Bonaparte's invasion of Egypt, nominally a part of the Ottoman Empire, in the following year, 1798, brought the godless and seditious doctrines of the French Revolution to the very borders of the Empire. The Serbian revolt of 1804, initially a reaction against intolerable oppression by the janissaries but gradually acquiring the character of a national uprising, was an encouraging demonstration of Ottoman vulnerability which was seized upon by the anonymous author of the *Hellenic Nomarchy* (1806), the most remarkable political tract of the independence period. When the Ionian islands, as part of the settlement at the Congress of Vienna, were in 1815 established as a nominally independent state, under British protection, they afforded a suggestive example of an area of Greek territory not under Ottoman rule.

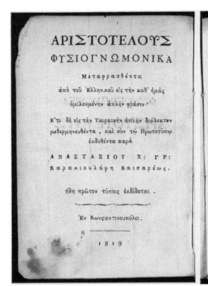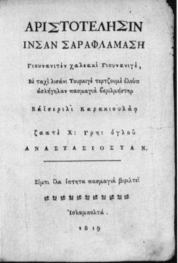

7 The title-page, in both Greek and Turkish, of an edition of Aristotle's *Physiognomonica*, printed in 1819 in Constantinople, or *Islambol* (literally 'Abounding in Islam') as the Turkish text has it. The book, translated by Anastasios Karakioulaphis, from Caesarea of Cappadocia (now Kayseri in Turkey), gives the text in the ancient Greek original, in 'our simple spoken tongue' (i.e. modern demotic Greek), and in Turkish printed with Greek characters, for the benefit of the *karamanli* Greeks. These were Turkish-speaking Orthodox Christians, mainly to be found in Asia Minor, who used the Greek alphabet to write Turkish and for whom a substantial literature was printed in the eighteenth, nineteenth and early twentieth centuries. This edition of the *Physiognomonica* (a work subsequently demonstrated not in fact to have been written by Aristotle) is one of a number of books published in the last decades of the eighteenth century and the first two of the nineteenth which reflected a revival of interest, amounting by the eve of the war of independence almost to an obsession, in the language, history and civilisation of ancient Greece on the part of the small nationalist intelligentsia. Knowledge of the ancient world had largely died out in the Greek lands during the centuries of Turkish rule. Adamantios Korais (1748–1833), the best known of these nationalist intellectuals and himself a great classical scholar, was indefatigable in editing ancient Greek texts for the edification of

The two reasons, o my dear Greeks, why up to now we are bound with the fetters of tyranny, are the ignorant priesthood and the absence abroad of the best of our fellow countrymen.

Anonymous, *Elliniki Nomarkhia* [Hellenic Nomarchy] (1806)

Rigas Velestinlis' martyrdom was to prove an inspiration to the three young Greeks who came together, significantly enough in the diaspora community of Odessa in southern Russia, with ambitious plans to mobilise the nation's resources in an armed revolt against its Ottoman overlords. The three, Emmanouil Xanthos, Nikolaos Skouphas and Athanasios Tsakaloff, were somewhat marginalised members of the mercantile diaspora. The vehicle for their conspiracy was the *Philiki Etairia*, or Friendly Society, founded in 1814 with the single aim of liberating the 'Motherland' from the Ottoman yoke through an armed and co-ordinated revolt.

Strongly influenced by Freemasonry, the society insisted on elaborate initiation rituals for its four basic categories of membership. Betrayal of its mysteries was punishable by death. In the early years the society's recruitment efforts met with little success. But from 1818 its membership grew more rapidly, particularly in the diaspora communities, although there were never more than a thousand or so members until the months immediately before the outbreak of the revolt. Merchants formed the largest single category in its membership, even if few of the mercantile grandees enlisted.

From the outset the leadership of the society put it about, misleadingly if plausibly, that the conspiracy enjoyed the support of Russia, the Orthodox power which most Greeks looked upon as their most likely saviour. Two attempts, indeed, were made to enlist as overall

---

Caption for Plate 7 (*cont.*).

his fellow countrymen. He urged them to emulate the worthies of ancient Greece and, through education, to show themselves to merit emancipation from the Turkish yoke. A characteristic manifestation of this revived 'sense of the past' was the practice, dating from the first decade of the nineteenth century and much frowned upon by the Church authorities, of giving children ancient Greek names such as Aristotle, Calliope, Socrates, Plato, Aspasia and Leonidas in place of traditional Christian baptismal names.

leader Count Ioannis Kapodistrias, the Corfiote Greek who had served, since 1816, as the joint foreign minister of Tsar Alexander I and who was thoroughly versed in the ways of international diplomacy. These failed, for Kapodistrias considered the whole venture to be misguided and counselled instead that his compatriots await the next in the seemingly interminable series of wars between Russia and the Ottoman Empire, when they might then hope to achieve an autonomous status similar to that already secured by the Serbs. Despite his conviction that the plans of the *Philiki Etairia* were foolish and doomed to failure Kapodistrias did not betray the conspiracy and the leadership was offered instead to the less impressive General Alexandros Ypsilantis, a Phanariot serving as aide-de-camp to Tsar Alexander. Optimistic schemes to enlist the support of the Serbs and Bulgarians aroused little enthusiasm among peoples who were becoming increasingly resentful of Greek ecclesiastical and cultural hegemony and whose own national movements were in train.

Nature has set limits to the aspirations of other men, but not to those of the Greeks. The Greeks were not in the past and are not now subject to the laws of nature.
Benjamin of Lesvos, *Stoikheia tis Metaphysikis* [Elements of Metaphysics] (1820)

But if attempts to create a common Balkan front failed, the *Philiki Etairia* was nonetheless able to exploit the opportunity opened up by Sultan Mahmud II during the winter of 1820/1 when, as part of his efforts to restore the depleted authority of the Ottoman central government, he sought to destroy Ali Pasha, the Muslim warlord who held sway over much of mainland Greece. Since such a campaign would necessarily tie up a substantial portion of the imperial armies, this was clearly a chance not to be missed. Consequently Ypsilantis, in March 1821, launched his small and motley army across the river Pruth which marked the border between Russian Bessarabia and Moldavia. As he did so he invoked the shades of Epameinondas, Thrasyboulos, Miltiades, Themistocles and of Leonidas in the struggle to bring 'liberty to the classical land of Greece'.

Ypsilantis also hoped to take advantage of the concurrent uprising, led by Tudor Vladimirescu, of the Romanian inhabitants of the Principalities against the native *boyars*, or notables. But the

Romanians showed no greater enthusiasm than did the Serbs and Bulgars for making common cause with the Greeks, whom they identified with the oppressive rule of the Phanariot *hospodars*. Following the defeat of his ragged army at the hands of the Ottoman forces at the Battle of Dragatsani in June 1821, Ypsilantis was forced to flee into Habsburg territory and the invasion petered out.

Not long after Ypsilantis' initial incursion across the Pruth river sporadic outbursts of violence in the Peloponnese towards the end of March assumed the form of an all-out revolt, although the degree to which the two uprisings were co-ordinated is not clear. The heavily outnumbered Turks, thrown on to the defensive, withdrew to their coastal fortresses after vicious fighting marked by atrocities on both sides. The traditions of kleftic warfare were to prove invaluable to the insurgent Greeks, while their nautical skills enabled them swiftly to dominate the Aegean. The Greeks having seized the initiative, the struggle fairly quickly settled down to a military stalemate. When news of the revolt reached western Europe there was much enthusiasm on the part of liberal opinion and, before long, philhellene volunteers, the best known of whom was the poet Byron, enlisted in the cause of Greek freedom. Nurtured on an idealised picture of ancient Greece, some of them rapidly became disillusioned when they discovered that the modern Greeks had little in common with the worthies of Periclean Athens. Others saw in insurgent Greece a testing ground for their pet hobby-horses; still others were genuine idealists. Some, indeed, made a valuable contribution to the military prosecution of the war. Philhellenic committees throughout Europe raised money for the conduct of the war and for the relief of its victims, particularly as news spread of the great massacre of Christians on Chios in April 1822. If the practical consequences of all this activity were limited, philhellenic agitation nonetheless had some small effect in finally moving the governments of the Holy Alliance, whose initial reaction to the revolt had been one of ill-disguised alarm at the threat to the established order, to intervene in the conflict.

The early successes of the insurgents raised the question of how the territories under their control should be governed. Within a matter of months three provisional regional governments had come into existence, and early in 1822 a constitution was adopted. In the context of the times this was a highly liberal document and was clearly

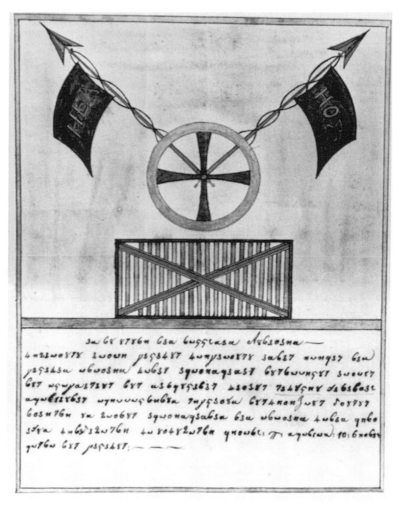

8 Letter of commendation of a *ierefs* (priest) of the *Philiki Etairia* (Friendly Society). This was the secret society that prepared the way for the outbreak of the war of independence in 1821. Founded in Odessa in 1814 by three impoverished young Greeks, Emmanouil Xanthos, Nikolaos Skouphas and Athanasios Tsakaloff, it sought the 'liberation of the Motherland' through armed revolt and recruited widely throughout the Greek world. It had four grades of membership: the *vlamis* (brother), the *systimenos* (recommended one), the *ierefs* (priest) and the *poimin* (shepherd). There were in addition

intended by its framers to appeal to enlightened opinion in Europe. The following year, 1823, the constitution was revised and the three local governments were merged into a single central authority. But the creation of a unified government brought factional intrigue in its wake and by 1824 the feuding among the insurgents had degenerated into civil war, as was to happen at other times of grave national crisis. As General Makriyannis, one of the leading protagonists of the war, plaintively put it: 'I took an oath to fight against Turks, not Greeks.'

During the course of the war alliances and alignments on the insurgent side fluctuated. The Peloponnesian *kodjabashis*, or notables, fought to retain the power and privileges that they had enjoyed under the old dispensation, while former *klefts* turned military leaders, of whom the most prominent was Theodoros Kolokotronis, were no less determined to appropriate a share of political power commensurate with their vital role in the prosecution of the war. Likewise the island shipowners, whose contribution to the war at sea was substantial, wanted their share of the political spoils. The small group of westernising intellectuals may have lacked military muscle, but

---

Caption for Plate 8 *(cont.)*.

two military grades, while the highest authority was held by the 'Great Priests of the Eleusinian Mysteries', grouped in the *Anotati Arkhi* (Supreme Authority). The *Etairia* had elaborate initiation rituals which were influenced by Freemasonry and provided for death in the event of betrayal of its plans. The letter of commendation is headed by crossed flags bearing the initials of the slogan '*I E[leftheri]a i Th[anato]s*': 'Freedom or Death'. The ciphered text, made up of letters and numbers, reads as follows:

In the name of the future salvation [of Greece], I dedicate as a priest of the Society and commend to the love of the *Philiki Etairia* and to the protection of the Great Priests of the Eleusinian Mysteries my fellow citizen Nikolaos Spetziotis, the son of Dimitrios, by trade a seaman, thirty years old, a wholehearted defender of the Society and of the Motherland, catechised and sworn by myself P: Spetses 10 March, [year] five of the Society [i.e. 1819].

By 1821 almost a thousand members are known to have been initiated into the society.

9 A contemporary print depicting the hanging by the Turks on 10 April 1821 of the Ecumenical Patriarch, Grigorios V, at one of the gates of the Patriarchate in Constantinople. The gate, considerably less grandiose in reality than in this imaginary reconstruction, has remained closed from that day to this. A number of bishops and Phanariot grandees, including Konstantinos Mourouzis, the Grand Dragoman of the Porte, were likewise executed in reprisal for the outbreak of the war of independence. Grigorios V and the Holy Synod, composed of the senior metropolitans of the Orthodox Church, had issued encyclicals vigorously denouncing Alexandros Ypsilantis, Mikhail Soutsos and the Greek insurgents in Moldavia as rebels not only against the Ottoman sultan but against God's divine will. The patriarch was executed nevertheless, for in Ottoman eyes he had failed to observe the implicit contract whereby in return for religious freedom the patriarch was expected to act as the guarantor of the loyalty of the Orthodox *pliroma*, or flock. The execution of this *ethnomartyras*, or national martyr, caused outrage in the West and contributed to the powerful upsurge of sympathy for the insurgent Greeks that developed in liberal circles in western Europe. After three days Grigorios' body was cut down, handed to a Jewish mob, for there had long been animosity between Greeks and Jews in the city, and dragged to the Golden Horn. The corpse was picked up by the

they enjoyed a disproportionate influence and were able to ensure that the embryonic state was equipped with the trappings of liberal constitutionalism.

The factionalism that was the background to the war can broadly be interpreted in terms of a power struggle between the 'military' or 'democratic' party and the 'civilian' or 'aristocratic' party. Whereas the former kleftic leaders who dominated the 'military' party could, after a fashion, be said to represent the mass of the people, the 'civilian' party reflected the interests of the Peloponnesian notables, the island shipowners and the small group of Phanariots who had gained their early political experience under the Ottomans but who had thrown in their lot with the insurgents. Cutting across this cleavage was the gulf between the modernisers and the traditional elites.

For the most part western-educated and dressing in the European fashion, *alafranga*, the modernisers, replete with the rhetoric of romantic nationalism, sought to import western institutions lock, stock and barrel, oblivious to the fact that Greek society under Ottoman rule had evolved in a manner very different from that of the states of western Europe that were their model and whose institutions they wanted to adopt rather than adapt. The traditional elites, whose style of dressing symbolised their commitment to the old order (minus the incubus of the Turks), had dominated society during the pre-independence period. With little in the way of an articulated nationalist programme, they were determined, come what may, to hang on to their prerogatives under the new, independent dispensation. Essentially they thought of independence in terms of substituting their own oligarchical rule for that of the Turks. No wonder that the *kodjabashis*, the Peloponnesian notables, were

---

Caption for Plate 9 (*cont.*).

Greek crew of a Russian ship and taken to Odessa. Fifty years later, in 1871, the body was returned to Greece, and on the hundredth anniversary of his martyrdom, in 1921, Grigorios was formally proclaimed a saint of the Orthodox Church. The fact that Grigorios was three times patriarch (in 1797–8, 1806–8 and 1818–21) is a reflection of the corruption and factionalism that characterised the upper reaches of the Orthodox hierarchy during the *Tourkokratia*.

10 The arrival of Lord Byron in Mesolongi on 4 January 1824, as painted by Theodoros Vryzakis. The outbreak of the war of independence struck an immediate and responsive chord with liberal opinion throughout the western world, a reaction that was in sharp contrast to that of the conservative governments of the Holy Alliance. Philhellenic committees were established, funds were solicited for the relief of war victims and (expensive) loans raised for the prosecution of the war. Philhellene volunteers (including a substantial leavening of do-gooders, misfits and cranks) flocked to Greece from western Europe and the United States (a solitary Cuban is recorded). The best known of these was Byron, who died of fever at Mesolongi in April 1824 before he could participate more actively in the war. But his death in the cause of Greek freedom helped to keep interest in the plight of the insurgents alive among an admiring European readership. Moreover, unlike a number of other would-be philhellenes, the Russian poet Pushkin among them, Byron, who had travelled extensively in the Greek lands before the outbreak of the revolt, was not disillusioned by the failure of the Greeks to measure up to an idealised image of their ancient forebears. If the propaganda value of the philhellenes was greater than their military contribution to the insurgent war effort, some, such as Leicester Stanhope, a follower of Jeremy Bentham and dubbed by Byron 'the Typographical Colonel' on account of

disparagingly referred to as 'Christian Turks'. One hero of the war of independence, Photakos Khrysanthopoulos, said that the only difference was one of names: instead of being called Hasan the *kodjabashi*, he would be called Yanni; instead of praying in the mosque he would go to church.

While the insurgent Greeks were quarrelling, and at times fighting, among themselves, their military situation took a drastic turn for the worse, for Sultan Mahmud II had found a new ally in his attempt to crush the rebellion. This was his nominal vassal Mehmet Ali, the ruler of Egypt, and Mehmet's son, Ibrahim Pasha. In return for their support they were promised a large share of the spoils. Ruthless control was established over Crete, and Ibrahim Pasha, having built up strong forces in the Peloponnese in 1825, harried the insurgents without mercy. Under serious military threat, the increasingly desperate Greeks turned to the Great Powers for a solution to their plight. By this stage of the war the Powers were more inclined to an interventionist role, for not only were their trading interests seriously affected but each was fearful lest the other might be able to turn the festering conflict to its own political advantage. In 1825 the British foreign secretary, George Canning, who had a genuine sympathy for the Greek cause, rejected the proposal of some of the leaders for an 'Act of Submission' which would have placed insurgent Greece under British protection. Instead a mission by the Duke of Wellington resulted in the Protocol of St Petersburg, by which Britain and Russia undertook to mediate in the conflict, a venture to which France became a party through the Treaty of London of 1827. This policy, characterised by Canning as one of 'peaceful interference', culminated in October 1827 in the Battle of Navarino, the last great battle of the age of sail. The combined British, Russian and French

---

Caption for Plate 10 (*cont.*).

his enthusiasm for the benefits of printing, assisted the cause in other ways. Not the least of Greece's foreign benefactors at this time was the Irishman William Stevenson, who introduced potato cultivation. Vryzakis (1814–78), one of the leading painters of nineteenth-century Greece, was heavily influenced by western and, in particular, German romantic models.

11 The kleftic leader Nikitas (Nikitaras) Stamatelopoulos,
known as the *Tourkophagos* (Turk-eater), attacking a Turkish
cavalryman during the battle of Dervenakia of August 1822.
In this battle Greek irregular forces inflicted a major defeat
on Mahmud Dramali's army at a critical stage of the war of
independence. Nikitas was the nephew of another *kleft*,
Theodoros Kolokotronis, the principal Greek commander.
The *klefts* (literally 'thieves') were brigands with a long tradition
of defiance of Ottoman authority. They formed an essential, if

fleets, under the command of Admiral Sir Edward Codrington, destroyed the Turco-Egyptian fleet. The Ottoman position was to be further weakened by the outbreak in April 1828 of yet another war with Russia in which the Turkish armies experienced severe setbacks. The 'untoward event', as the Duke of Wellington termed it, of Navarino, if not wholly planned, nonetheless proved decisive and Great Power intervention made some form of independent Greece inevitable. Establishing the borders of the new state and the terms of its governance and sovereignty, however, were to occupy the insurgent Greeks and the representatives of the Powers for some time to come.

In May 1827, the insurgents had enacted a third constitution. This was promulgated by the assembly of Troezene, which elected Count Ioannis Kapodistrias as the first *kyvernitis*, or president, of Greece, an office which he assumed in January of 1828. Kapodistrias was a master of the diplomatic craft, but schooled as he was in the traditions of Russian autocracy he had little time for the liberal provisions of the Troezene constitution or the factionalism of the assembly. This last he replaced by a twenty-seven member *Panhellenion*, which was

---

Caption for Plate 11 (*cont.*).

ill-disciplined and frequently brutal, reservoir of military talent without which there would have been little chance of the successful prosecution of the war. Although their depredations during the pre-revolutionary period had been directed as much against Greek as Ottoman elites, they had become symbols in the popular imagination of a primitive pre-national resistance to the Turks. Their physical prowess was legendary (one was credited with the ability to leap over seven horses in a row, while Nikitas himself was reputed to be able to outrun a horse) and many of the kleftic ballads recorded their heroic defiance of Turkish torture. The lawlessness of the *klefts* is testimony to the fact that in many of the remote mountainous areas of the Greek lands the authority of the Ottoman central government before 1821 had been tenuous. The picture is taken from a series of lithographs based on paintings by the Bavarian painter Peter von Hess, who had been commissioned by King Ludwig I of Bavaria to record his son Otto's arrival in Greece in January 1833 to take up the throne of Greece.

Map 2 The expansion of the Greek state, 1832–1947

under his direct control. He had a two-fold mission: to create the foundations of a state structure in a country ravaged by years of savage fighting and to secure as favourable borders as possible for the new state. The problems that he faced were legion. During the three and a half years of his presidency he struggled to create a national army, to endow the state with an administrative structure and an educational system, to improve communications and to restore the shattered economy. He also sought to get to grips with the question of the 'national lands', the properties that had been vacated by the fleeing Turks. Kapodistrias hoped that peasant proprietors would form the stable backbone of the new state but he ran up against the opposition of the military leaders and the Peloponnesian notables who were determined to secure as large a share as possible of the available lands.

[Kapodistrias] ruined Greece because he immediately made it Frankish [western], while to begin with he should have made it three parts Frankish and seven Turkish, later half and half, and afterwards entirely Frankish.

Theodoros Kolokotronis (1836)

After prolonged negotiations, involving the ambassadors to the Ottoman Porte of the three 'mediating' powers, Britain, Russia and France, a frontier was agreed running from Arta in the west to Volos in the east. The new state, embracing the Peloponnese, southern Roumeli and a number of islands near to the mainland, was thus to be larger than the Powers had originally envisaged but nonetheless was to contain fewer than a third of the Greek inhabitants of the Ottoman Empire at the time of the outbreak of the war. As part of the price of agreeing to independence the Powers had also determined that Greece should be an hereditary monarchy, whose king should be drawn from one of the royal houses of Europe not directly connected with those of Britain, Russia or France. After Leopold of Saxe-Coburg, discouraged by Kapodistrias' gloomy reports, had turned down the throne, the Powers' choice lighted on Otto of Wittelsbach, the seventeen-year-old second son of King Ludwig I of Bavaria.

Meanwhile, despite his not inconsiderable achievements on the diplomatic front, Kapodistrias' authoritarian style and his belief that the Greeks were not yet capable of self-government had provoked the opposition of influential sections of society. He made no secret of his contempt for the elites of Greek society. He dismissed the primates as 'Christian Turks', the military chieftains as 'robbers', the intelligentsia as 'fools' and the Phanariots as 'children of Satan'. Having comprehensively alienated those who had played a major role in prosecuting the war and who naturally expected power and recognition under the new dispensation, he also managed to incur the wrath of the powerful Mavromikhalis clan in the Mani in the southern Peloponnese. Two members of the clan assassinated Kapodistrias as he entered a church in Nafplion, the provisional

12 The assassination of President Ioannis Kapodistrias on his way
to church in Nafplion on 9 October 1831, as depicted by an
anonymous contemporary artist. Count Kapodistrias, a Corfiot
Greek, had been approached in 1817 and 1820 with the offer of
the leadership of the *Philiki Etairia* while serving as joint foreign
minister to Tsar Alexander I of Russia. This he declined, counselling that the best hope for his fellow countrymen lay not in armed
revolt but in a war between Russia and the Ottoman Empire from
which Greece might hope to emerge with an autonomous status. In
1822 he resigned from the tsar's service. In 1827, at the assembly
of Troezene, he was elected president of Greece. By the time he
arrived on Greek soil in January 1828, independence had effectively been secured as a consequence of the defeat of the Ottoman
navy by a combined British, French and Russian fleet at the Battle
of Navarino in October 1827. Frontiers had not yet been drawn
and Kapodistrias deployed his great experience of European diplomacy to secure as much territory as possible for the new state. He
also sought to lay the foundations of a state structure in a land
ravaged by seven years of warfare. Schooled in the tradition of
Russian autocracy he was temperamentally out of sympathy with
the elites of Greek society. With attitudes such as these it is not
surprising that he made powerful enemies. He met his death at the
hands of Georgios and Konstantinos Mavromikhalis, whose
powerful clan in the Mani in the southern Peloponnese he had
offended.

capital, on 9 October 1831. If Kapodistrias was not mourned by the would-be power brokers in the new state, his paternalist ways had nonetheless secured him some affection among the population at large. With his death the small rump of a Greece whose independence was now assured relapsed into the anarchy that was not far beneath the surface.

3

Nation building, the 'Great Idea' and National Schism 1831–1922

It was symptomatic of the dependent nature of the new state that the Greeks were not a party to the treaty of May 1832 between Britain, France, Russia and Bavaria which settled the terms under which King Otto was to accept the throne and which placed Greece under the 'guarantee' of the 'Protecting' Powers. If the welcome which awaited the young king on his arrival in the provisional capital of Nafplion in February 1833 was genuine enough, the problems that confronted him and his extensive Bavarian entourage were legion. In addition to the inevitable problems attaching to the creation of the basic infrastructure of a state where none had previously existed, there was also the pressing need to create a shared sense of Greek identity. The intermittent prosecution of the war over a period of almost ten years had certainly helped to establish a sense of nationhood extending beyond the intelligentsia and those primarily responsible for fighting the war. But the new rulers of Greece were essentially faced with the problem of constructing a nation as well as a state. Creating a sense of loyalty to the state that would transcend traditional loyalties to family, to native village and to region was no easy task.

The fact that the kingdom embraced within its borders such a small proportion, less than a third, of the Greek population of the Ottoman Empire was to create tensions that were only to be resolved when, some ninety years after the granting of independence, the irredentist project of the *Megali Idea* was consumed in the ashes of Smyrna in 1922. Proponents of this 'Great Idea' aspired to unite within the bounds of a single state, whose capital would be Constantinople, all the areas of Greek settlement in the Near East. The term 'Great Idea' was first coined by Ioannis Kolettis, a Hellenised Vlach who, from being doctor to Ali Pasha's son, had emerged as one of the most influential political figures of the first two decades of the independent kingdom. In 1844, in the debates that gave rise to the first constitution, Kolettis vigorously championed the cause of the *heterochthons*, the Greeks from the areas outside the initial confines of the kingdom, against the hegemonistic pretensions of the *autochthons*, the 'natives' from the heartland of the struggle for independence. Not only, he insisted, were inhabitants of the kingdom Greeks but so too were those who lived in any land associated with Greek history or the Greek race. There were two main centres of Hellenism: Athens, the capital of the kingdom; and the 'City' of Constantinople, 'the dream and hope of all Greeks'.

> The Greek kingdom is not the whole of Greece, but only a part, the smallest and poorest part. A native is not only someone who lives within this Kingdom, but also one who lives in Ioannina, in Thessaly, in Serres, in Adrianople, in Constantinople, in Trebizond, in Crete, in Samos and in any land associated with Greek history or the Greek race . . .
>
> Ioannis Kolettis before the constituent assembly in 1844

The 'Great Idea', reflecting and reinforcing as it did the messianic longings of the prophecies that enjoyed such wide currency during the period of Ottoman rule and, indeed, into modern times, was to be the dominant ideology of the emergent state. It was by no means a unique phenomenon in the nineteenth-century Balkans. Serbs, Romanians, Bulgarians and Albanians all aspired to their own equivalent of the dream of a 'Greater Greece'. But whereas the other Balkan peoples were relatively compactly settled, the Greeks were widely scattered throughout the Near East. There were the Greek populations settled over a wide swathe of the southern Balkan peninsula extending from Valona (now Vlorë in Albania) in the west to Varna, in present-day Bulgaria, in the east. Towards the north these were inextricably intermixed with Serbs, Bulgarians, Albanians, Turks and Vlachs. When rival Balkan nationalisms contested this region at the turn of the nineteenth and twentieth centuries as the Ottomans were forced out of Europe, the ensuing struggles were bloody and the eventual frontiers were, not surprisingly, imperfect.

While there were substantial Muslim minorities in Cyprus and Crete (where the Muslims were Greek-speaking), the inhabitants of the islands of the Aegean were very largely Greek, although only a few of them had been incorporated within the 1832 boundaries. There were in addition very large Greek populations in the Ottoman capital itself, around the shores of the Sea of Marmara, and along the western littoral of Asia Minor, with a particularly large concentration in Smyrna, and in Cappadocia, in the centre of Anatolia. Here, as in other parts of Asia Minor, and, indeed, in Constantinople itself, many of the Greeks were Turkish-speaking. Another great concentration of Greeks had settled in Pontos, between the Pontic Alps and the southern shores of the Black Sea. Cut off from the mainstream of Greek life, the Pontic Greeks, large numbers of whom in the nineteenth century migrated to the more welcoming Russian shores of the Black Sea, spoke a form of Greek that was scarcely intelligible in other parts of the Greek world.

The immediate concern of the new kingdom was to repair the ravages inflicted by the years of fighting and to create an institutional infrastructure for the new state, a process that had begun during Kapodistrias' short presidency. Commerce had been devastated by the war. All the major centres of Greek mercantile enterprise such as Smyrna, Salonica and Constantinople remained within the Ottoman Empire and, indeed, continued throughout the nineteenth century to attract migrants from the kingdom. The question of the disposition of the 'national lands' remained to be resolved and a major threat to the stability of the new kingdom was caused by the existence of large bodies of armed irregular troops. Resentful of the lack of recognition of their contribution to the war effort, only a small number were integrated into the regular army under Bavarian officers. Many lapsed, or relapsed, into the brigandage which was to constitute a major social and political problem throughout the nineteenth century. Brigands, however, had their uses to the government when, at times of crisis in relations with Turkey – and these were numerous – they could be used to stir up trouble across the frontier. The frontier also afforded a convenient refuge to brigands when they were being harassed by the forces of law and order. It was by no means unknown for brigands to enjoy the protection of politicians, who found them a useful means of exerting pressure on intractable voters. As Otto was a minor when he ascended the throne, the country was governed until 1835 by a regency council consisting of three Bavarians who had arrived in the king's large and resented Bavarian retinue. The regents had little sympathy for the aspirations of those who had actually fought for independence and who felt cheated of the spoils of victory. They showed little sensitivity to Greek tradition in fashioning the institutions of the new state after western European models. The educational system, for instance, was based on French and German prototypes. Criminal and civil law codes were introduced which reflected the Roman legal traditions of continental Europe and took little heed of existing customary law. The Church settlement of 1833, by which ties with the Ecumenical Patriarchate were severed, and the Church was declared autocephalous and subject to a considerable degree of government control, constituted another breach with tradition. Relations with the Patriarchate were not formally restored until 1850, when Constantinople recognised the 1833 settlement.

The choice of Athens as capital, a town dominated by the imposing ruins of the Parthenon and with its associations with the glories of the Periclean age but in the early 1830s little more than a dusty village, symbolised the cultural orientation of the new state towards the classical past. It was only towards mid-century that interest developed in Greece's medieval, Byzantine past and attempts were made to link the classical, medieval and modern periods of Greek history in a theory of unbroken continuity. The fixation on the classical past was reflected in the great emphasis that was laid in the schools and in the University of Athens on the study of the culture of ancient Greece and on the *katharevousa*, or 'purifying' form of the language, a stilted construct that blighted the schooling of generations of children. The university, founded in 1837, was seen as the power house of the attempt to 're-Hellenise' the unredeemed Greek populations of the Ottoman Empire. It attracted students not only from the kingdom but from throughout the Greek world who then returned to their homelands to spread the pure gospel of Hellenism. Not until the end of the century did the Ottoman authorities begin to restrict educational propaganda among the 'unredeemed' Greeks.

Even after the formal termination of the regency in 1835, Bavarian influence remained both strong and much resented. A further source of tension was the continued refusal of Otto to grant a constitution, as the settlement from which an independent Greece had emerged had provided. Nonetheless, rudimentary parties, which had their roots in the period of the war of independence, were the focus of an intense political life. Significantly, these were known as the 'English', 'French' and 'Russian' parties and their leaders retained close contacts with the ministers in Athens of the three Protecting Powers. The 'English' party attracted the support of those who most resented Otto's refusal to concede constitutional government. The 'French' party likewise advocated constitutionalism but its supporters were advocates of a more forward policy in achieving the 'Great Idea'. The 'Russian' party, whose supporters were not so much concerned with the lack of constitutional government as with the breaking of links with the Patriarchate, served as the rallying point for the conservative elements in society. Boundaries between the parties were fluid and intrigues could be neutralised by the judicious dispensation of favours. But towards the end of the first decade of independence there were increasing manifestations of discontent.

To the degree that a person feels himself to be weak or strong, he either becomes a follower of some powerful man or groups his supporters round his own self. In this fashion every prominent man has a more or less numerous cohort of dependants who consort with him, listen to him, seek his advice, carry out his wishes and defend his interests, ever anxious to secure his favour and to win his confidence. Such is the origin and nature of the innumerable coteries with which Greece abounds . . . it is through the grouping together of these coteries that parties are formed.

Friedrich Thiersch, *De l'état actuel de la Grèce* (1833)

In 1839 an obscure 'Philorthodox' conspiracy came to light, seemingly aimed at forcing Otto either to convert from Catholicism to Orthodoxy or to abdicate. There was disquiet, too, that Otto and his queen, the autocratic Amalia of Oldenburg, had not produced an heir. Since 1837 the prime minister had always been a Greek and the last Bavarian troops left the country in 1838, but Bavarian influence remained strong and the minister of war was a Bavarian. Resentment had also built up against the *heterochthons*, the Greeks who had moved to the kingdom only after independence, and who, by virtue of their better education, had secured a disproportionate share of the high offices of state, to the chagrin of the veterans of the war of independence who felt cheated of their inheritance. Onerous tax burdens, with a large part of the state's modest revenues being swallowed up by excessive military expenditures and the servicing of the loan granted by the Powers on independence, contributed to the growing groundswell of opposition.

This culminated in the *coup d'état* launched on 3 September 1843, the first, but by no means the last, instance of military intervention in the political process. In this case the virtually bloodless coup enjoyed widespread popular support. Otto quickly conceded the principal demand of the politicians and army officers behind the coup and a constituent assembly was charged with drafting a constitution. This was promulgated in March 1844. Thus, at an early stage, Greece was equipped with the trappings of liberal parliamentary democracy. The 1844 constitution, for instance, granted virtually universal manhood suffrage (although women were not to gain the right to vote until 1952). But from the outset problems arose from the grafting of the forms of western constitutionalism, which had evolved over centuries in societies with a very different historical experience, onto a traditional society, whose values had been critically influenced by the centuries of Ottoman rule and differed significantly from those prevailing in the industrialising societies of western Europe. The ensuing tension between democratic forms and traditional attitudes and practices, as elsewhere in the Balkans, distorted the evolution of parliamentary institutions. Moreover, Otto quickly manifested a disinclination to abide by the rules of the constitutional game, and with the connivance of the agile Vlach politician, Ioannis Kolettis, instituted a kind of parliamentary dictatorship. Kolettis' energetic dispensation of *rouspheti* (favours), combined with brute force, was enough to ensure that the existence of a parliament need not inhibit the exercise of the royal prerogative.

By the early 1850s, however, a new generation was coming to maturity which had no involvement in the war for independence and which felt alienated from the ruthless pursuit of office by politicians whose main object was to gain control of the state, by far the largest employer in the country, so as to be able to dispense patronage to their electoral clienteles and their extended families. At the same

13   A water colour of 1836 by the Bavarian artist Hans Hanke,
after the original by L. Kollnberger, depicting the café *Oraia
Ellas* (Beautiful Greece), situated at the corner of Aiolou
and Ermou Streets. This was for long the centre of Athenian
political gossip and intrigue and was an exclusively male preserve, as such *kapheneia* have remained until recently. On
the left is a group of Greeks dressed in European style, *alafranga*,
and apparently drinking beer (a fashion that arrived with
the Bavarian entourage of King Otto). They are sitting apart
from the group on the right, traditionally dressed *foustanello-
phoroi* or kilt-wearers, one clad in the richly embroidered waist-
coat and leggings of the kleftic leaders. They appear to be
drinking *raki* (a grape spirit flavoured with aniseed) and are
smoking a *tsibouki* or traditional pipe in contrast with the
group of Bavarian soldiers by the door who, besides drinking
beer, are smoking cigars or cigarettes, like the billiard table
another western import. In the centre a man dressed in a *redin-
gota* (literally 'riding coat') or frock coat talks to another wearing the *kapa*, the thick woollen cloak of the shepherd. This
charming water colour neatly epitomises a wider dichotomy in
society arising from the importation of western models in many
fields. In architecture, for instance, the neoclassicism that was the
mode in western Europe tended, in the cities at least, to displace
traditional architectural forms. In art western, and particularly

time the old political groupings, based on the 'English', 'French' and 'Russian' parties, faded away. Otto experienced a short-lived upsurge in popularity at the time of the Crimean war through his ardent espousal of the 'Great Idea'. The outbreak of this war in 1854, yet another in the endless series of wars between Russia and Turkey, appeared to offer Greece a chance to exploit the discomfiture of the Ottoman Empire. Guerrilla bands, in which bandits and university students played a noteworthy part, were infiltrated across the border with Turkey into Thessaly, Epirus and Macedonia. But the European powers rallied to defend the integrity of the Ottoman Empire and Britain and France occupied Piraeus, the port of Athens, between May 1854 and February 1857, in order to apply pressure on Greece to desist from stirring up trouble across the frontier.

A truly independent Greece is an absurdity. Greece can either be English or Russian, and since she must not be Russian, it is necessary that she be English.

                    Sir Edmund Lyons, British minister to Greece (1841)

Coming just four years after Lord Palmerston's naval blockade of Piraeus in January 1850 as a result of the Don Pacifico incident, a notorious exercise in 'gunboat diplomacy', this was one of the most flagrant instances of intervention in Greece's internal affairs by the 'Protecting' Powers until the guarantee of 1832 was formally abolished in 1923. Otto's forward policy in pursuit of the 'Great Idea' not only proved fruitless but contrasted with his sympathy with Austria in opposing Italian unification, an unpopular attitude in a country besotted with romantic nationalism. All the old resentments that had acted as the catalyst for the 1843 coup once again came to

---

Caption for Plate 13 (*cont.*).

German romantic, models overlaid an artistic tradition dating back to Byzantine times. Such western prototypes influenced music, law, education and, above all, politics. The tensions that arose from the grafting of western parliamentary institutions and the forms of European constitutional government onto a deeply traditional society, whose political culture had evolved in wholly different circumstances, were a persistent feature of nineteenth-century political life.

14 *Hadji Oustas Iordanoglou of Cappadocia and his son Homer* painted by Photis Kontoglou in 1927. Until the exchange of populations between Greece and Turkey in 1923–4 there were very large Greek populations scattered throughout Asia Minor. In the large seaport cities such as Constantinople, Smyrna and Trebizond many of these were prosperous, educated and westernised. Elsewhere, however, particularly in the interior, their lifestyle was little different from that of their Turkish peasant neighbours. While they clung tenaciously to

the fore. Following an unsuccessful attempt against the life of Queen Amalia, a coup by the Athens garrison led to Otto's overthrow in 1862, while he and his consort were on a tour of the Peloponnese. On the advice of the ministers of the Powers Otto put up no resistance and retired to his native Bavaria where, until his death in 1867, he manifested a genuine, if largely unrequited, affection for his former subjects. He frequently wore the *foustanella*, the traditional Greek dress, and one of his last acts was to make a contribution on behalf of the insurgent Cretans in 1866.

With Otto's forced departure, the Powers were once again faced with the need to choose a sovereign for Greece, not the easiest of tasks given the way in which Otto had been treated by his reluctant subjects. The Greeks themselves, in an unofficial plebiscite, expressed a strong preference for Prince Alfred, the second son of Queen Victoria. But as a member of the dynasty of one of the Protecting Powers his candidature was ruled out. The choice of the Powers fell on Prince Christian William Ferdinand Adolphus George of the Danish Glücksburg dynasty and the Greek branch of the dynasty

---

Caption for Plate 14 (*cont.*).

their Orthodox religion, many, particularly the womenfolk, spoke only Turkish. In the early nineteenth century few of these Turkish-speaking Greeks, the *karamanlides*, had much consciousness of being Greek and strenuous efforts, which were strongly supported by the Greek kingdom, the 'national centre', were made later in the century to instil in them a sense of Greek ancestry. Kontoglou emphasises the oriental lifestyle of many of these *karamanli* Christians, who at the time of the 1923 exchange of populations numbered as many as 400,000. The father has a largely Turkish name (*usta* means 'master craftsman') while his son has been named Homer in deference to the heavy emphasis on the ancient Greek heritage in the educational propaganda emanating from the kingdom. The title *Hadji* was used by Christians who had made the pilgrimage to the Holy Places in Palestine as well as by Muslims who had visited Mecca. Photis Kontoglou (1895–1965), a native of Ayvali in Asia Minor, consciously turned his back on the western influences that had hitherto dominated the artistic life of the independent state and sought his inspiration in the Byzantine and post-Byzantine traditions of popular art.

was to reign intermittently between 1864 and 1974. He assumed the throne with the title of King George I of the Hellenes. George's long reign lasted almost fifty years, ending with his assassination by a madman in 1913. As a kind of dowry, designed (unsuccessfully) to dampen irredentist fervour, Britain yielded the Ionian islands to Greece. This acquisition, the first accession of territory since independence, added some quarter of a million to the population and brought into the kingdom a region that had been more exposed to western influences than any other part of the Greek world. In the

---

Caption for Plate 15.

15 A portable icon, dated 1838, depicting the 'neo-martyr' St George the Younger of Ioannina. 'Neo-martyrs' were those who chose to die, often in horrible circumstances, rather than compromise their Orthodox Christian faith. Most commonly they had reverted to Christianity after embracing Islam and thus were regarded by the Turks as renegades. St George the Younger, an orphan from a village near Grevena, had served as a groom to a Turkish officer, Hadji Abdullah. Known as Hasan, he was generally considered to be a Muslim by the Turks, whose wrath had been aroused when he married a Christian in 1836. On this occasion he was saved through the intervention of Hadji Abdullah, who testified that Hasan/ George was indeed a Christian. Trouble again broke out two years later, however, when he had his son baptised. This time he was imprisoned, brutally tortured to make him renounce his faith and, when he refused, was hanged in Ioannina on 17 January 1838. Almost immediately his tomb was reported to be miraculous and he was popularly recognised as a saint some time before the Church gave recognition to his cult. St George the Younger, the patron saint of the royal (now presidential) *evzone* guard, was the last of the 'neo-martyrs', for soon afterwards the Ottoman Porte, under British pressure, abandoned executions for apostasy. The staunch faith of the often humble 'neo-martyrs' stands in contrast to the worldly ambition and corruption that had penetrated the higher levels of the Church hierarchy. This portable icon was painted within a few days of St George's death by Mikhail Zikos from the village of Khionades in Epirus, known for its itinerant religious and decorative painters. Other villages were known for their travelling stonemasons, builders, carpenters, waterworkers, woodcarvers and so on.

16 'A very Greek coup'. An engraving published in 1847, after a painting by H. Martens. It depicts the handing over to King Otto by General Dimitrios Kallergis, the commander of the Athens cavalry, of the demand for a constitution on 3 September 1843. Otto is dressed in traditional costume, which he continued to wear even after he had been driven into exile in his native Bavaria. In the background is his wife, the strong-willed Amalia of Oldenburg. At an adjacent window of the newly built royal palace (now the parliament building) is Major Hess, a particularly unpopular member of the king's Bavarian entourage. The virtually bloodless coup of 3 September enjoyed a wide measure of popular support and the demand for a constitution reflected discontent arising from a number of factors. These included the continuance of royal absolutism ten years after Otto's accession to the throne; the unpopularity of measures of retrenchment imposed by the Protecting Powers (Britain, France and Russia) in an effort to secure repayment of the loan which they had guaranteed when Greece was granted independence; Otto's failure to convert from Catholicism to Orthodoxy; and uncertainty over the succession occasioned by the fact that he had no children. The continued influence of Bavarians at the court offended those who had fought for independence and felt excluded from political power. Otto put up no resistance, and in 1844 a remarkably liberal constitution

same year a constituent assembly adopted a new constitution. This amplified the democratic freedoms conceded in 1844, although the sovereign retained considerable prerogatives and had substantial, if vaguely defined, powers in matters of foreign policy. These King George did not hesitate to use, travelling frequently and exploiting his wide-ranging dynastic connections.

During the early part of George's reign political life remained much as it had been under Otto. Political parties were essentially fluid groupings, crystallising around prominent politicians rather than ideologies, and engaged in the unending pursuit of office. The perquisites of power were essential if politicians were to have any chance of satisfying the insatiable demands of their voters-cum-clients. Given the rudimentary development of the economy, the state assumed a disproportionate importance as a source of employment, and the proportion of bureaucrats to citizens was far higher than in western Europe. Characteristically, the number of deputies in parliament was also disproportionately large. In the never-ending competition for political power, and hence access to patronage, politicians were ever willing to form kaleidoscopic and shifting coalitions. Elections were fiercely, and frequently roughly, contested, for on each change of government hinged a myriad positions in the public service. Stable government proved elusive. Between 1870 and 1875, for instance, there were no fewer than four elections and nine administrations.

Elsewhere parties come into existence because people disagree with each other, each wanting different things. In Greece, the exact opposite occurs: what causes parties to come into existence and compete with each other is the admirable accord with which all seek the same thing: to be fed at the public expense.

Emmanouil Roidis (1875)

Patron–client relationships permeated society at all levels and, indeed, have continued to be a pronounced feature of society until

---

Caption for Plate 16 (*cont.*).

was promulgated. The 1843 coup was the first instance of military intervention in the country's political life but it was by no means the last.

17 The swearing-in of the Greek volunteer legion, under the flag of Orthodoxy and the command of Panos Koronaios, to assist in the Russian defence of Sebastopol during the Crimean war, as depicted by a French artist. For the first century of its independent existence the foreign policy of the new Greek state was dominated by the *Megali Idea*, or 'Great Idea', the grandiose vision of restoring the Byzantine Empire through the incorporation within the bounds of a single state of all the areas of compact Greek settlement in the Near East, with Constantinople as the capital. For much of the period of the *Tourkokratia*, the Russians, the *xanthon genos* or fair-haired race of the prophecies and the sole Orthodox power, had been looked upon as the future liberators of the Greeks. In the first decades after independence had been achieved Russia was seen as the power most likely to assist Greece in achieving her irredentist ambitions. When Russia, putting herself forward as the protector of the sultan's Orthodox subjects, became embroiled in the Crimean war (1853–6) with the Ottoman Empire and its British and French allies there was great enthusiasm in the Greek kingdom for the Russian cause. Guerrilla bands, several led by veterans of the war of independence, were infiltrated across the border into Ottoman Thessaly and Epirus, prompting a much-resented British and French occupation of Piraeus, the port of Athens, between 1854 and 1857 to ensure

the present. Having the right *mesa*, or contacts, who could mitigate the inertia and inefficiency of the bureaucracy, was all-important, while *rouspheti*, the reciprocal dispensation of favours, was the essential lubricant of a cumbersome and unresponsive state machine. Theodoros Deliyannis, a consummate master of the 'old' politics and a dominant figure in political life during the second half of the century, actually kept ledgers in which he carefully noted the favours he had granted so that, in due course, he could reap the appropriate return. Laws, which parliament, like other Balkan legislatures, spewed out in large quantities, were there essentially to be got round rather than obeyed.

Patronage had originally developed as a kind of defence mechanism against the harshness, and particularly the arbitrariness, of the Ottoman system of government. There was a need for patrons and protectors to mediate with the Ottoman authorities and to mitigate the capriciousness of the judicial system. Many Greeks regarded the impositions of the new state as scarcely less oppressive than those of the Ottomans, and values and attitudes shaped under Ottoman rule persisted into the independence period. Patronage, indeed, proved wholly compatible with the formal institutions of parliamentary democracy. The local *kommatarkhis* or political boss simply took over the role of the Ottoman *ağa*. Until modern times a parliamentary deputy has seen it not only as an obligation but as the indispensable precondition of political survival to secure favours for his voters.

Undoubtedly there was a considerable divergence between the outward forms of politics and the substantive practice in the nineteenth century, yet Greek society was essentially open. The 'political world' may have been something of a self-perpetuating oligarchy but few avenues of advancement were closed off on grounds of social origins alone, as the career of Deliyannis itself demonstrated.

Caption for Plate 17 (*cont.*).

that Greece remained neutral in the conflict. In the decades after the Crimean war, as Russia championed the cause of the south Slavs, and, in particular, that of the Bulgarians, the chief rivals of the Greeks for hegemony in Macedonia, Greek enthusiasm for the Russian cause waned.

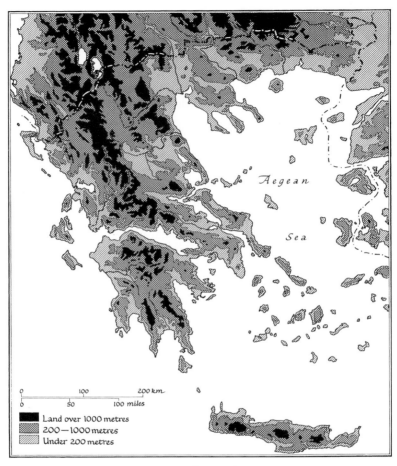

Map 3 Relief map of Greece

The demands on politicians were such that relatively few prospered at the public expense. In addition, from the prime minister down-wards, political figures were expected to, and did, make themselves available to the humblest supplicant. One politician prominent at the end of the nineteenth and in the early twentieth century, Dimitrios Rallis, is reputed to have had a thousand god-children, all of whose name-days had to be remembered and many of whom had to be found jobs when they came of age. Moreover, a lively and voluminous press, which enjoyed a freedom amounting to licence, acted as a check against the more flagrant abuses.

Towards the end of the nineteenth century, progress, hesitant perhaps but nonetheless real, was made in the direction of the modernisation of the political system. During the early part of King George's reign there was increasing dissatisfaction with personalistic and essentially 'issueless' politics. The turning-point came in 1875 when the king accepted the principle that he would invariably call upon the party leader enjoying the support of a majority of deputies in parliament to form a government. It was not until 1881, however, that Kharilaos Trikoupis, a rising star in the political firmament, the leading moderniser of the second half of the century and the principal proponent of this particular reform, was able to secure a majority for his New Party. For much of the remaining two decades of the century the essence of a two-party system operated, with Trikoupis alternating in power with his arch-rival, Deliyannis.

Trikoupis essentially represented the westernising tradition in political life; Deliyannis the traditional. Trikoupis believed that the state needed to be strengthened politically and economically before it could contemplate engaging in irredentist adventures. He therefore sought to establish the country's international creditworthiness, to encourage incipient industrialisation, to improve communications through railway construction and the building of the Corinth canal, and to modernise the army and navy. Such a programme, however, was costly and entailed increased taxation. This afforded an easy target for the popular but demagogic Deliyannis, who made no secret of the fact that he was against everything that Trikoupis stood for. Deliyannis' flamboyant populist rhetoric and his enthusiastic championship of a 'Greater Greece' undoubtedly reflected more faithfully the enthusiasms and prejudices of the man in the street than did the austere reforming programmes of Trikoupis. But Deliyannis' adventurist policies when in power were to place a severe strain on a weak economy, as happened with the abortive mobilisation during the Bulgarian crisis of 1885 which resulted in a Great Power blockade. Moreover, his belligerence was to result in defeat during the disastrous thirty-day war with Turkey of 1897.

18 A cartoon by Alphonse Daumier satirising Greece's indebtedness to the Great Powers. The caption reads:

Greece owes England	
Capital	1,000,000
Expenses	50,000
False expenses	225,775
Interest	20,000
Interest on interest	137,000
Purchase of pistols	375,000
Total	Four Millions

The insurgent Greeks had contracted loans, on disadvantageous terms, in the City of London during the war of independence and in 1832, the three Protecting Powers, Britain, France and Russia, guaranteed a loan of 60 million francs, much of

Much as Trikoupis may have sought peace as the precondition for the successful implementation of his reform project, issues of foreign policy tended to dominate domestic politics in the later nineteenth century to the exclusion of all else, as they have done in more recent times. Periodic uprisings in the island of Crete (1841, 1858, 1866–9, 1877–8, 1888–9 and 1896–7) in pursuit of the *enosis* or union of the 'Great Island' with the kingdom were to place a permanent strain on relations with the Ottoman Porte and were to provoke the intermittent intervention of the Powers. During the last decades of the century the main focus of foreign policy lay in the provinces to the north of the border with the Ottoman Empire. Greece's involvement in the great crisis that convulsed the Balkans between 1875 and 1878 and which was the focus of intense Great Power interest and rivalry was marginal. But Greece, no less than Britain and Austria-Hungary and, indeed, Serbia, was thoroughly alarmed by Russia's sponsorship, in the wake of her crushing victory over the Ottoman Empire in the war of 1877/8, of an autonomous 'Big Bulgaria', for this embraced territories long coveted by Greek nationalists. Greece was not directly represented at the Congress of Berlin in the summer of 1878 which

---

Caption for Plate 18 (*cont.*).

the proceeds of which were expended on the army, on King Otto's Bavarian bureaucracy and on the service of the loan. In the 1880s, further loans, totalling 630 million drachmas, were contracted, the service of which came to consume a third of the revenues of the state. When, in 1893, there was a collapse in world demand for her principal export, currants, Greece was forced greatly to reduce interest payments and was effectively bankrupt. Her economic condition was further weakened by defeat in the Greek–Turkish war of 1897, which resulted in the payment of a war indemnity of 4,000,000 Turkish pounds. The servicing of the loan raised to pay this indemnity and of Greece's existing loans was placed in the hands of an International Financial Commission. This was based in Athens and consisted of representatives of the six 'mediating' powers, Britain, Russia, Austria-Hungary, Germany, France and Italy. The repayment of these loans was to be assured by the assignment of receipts from government monopolies, tobacco duties, stamp taxes and the customs duties levied in the port of Piraeus. The arrangement, virtually without precedent, amounted to a serious breach of Greece's financial sovereignty.

19 Members of the band of brigands who, in April 1870, kidnapped and subsequently murdered at Dilessi in Boeotia a party of English aristocrats. The outrage provoked a crisis in relations with Britain, led to the downfall of the government and focused international attention on the endemic lawlessness of much of rural Greece, including the neighbourhood of the capital, in the nineteenth century. The party, on an excursion from Athens to Marathon, was held to ransom but negotiations were bungled and opposition politicians, in the hope of bringing down the government, encouraged the brigand leaders to hold out for an amnesty which the king, under the 1864 constitution, was not empowered to grant. When the band was ambushed by government troops the hostages were killed. Much obloquy was heaped on Greece, particularly in the British press. Greeks of all parties rallied in defence of the national honour and attempts were made to pin the blame on Albanians and Vlachs. Throughout the nineteenth century brigandage, which had deep roots in the pre-revolutionary period, was a major social problem. The irregulars who had made such an important military contribution to the war for independence proved difficult to assimilate into the regular army that was created by King Otto and they enjoyed an uneasy toleration by politicians who found their services useful whenever there was a need to stir up trouble across the Turkish frontier in pursuit of irredentist objectives. Outright brigandage was widespread and proved difficult to suppress on account of poor communications, mountainous terrain and the ease with which fugitives could slip across the frontier. Moreover, politicians were not averse to exploiting brigandage for their own ends. In the 1894 trial of a deputy

cut 'Big Bulgaria' down to size, but a Greek delegation was allowed to state its case. As a result the Powers decreed that the Ottoman Empire cede the fertile province of Thessaly, together with a part of Epirus, to Greece. A further consequence of the Balkan crisis was the acquisition by Great Britain, through the Cyprus convention of 1878, of the administration of the predominantly Greek-populated island of Cyprus. The island remained under Ottoman sovereignty until 1914. It was then annexed by Britain after the Ottoman Empire had entered the First World War on the side of the Central Powers.

The annexation of Thessaly, the second extension of Greece's borders and, like the first, the cession of the Ionian islands in 1864, the result not of irredentist agitation but of Great Power mediation, brought the frontier to the borders of Macedonia. For the last two decades of the nineteenth century and the first of the twentieth, Macedonia, with its inextricably mixed populations of Greeks, Bulgars, Serbs, Albanians, Turks and Vlachs, was to be the focus of the competing nationalisms of Greece, Bulgaria and Serbia, as each sought to carve out as large a stake as possible of the crumbling Ottoman possessions in the Balkans. Confrontation with the Bulgarians, in particular, was frequently more violent than with the Ottomans, who, wherever they could, sought to divide and rule. The creation of an independent Bulgarian Church (known as the Bulgarian Exarchate) in 1870, a critical stage in the progress towards Bulgarian nationhood, weakened the Greek dominance of the hierarchy of the Church in the region and created bitter rivalries between the adherents of the Ecumenical Patriarchate and of the Bulgarian Exarchate. Initially these rivalries were played out in ecclesiastical, educational and cultural propaganda. But at the turn of the century this war of words gave way to armed struggle between guerrilla bands supported and subsidised by the governments of the respective motherlands.

Against the background of the struggle for Macedonia, revolt once again erupted in Crete in the mid-1890s. This was supported

---

Caption for Plate 19 (*cont.*).

from Thessaly it emerged that the pickings of one brigand band had been shared with the Church and the deputy and his brothers.

20 The Corinth canal under construction in the 1880s. Begun
in 1882 and completed in 1893, the canal, a major feat of
engineering in its day, shortened the sea route from Piraeus,
the port of Athens, to Italy by a half, although its economic
benefits failed to live up to expectations. The cutting of the canal
was one of a number of important public works projects undertaken in the later nineteenth century. These are principally
associated with Kharilaos Trikoupis, the modernising prime
minister between 1882 and 1885, 1887 and 1890, and 1892
and 1895. He was well aware that improved communications
were the essential precondition for economic growth. During
the 1880s roads suitable for wheeled traffic increased threefold.
This gave a significant boost to the internal market, although
communications by land throughout much of the kingdom
remained poor. Much of the railway network of 'Old' Greece
as it exists today was established during the last two decades of
the century. When Trikoupis first became prime minister there
were only 12 kilometres of railway, linking Athens to Piraeus.
By the time of his death in 1896 almost 1,000 kilometres had
been constructed, often in difficult terrain, although it was not
until 1916 that the railway system was connected to that of
Europe. Another project begun in the 1880s was the draining
of Lake Copais in Thessaly, which yielded many thousands of
acres of fertile land. Some tentative steps were also made in the
direction of industrialisation, with the establishment of cotton,
wool and olive oil refining mills.

by the nationalist enthusiasts of the *Ethniki Etairia* or National Society. But despite his identification with an aggressive policy in foreign affairs, prime minister Deliyannis was initially cautious, for the Powers had blockaded Greece when he had sought to exploit Serbia's attack on Bulgaria in 1885, and on this occasion had sent a fleet to Crete. But, responding to intense popular pressure, he sent ships and troops to the island early in 1897. This was followed by a general mobilisation and, in April, the outbreak in Thessaly of the disastrous 'Thirty Day War' with the Ottoman Empire. Rapid and humiliating defeat starkly highlighted the gulf between Greece's irredentist aspirations and her modest military capabilities. In the words of one contemporary observer, Greece combined the appetites of a Russia with the resources of a Switzerland.

The ensuing peace settlement was not especially onerous for Greece. Crete was granted autonomous status under Ottoman suzerainty and Prince George, King George's second son, was appointed high commissioner. Greece was forced to make marginal frontier adjustments in favour of Turkey and to pay a war indemnity. At the insistence of the Powers an International Financial Commission was established to oversee the repayment of her large external debts, for in 1893 Trikoupis, the then prime minister, had been forced to declare the effective bankruptcy of the state. Poor economic prospects at home were the main impetus underlying the wave of emigration, principally to the United States, that got under way in the 1890s. It has been estimated that between 1890 and 1914, some 350,000 Greeks, almost all male and amounting to nearly one-seventh of the entire population, emigrated. The great majority left with the intention of returning to the homeland after working abroad for a few years to build up modest savings, but in the end most of the migrants became permanently established in their adopted countries. From now on the remittances which these frugal, hard-working and enterprising migrants sent back to their families were to constitute a key element in the balance of payments.

The crushing defeat of 1897 was to usher in a period of introspection and self-doubt, for the clear lesson of the war was that the single-handed pursuit of the 'Great Idea' was doomed. Whatever the weakness of the Ottoman Empire in its decline, Greece was likely to

21 The Greek representatives at the Congress of Berlin of June/
July 1878. Seated in the centre is their leader, Theodoros
Deliyannis, a strong champion of Greek irredentism, several
times prime minister and, with Kharilaos Trikoupis, the dominant
figure in the politics of the later nineteenth century. To his right
is Alexandros Rizos Rangavis, a scholar-diplomat, who was
Greece's envoy to Germany. Standing between the two is another
scholar-diplomat, Ioannis Gennadius, the chargé d'affaires in
London. The Congress of Berlin had been convened as a result of
the crisis that had convulsed the Balkans since 1875. The ensuing
war between Russia and Turkey had led to the creation, through
the Treaty of San Stephano (1878), of a 'Big Bulgaria' under
Russian patronage which embraced territories coveted, among
others, by Greece. Fortunately for Greece both Britain and
Austria-Hungary viewed such a development with alarm, and the
Congress was convened to cut San Stephano Bulgaria down to size.
Although Greece was not formally a party to the Congress, its
representatives were permitted to state their case for the incorporation of Crete, Thessaly and Epirus into the kingdom. The
Congress 'invited' the Ottoman Empire, whose chief representative
was an Ottoman Greek, Alexandros Karatheodoris Pasha, to
revise its frontiers in favour of Greece. Accordingly, in 1881,
Thessaly and the Arta district of Epirus were ceded to Greece.
Irredentism, enshrined in the 'Great Idea', was the dominant

come off worse in any armed conflict. Some intellectuals, indeed, argued that the country's future lay in some kind of condominium with the Ottoman Turks. They urged that every effort should be made to build on the already remarkable extent to which the Greeks still subject to Ottoman rule, who constituted over half of the total number of Greeks in the Near East, had managed to re-establish much of the economic, and even some of the political, power that they had enjoyed in the Ottoman Empire before 1821. During the later part of the century strenuous efforts, mostly inspired from within the kingdom, were made to inculcate a sense of Hellenic identity not only in the Greeks (and some non-Greeks) of Macedonia but in the large, and frequently Turkish-speaking, Greek populations of Asia Minor. However, most of these cultural propagandists envisaged eventual liberation by the kingdom rather than power-sharing with the Ottomans. Others advocated building up the resources of the kingdom as the essential precondition for further onslaughts on the Ottoman Empire, for such a strategy of confrontation had so far proved unsuccessful.

Following the death of Trikoupis and the defeat of 1897 the politics of the kingdom relapsed into their old malaise. Once again widespread disillusion set in at the jobbery and demagogy of traditional politics. Remarkably, however, within fifteen years of humiliating defeat at the hands of the Turks, Greece was to emerge as the up-and-coming power in the eastern Mediterranean. Her aspirations for the realisation of the 'Great Idea' and her self-proclaimed civilising mission in the East were no longer to appear to lie in the realms of fantasy. This restoration of self-confidence after the traumas of defeat was to be the work of Eleftherios Venizelos, the most charismatic politician of the first half of the twentieth century. He had gained his early political experience in autonomous Crete but was now to be projected to the forefront of the national political stage as a consequence of the military coup at Goudi of 1909.

Caption for Plate 21 (*cont.*).

ideology in the nineteenth-century kingdom. But, until the Balkan wars of 1912–13, Greece's hopes for territorial expansion were dependent on the goodwill of the Great Powers, as in the case of the incorporation of the Ionian islands in 1864 and of Thessaly in 1881.

22 A band of *Makedonomakhoi*, guerrilla fighters who, in the
early years of the twentieth century, pursued by armed force
the Greek claim to Macedonia as Ottoman rule in European
Turkey crumbled. This particular band, composed partly of
Cretans and partly of local men, was led by a Cretan officer in
the Greek army, Georgios Tsontos, who fought under the
nom de guerre of Captain Vardas. Other contenders to all or
part of Macedonia were the Bulgarians (the chief rivals of the
Greeks), the Serbs and the Albanians. Initially the struggle was
waged through religious and educational propaganda, with
fierce rivalry developing between those who accepted the religious authority of the Greek-controlled Ecumenical Patriarchate in Constantinople (the Patriarchists) and those who opted
for the jurisdiction of the Bulgarian Exarchate (the Exarchists)
which had been established by the Ottoman Porte in 1870.
Later the activities of the Bulgarian-inspired Macedonian Revolutionary Organisation (MRO), founded in 1893, were matched
by the Greek *Ethniki Etairia* or National Society and rival
bands fought for hegemony in the contested regions. A number
of Orthodox metropolitans, notable among them Germanos
Karavangelis, the bishop of Kastoria, patronised the armed
struggle and assisted it in various ways, as did the Athens government, which masterminded and supplied the struggle through
consular agents and undercover army officers. Gradually the

The Goudi coup which the Military League mounted in 1909 was in part a response to the Young Turk revolution of 1908 which had resulted in the restoration of the short-lived Ottoman constitution of 1876 and the overthrow of Sultan Abdul Hamid, or 'Abdul the Damned'. Initially, the Young Turks' promises of equality for all, whether Muslim, Christian or Jewish, aroused almost as much enthusiasm in Greece as in the Empire itself. But there were also fears that a revived Ottoman Empire might prove more difficult to dislodge from Macedonia, whose principal city, Salonica, had been the nerve-centre of the Young Turk conspiracy. Moreover, just as the Bulgarians responded to the Young Turk revolution by declaring their full independence from the Ottoman Empire and the Austrians by annexing Bosnia and Hercegovina, so the turbulent Cretans unilaterally declared *enosis* (union) with the kingdom of Greece.

The fumbling response of the politicians to this renewed Cretan crisis, combined with a faltering economy at home and the damaging effect on emigrant remittances (by now an important element in sustaining the economy) of an economic slow-down in the United States and in Egypt, another major outlet for Greek emigration, contributed to a groundswell of discontent against the traditional 'political world'. This acted as the catalyst for disgruntled army officers, commissioned and non-commissioned, to combine together in the Military League, headed by Colonel Nikolaos Zorbas. As so often in instances of military intervention, purely professional griev-ances provided the initial impetus for conspiracies which subse-quently acquired wider political objectives. There was resentment over promotion blockages, and a particular bone of contention was the feeling that the commander-in-chief, Crown Prince Constantine, was favouring his protégés within the armed forces.

From Goudi, on the outskirts of Athens, a sizeable proportion of the Athens garrison issued on 27 August 1909 a memorandum demanding the removal of the royal princes from the armed forces;

Caption for Plate 22 (*cont.*).

Greek bands got the upper hand, preparing the way for the annexation of large areas of Macedonia by the Greek armies at the time of the Balkan wars in 1912–13.

23 The interior of a bar in Piraeus, the seaport of Athens, towards the end of the nineteenth century. Seated on the right, a snappily dressed and heavily moustachioed *mangas*, or 'macho', holds his beer mug aloft. On the left, *doner* 'turning' kebab) or *gyro* is being prepared. Social life in town and country revolved around such institutions. As in the *Oraia Ellas* café (see p. 52) there are no women among either the staff or customers and such venues have remained an exclusively male preserve right up to modern times.

the ministries of war and the navy to be held by serving officers; and a programme of military and naval reconstruction. A number of other reforms of a non-military nature were sought. The League's demands received popular endorsement at a huge demonstration in Athens at the end of September. The prime minister, Dimitrios Rallis, resigned and his successor, Kyriakoulis Mavromikhalis, under the watchful eye of the Military League and following a threat to impose an outright military dictatorship, implemented a number of the desired reforming measures. The League, however, had little time for any of the old politicians and placed its faith instead in Eleftherios Venizelos, who had made a name for himself in the politics of his native Crete after the island had gained autonomous status in 1897. Aside from a clear genius for politics he had the inestimable advantage in the eyes of the League of being free of any association with the discredited 'political world' of the mainland. The members of the League could therefore step down in his favour without damage to their collective *philotimo*, or sense of honour, by appearing to capitulate to the political cliques of which they had been so critical.

Elections were held in August 1910 for a constituent assembly empowered to revise the 1864 constitution. Venizelos was not a candidate but his supporters emerged as the largest single bloc in parliament. In new elections, held in December of the same year, Venizelos did stand and his Liberal Party secured control of almost 300 out of 362 seats. He now had a clear mandate for his programme of domestic reform and economic and political modernisation, combined with the aggressive pursuit of the 'Great Idea'. To signal that he was no mere creature of the military, Venizelos reinstated Crown Prince Constantine to a high position in the army and released the officers who had been imprisoned for trying to thwart the Goudi putsch. In 1911 some fifty constitutional amendments were enacted. To reduce the scope for filibustering the parliamentary quorum was reduced from one-half to one-third of the total number of deputies. The legal basis for subsequent land reform was provided by measures for the expropriation of land and property in the national interest. Important educational reforms were introduced and, in an effort to reduce jobbery, appointment to posts in the civil service was made conditional on public examinations.

Modest measures of social reform were also initiated. These included minimum wages for women and children, the legalisation of trades unions and the outlawing of spurious 'company' unions. The innovation of a progressive income tax was widely evaded but it did symbolise a move away from earlier reliance on indirect taxes which bore disproportionately heavily on the poor. Venizelos already enjoyed the support of business interests and such measures helped to widen his electoral base by appealing to the incipient working class that had come into existence as a result of the modest degree of industrialisation over the previous thirty years. His mildly reforming measures helped to neutralise the development of strong socialist and agrarian movements such as appeared in some other Balkan

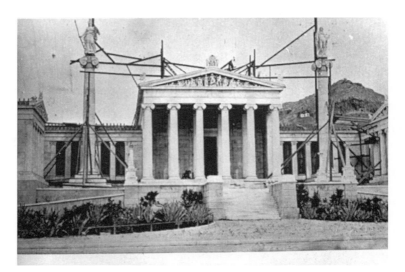

24 The Academy of Athens shortly before its completion in 1886. It was designed in an exuberant neo-classical style by the Danish architect Theophilos Hansen. The huge statues atop the columns were carved by Georgios Drosios and are of Athena and Apollo. The Academy is one of a complex of three such buildings (known as the 'Trilogy') designed by the Hansen brothers, the others being the university (1839–46), the work of Christian, and the national library (1885–1901), the work of Theophilos. They illustrate the extent to which the neo-classical idiom dominated the official architecture of the new state, an emphasis symbolic of its cultural orientation towards the heritage of ancient Greece. In the 1830s Athens was little more than a village, with a population of some 4,000, but its associations with the glories of the ancient past led to its being chosen as the capital in 1834. By the mid-nineteenth century its population had grown to 30,000, and the city had been endowed with some handsome public buildings. Besides the Hansen brothers, these were the work of Greek architects such as Lysandros Kaftantzoglou (the *Arsakeion* girls' school (1846–52) and the Eye Hospital (1852), the latter built, unusually, in the neo-Byzantine style) and Stamatis Kleanthis, the designer of the Duchesse de Plaisance's 'Ilissia palace' (1840–8), now the Byzantine Museum. Many of the public buildings of the capital (among them the Zappeion and the Averoff stadium built for the first modern Olympic games in 1896) were constructed with benefactions from wealthy Greeks of the diaspora. The Academy was built with a bequest from Simon Sinas, the hugely

countries. His commitment to the overhaul of the armed forces was symbolised by his taking personal charge of the ministries of the army and of the marine. A French military and a British naval mission assisted in the training of the armed forces, and the achievement of an overall budget surplus, after years of deficit, released funds for re-equipment.

> I steadfastly believe that . . . the material and moral resources of the Nation are enough, in the hands of committed workers for revival, to re-create a Greece worthy of the demands of present day civilisation, able to inspire the respect of the civilised world and to assume an honoured place in the family of civilised peoples, able finally, once it has become morally and materially strong, to contribute to the assurance of peace throughout the [Near] East under conditions assuring progress and prosperity to all the peoples of the East.
>
> Eleftherios Venizelos (1910)

After the years of drift Venizelos injected a new dynamism and optimism into public life and forged a new sense of national unity. His continuing popularity was demonstrated when, in elections held in March 1912, his supporters secured 146 seats in a 181-seat parliament (the 1910 parliament had been twice the size as it was a constituent assembly). But against this background of domestic renewal the clouds of war had been gathering. The early promise of equality for all ethnic groups in the Empire held out by the Young Turks soon gave way to a policy of forced 'Ottomanisation'. The question of the fate of Macedonia once again became a burning issue, made all the more acute by the emergence of the Albanian national movement. When Italy, seeking to demonstrate her credentials as a great power by acquiring a colonial empire of her own, struck against the Turks in Libya in 1911, the Slav states of the Balkans, Serbia, Bulgaria and Montenegro were keen to exploit the Empire's problems. Venizelos, however, was in something of a dilemma for, unlike the Serbs, Bulgarians and Montenegrins, the 'unredeemed' Greeks were not

---

Caption for Plate 24 (*cont.*).

wealthy son of Georgios Sinas, a Hellenised Vlach whose family came from Moschopolis in southern Albania, who had made his fortune in the Habsburg Empire and was himself the donor of Theophilos Hansen's observatory (1843–6).

25 A party at the Alexandrian home of Emmanouil Benakis, a Greek mercantile grandee, to mark the engagement, in 1887 or 1888, of his daughter. The bowler-hatted Benakis is standing immediately in front of the marquee. His daughter, Alexandra, is resting her arm on the shoulder of her Welsh fiancé, Tom Davies, who is sitting cross-legged in the centre. To the left, kneeling on the ground, is Alexandra's sister, Penelope, later, as Penelope Delta, a prolific writer of children's stories. Like many Egyptian Greeks she was a staunch Venizelist. Also in the photograph are members of the Khoremis family. Khoremis, Benakis and Company, founded in 1863 to exploit the boom in Egyptian cotton at the time of the American civil war, was by far the largest firm of Greek cotton brokers in Egypt. In Liverpool, where, as in Manchester, there was a thriving Greek community in the nineteenth century, they were represented by Davies, Benaki and Company. Emmanouil Benakis was closely associated with the modernising policies of Kharilaos Trikoupis and of Eleftherios Venizelos, who in 1910 placed him in charge of the newly founded ministry of national economy. During the nineteenth century there was a considerable migration, much of it from the Aegean islands (many of the wealthier merchants were from Chios), to Egypt where at the time of the First World War there were some 100,000 Greeks. The community, once the largest foreign colony in Egypt, went into a rapid decline with the rise to power of Nasser in 1952. During the late nineteenth and early twentieth centuries there were large and, for

compactly settled but were widely scattered throughout the Near East and were thus vulnerable to Turkish reprisals. If Greece stood aside, however, then she might miss out on the spoils in Macedonia.

Despite their conflicting interests, in the spring of 1912 treaties were concluded between Serbia and Bulgaria and between Greece and Bulgaria, while negotiations got under way for the Greek–Serbian treaty that was concluded in June 1913. During previous instances of Balkan turmoil, as in 1878, 1885 and at the time of the Greek–Turkish war of 1897, the Great Powers had not hesitated to intervene to protect their interests and the overall balance of power. In the summer of 1912 they likewise declared that they would not tolerate any disturbance of existing territorial boundaries. On this occasion, however, the Balkan states took no notice and, on 18 October 1912, Greece, Serbia and Bulgaria followed up Montenegro's prearranged attack by declaring war on the Ottoman Empire.

The Balkan allies, whose combined forces heavily outnumbered the Ottoman armies in Europe, achieved rapid and spectacular victories. By early November Greek forces had captured Salonica, beating by only a few hours the Bulgarians, who likewise laid claim to this rich commercial city with the best port in the northern Aegean. Greece's newly equipped navy quickly established superiority in the Aegean, liberating Chios, Mytilini and Samos in the process. The Dodecanese, however, had been 'temporarily' occupied by the Italians earlier in the year, in an attempt to put pressure on the Turks to withdraw from Libya. The 'twelve islands' were not to be incorporated into Greece until 1947. In February 1913, Greek troops captured Ioannina, the capital of Epirus. The Turks recognised the gains of the Balkan allies by the Treaty of London of May 1913.

The allies may have shared a common hostility towards the Ottoman Empire but their conflicting territorial claims in Macedonia rendered their alliance a fragile one. In June 1913, Greece and Serbia concluded a treaty in which they agreed to a division

---

Caption for Plate 25 (*cont.*).

the most part, prosperous Greek communities throughout the Near and Middle East, *I kath'imas Anatoli* (Our East) to use the evocative Greek phrase.

26 A painting of a travelling strongman, Panagis Koutalianos, the *New Hercules*, painted in 1910 by Theophilos Khatzi-mikhail on the wall of a bakery in Velentza near Volos. Born some time between 1866 and 1873, Theophilos, as he was gen-erally known, trained as a plasterer but for most of his life worked as a journeyman painter, decorating the walls of coffee shops, tavernas, shops and houses, first of all in Smyrna, with its very large Greek population, and then, for some thirty years, in the villages of Mount Pilion near Volos in Thessaly. Latterly he moved to his native island Mytilini (Lesvos) where he died in 1934. He drew his themes from ancient history, from the war

of the spoils in Macedonia at the expense of Bulgaria. The Bulgarians, geographically the closest to the Ottoman capital, for their part felt that they had borne the brunt of the fighting and that their gains had not been commensurate with their sacrifices. They now turned against Greece and Serbia. Romania, which had stood aloof from the first Balkan war, now entered the fray by attacking Bulgaria. The second Balkan war was of short duration and the Bulgarians were soon forced to the negotiating table. By the Treaty of Bucharest (August 1913) Bulgaria was obliged to accept a highly unfavourable territorial settlement, although she did retain an Aegean outlet at Dedeagatch (now Alexandroupolis in Greece). Greece's sovereignty over Crete was now recognised but her ambition to annex northern Epirus, with its substantial Greek population, was thwarted by the incorporation of the region into an independent Albania.

Despite this setback, Greece's territorial gains had been truly dramatic. The territories of 'New' Greece added some 70 per cent to her land area, while her population increased from approximately 2,800,000 to 4,800,000. But by no means all these new citizens were Greeks. The largest community in Salonica, for instance, comprised the Sephardic Jews, the descendants of the Jews expelled from Spain in 1492 and still Spanish-speaking. Far from looking upon the Greeks as liberators the Jews saw them as competitors for the control of the prosperous commerce of the city. Elsewhere in the newly acquired territories there were substantial numbers of Slavs, Muslims (mainly Turks) and Vlachs, speaking a form of Romanian. At the best of times, the integration of these newly acquired territories with their ethnically diverse populations would have posed problems,

---

Caption for Plate 26 (*cont.*).

for independence and from everyday life. Itinerant strongmen, the climax of whose act is to hold aloft exploding cannons, can still from time to time be encountered in Greece. For much of his life Theophilos' talent as a primitive painter went unrecognised and he lived in poverty, but a few years before he died he was patronised by the Paris-based art critic Tériade (Efstratios Eleftheriadis), who helped introduce him to a wider audience in Greece and abroad. In the 1960s Tériade built a museum in Mytilini to house paintings by Theophilos.

27 'The discreet charm of the Ottoman Greek bourgeoisie.' The
wedding reception in 1905, at the splendid Zarifis mansion on
the Bosphorus, of Eleni Zarifi and Stephanos Evgenidis, members of two of the foremost banking families in nineteenth-
century Constantinople. Contrast the luxury of the Zarifi/
Evgenidis wedding with the simplicity of the Marcellas/
Mouskondis wedding in Salt Lake City sixteen years later
(page 110). Eleni Zarifi's father, Georgios, one of the founders
of the Zafiropoulos and Zarifis bank, had amassed a huge
fortune in supplying coal (and eggs) to the British fleet and
army during the Crimean war (1853–6). He played an important role in the management of the Ottoman public debt and,
as the personal banker and close confidant of Sultan Abdul
Hamid (1876–1908), he was a man of immense wealth and
influence. Among other benefactions he paid for the Greek
school of Philippoupolis (now Plovdiv in Bulgaria) and for
the reconstruction of the *Megali tou Genous Skholi* (Great
School of the Nation) which dominates the Phanar quarter of
Constantinople. Another very rich Greek banker, Christaki
Efendi Zographos, built the most important Greek boys' school
in the Ottoman capital, known as the *Zographeion*. One of
the more remarkable aspects of the history of the Greeks during
the nineteenth century is the way in which they were able to

but the process was to be complicated by the consequences for Greece of the outbreak of the First World War.

By the summer of 1913 Greece had emerged as a significant Mediterranean power. Under Venizelos' inspired leadership, the hitherto elusive vision of the 'Great Idea' appeared to have moved beyond the vapourings of romantic nationalists to the realms of possibility. King George I had died at the hands of a madman while on a visit to Salonica in March 1913. It was widely, though in the event erroneously, expected that his successor, Crown Prince Constantine, would adopt the style of Constantine XII rather than Constantine I, to demonstrate that he was the direct heir and successor of Constantine XI Palaiologos, the last emperor of Byzantium. But during the period of the First World War the 'Great Idea' ceased to be the sole ideology around which the great mass of the nation could unite, and became instead one of the sources of the massive cleavage in society known as the *Ethnikos Dikhasmos*, or National Schism, which split the country into two rival, and at times warring, camps. Not for the first and certainly not for the last time Greece was to be riven with domestic dissension at a time of grave international threat.

A major contributory factor in destroying the remarkable and unprecedented consensus established by Venizelos between 1910 and the period of the Balkan wars was a fundamental dispute between Venizelos and King Constantine over the question of participation in the World War. Venizelos had a strong emotional attachment to Britain and France, which, with Russia, made up the *Entente*

Caption for Plate 27 (*cont.*).

re-establish not only much of the economic but also a good part of the political power in the Ottoman Empire that they had enjoyed during the century or so before the outbreak of the war of independence in 1821, a power that they were to lose once again with the Empire's collapse in the aftermath of the First World War. The first Ottoman minister to independent Greece was an Ottoman Greek, Kostaki Mousouros Pasha. He was a vigorous defender of the interests of his Turkish masters not only in Athens but in Vienna, Turin and London, where he served as ambassador for almost thirty years (1851–79) before his death in 1891. Another Ottoman Greek, Alexandros Karatheodoris Pasha, served as Ottoman foreign minister.

Treaty of Bucharest
August 1913

- Bulgaria to Romania
- Turkey to Montenegro
- Turkey to Serbia
- Turkey to Albania
- Turkey to Bulgaria
- Turkey to Greece

AUSTRIA-HUNGARY

RUSSIA

ROMANIA

MONTE-NEGRO

S E R B I A

BULGARIA

Black Sea

ALBANIA

T U R K E Y

I o n i a n   S e a

GREECE

Aegean Sea

150 km

miles 100

Map 4 The outcome of the Balkan wars, 1912–13

Powers. He saw them both as the probable victors and as the powers most likely to look with favour on the achievement of the country's remaining territorial ambitions. Constantine, however, an honorary field marshal in the German army and married to the sister of Kaiser Wilhelm II, had a greater respect for the military capability of the Central Powers, Germany and Austria-Hungary. Aware of the vulnerability of Greece to British naval power, the king advocated neutrality. From the outset of the war Venizelos was anxious to commit Greek troops alongside those of the *Entente*. The British foreign secretary, Sir Edward Grey, declined the offer, for he was anxious to keep both the Ottoman Empire and Bulgaria out of the war. To have accepted Greece, which was hostile to both, as an ally might have precipitated their alignment with the Central Powers.

In fact, in November 1914 the Ottoman Empire sided with Germany and Austria-Hungary (prompting, *inter alia*, the formal annexation of Cyprus by Britain). But this served only to increase the strategic importance of Bulgaria. Therefore, in January 1915, Grey proposed that Greece cede to Bulgaria the recently acquired region of Kavala, Drama and Serres in return for compensation in northern Epirus and the even more attractive, if vague, promise of 'important territorial concessions on the coast of Asia Minor', which with its large Greek population was a major focus of irredentist ambition. Grey was reluctant to be more specific, for he was also wooing Italy, which likewise cast a covetous eye on parts of Asia Minor. Venizelos was nonetheless willing to go along with Grey's proposal. The king and his military advisers, however, wanted more concrete assurances before consenting to give up territory so recently won. Matters were further complicated when, in February 1915, the *Entente* allies launched the ill-fated Dardanelles campaign. Venizelos was anxious to participate, although Constantinople, the eventual objective of the landings, had already been promised to Russia in the event of success. The king, having initially agreed to Greek participation, changed his mind, influenced by the resignation of the acting chief of staff, Colonel Ioannis Metaxas, a future military dictator, who feared that Bulgaria would take advantage of any Greek involvement.

Confronted by this volte-face on the part of a king whose constitutional powers over the conduct of foreign policy were substantial but ill-defined, Venizelos resigned on 6 March 1915. Thus began a process which was to result eighteen months later in the existence of two rival governments. Venizelos regarded the clear majority he received in new elections held in June as a mandate for his pro-*Entente* policies. When he returned to office, however, he once again found himself embarked on a collision course with the king, for, in September 1915, Bulgaria, now aligned with the Central Powers, attacked Serbia. This raised the question as to whether Greece was bound, as Venizelos and his supporters insisted, to go to Serbia's aid under the terms of the June 1913 treaty. Venizelos invited Britain and France to send an expeditionary force to Salonica in support of the Serbs. Once again this was a move which the king had originally sanctioned, only subsequently to change his

H ΚΑΤΑΛΗΨΙΣ ΤΗΣ ΧΙΟΥ   L' OCCUPATION DE L'ILE DE CHIO

28 A *laiki gravoura*, a popular engraving such as would have adorned the walls of coffee shops and the homes of patriots, depicting the capture of the island of Chios on 24 November 1912 during the first Balkan war. The war had got under way in October when Montenegro, Serbia, Bulgaria and Greece, temporarily sinking their territorial rivalries and defying attempts by the Great Powers to maintain the peace, combined to drive the Ottoman Empire out of Europe. Enjoying a massive numerical superiority, the Balkan allies made rapid headway. Hostilities broke out on 18 October and within a few days Elasson (23 October) and Kozani (25 October) had been captured. On 8 November, the feast of St Dimitrios, the patron saint of the city, Greek troops entered the port of Salonica, the greatest prize in Macedonia, just a few hours ahead of a large Bulgarian contingent. Greek command of the sea led to the capture of the islands of the eastern Aegean, while Crete was formally annexed to the kingdom.

mind. As a consequence Constantine, for the second time within six months, called upon Venizelos to resign as prime minister.

The gulf separating the king and his charismatic former prime minister was now total. Venizelos and his supporters claimed that the king had grossly exceeded his constitutional powers. They accordingly abstained from new elections held in December 1915, in which the turn-out was scarcely a quarter of that in the previous June. But there were other dimensions to the 'National Schism'. Venizelos was by now wholly identified with an aggressive policy in the prosecution of the 'Great Idea', whereas the king and his supporters were advocates of 'a small but honourable Greece', which should first consolidate its hold over the new territories before engaging in hazardous irredentist adventures. Royalists, too, most strongly entrenched in 'Old' Greece, the original heartland of the independent kingdom, were fearful of Venizelos' identification with capitalist modernisation and social reform. Backward looking, they represented the large constituency that was fearful of the prospect and pace of change.

There were Venizelist nationalists and anti-Venizelist nationalists, Venizelist marxists and anti-Venizelist marxists. And it was a thousand times easier for a Venizelist nationalist to reach an understanding with a Venizelist marxist than with an anti-Venizelist nationalist.

Georgios Theotokas, *Argo* (1936)

The deterioration in relations between Constantine and Venizelos was paralleled by mounting discord between the *Entente* and the royalist government. The Salonica front had been established by British and French troops in October 1915 in a country that was still neutral, as remained the case when the *Entente* occupied the island of Corfu in January 1916 to provide a secure haven for the Serbian army in retreat through Albania. Friction increased when the Athens government refused to allow the Serbs to cross by land from Corfu to Salonica to reform their front and when Greece surrendered to the Bulgarians, without resistance, the strategically important Fort Rupel in Macedonia.

In August, pro-Venizelist army officers in Salonica, backed by the pro-*Entente Ethniki Amyna*, or National Defence, organisation, launched a coup against the royalist government. A few weeks later, Venizelos left the capital for his native stronghold of Crete and, subsequently, after a triumphant procession through the newly liberated islands, made for Salonica. The principal city of 'New' Greece, Salonica, like the rest of the territories recently freed from the Turks,

29 A scene from one of the two elections held in 1915. A member
of the city's large Jewish community is casting his vote at a
temporary polling station erected in the church of *Aghia Sophia*
(Holy Wisdom) in Salonica. Some of the bystanders wear the fez,
for the city had been incorporated into the Greek state only three
years previously during the first Balkan war. No women are
visible; they were granted the vote only in 1952. The voting
system depicted was in force between 1864 and 1920. The
voter inserted his hand down the tube and dropped a lead
ballot into either the 'yes' (white) or the 'no' (black) sections of
a box. Some enthusiastic supporters of Venizelos were given to
demonstrating their devotion by arriving at the polling booths
with gold ballots (whether they actually cast them is another
matter). The voter could vote for or against all the candidates,
each of whom had a box. Depending on the number of seats
allocated to each constituency the successful candidates were
those with the largest number of 'yes' votes. Agents for the
candidates stood behind the rows of boxes. Their role was to

was passionately committed to the Venizelist cause. Here Venizelos made the split irrevocable by establishing a provisional government complete with its own army. Although this move enjoyed the blessing of the *Entente*, the Salonica government was not, initially, formally recognised for fear of provoking outright civil war. Meanwhile, increasing pressure was placed on the royal government in Athens. In December 1916 British and French forces landed in Piraeus and Athens to enforce the neutrality of the areas controlled by the royalist government, to back up demands for war materials and to secure control of the railway to the north. Shooting broke out and the allies were forced into an ignominious retreat. This was followed up by wide-ranging purges of known supporters of Venizelos in 'Old' Greece, southern Roumeli and the Peloponnese, which remained loyal to the king.

The allies, having gone out of their way to humiliate the royalists, exacted a severe revenge by recognising Venizelos' provisional government, by demanding reparations and by instituting a blockade which caused severe hardship in royalist-controlled areas. These increasingly flagrant violations of Greece's sovereignty culminated in June 1917 in the peremptory demand that King Constantine leave the country on the ground that he had violated his oath as a constitutional monarch. Constantine duly departed, without formally abdicating, being succeeded not by his eldest son, George, but by his second son, Alexander. Venizelos now became prime minister of a notionally unified but still bitterly divided Greece. One of his first acts was to recall the June 1915 parliament, in which he had enjoyed a hefty majority, arguing that the chamber elected in December of

---

Caption for Plate 29 *(cont.)*.

urge the voter to support their particular candidate and to try to determine in which section the ballot had been cast. This was not especially difficult, so that the secrecy of the ballot was somewhat notional, particularly in rural areas where all the voters would be known to the election agents. Since 1922, when the lead ballot was abandoned, the electoral system has changed with bewildering frequency, as governments of whatever political complexion have sought to manipulate it to their own advantage.

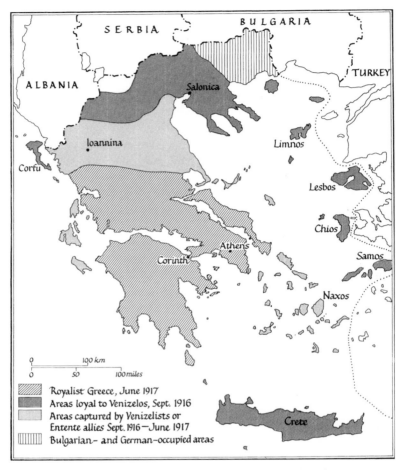

Map 5 The geography of the National Schism: 'Old' and 'New'
Greece in 1916/17

that year was fraudulent. Predictably, the 'Lazarus chamber', so
called because it had been raised from the dead, rewarded Venizelos
with a massive vote of confidence.

Prominent supporters of the deposed king were exiled as 'Ger-
manophiles'. Judges, civil servants and teachers were dismissed
wholesale. The most sensitive purges took place in the armed forces,

setting a precedent for the inter-war scourge of purge and counter-purge with rival factions, on gaining power, removing from the armed forces Venizelists or royalists as the case might be. As a mark of his commitment to the *Entente* cause, Venizelos deployed nine divisions on the Macedonian front, where they took part in the successful offensive launched in September 1918. This helped to precipitate the collapse on the western front that resulted in the 11 November armistice. Venizelos also committed two divisions to the ill-fated allied attempt to crush the Bolshevik revolution which, by removing Russia from the war in 1917, had simultaneously removed Greece's only competitor for hegemony over the Christian East. A further reason for the dispatch of these troops was that there were some 600,000 Greeks in southern Russia and the Pontos.

As leader of his country's delegation to the Paris peace conference Venizelos sought to reap the reward for his steadfast devotion to the *Entente* cause. His overriding objective was Smyrna (a city with more Greek inhabitants than Athens) and its hinterland. This was an area more or less comprising the Ottoman *vilayet* (province) of Aydin and was a long-cherished objective of Greek nationalists, although the statistics did not agree as to whether Greeks or Turks were in the majority. Greece also favoured international control (in the form of a League of Nations or American mandate) of Constantinople and sought the whole of western and eastern Thrace up to the vicinity of the Ottoman capital. If these demands could be achieved Venizelos was prepared to be flexible over claims to the Dodecanese, Italian sovereignty over which had been recognised by the 1915 Treaty of London, and over northern Epirus, the partially Greek-inhabited region that had been incorporated into Albania in 1913.

Before any settlement could be reached, however, contingents of Italian troops landed in Antalya in south-west Asia Minor and began to move in the direction of the Smyrna region. This alarmed not only the Greek, but the British, French and American governments as well. In advance of any clear understanding among the allies as to how the Ottoman Empire in general was to be liquidated or as to the future of Asia Minor in particular, Britain, France and America agreed to the landing of Greek troops in Smyrna. On 15 May

30 The Greek *Parthenagogeion*, or girls' school, in Ushak in the
interior of Asia Minor in 1921, shortly before the Greek presence in the region was to be extinguished forever. It was to
liberate the 'unredeemed' Greeks of Asia Minor that Greece
became embroiled in her ill-fated Anatolian entanglement
between 1919 and 1922. Outside the Ottoman capital itself
there were three main areas of Greek settlement: the coastal
regions of the Sea of Marmara and the Aegean; Cappadocia,
where many were Turkish-speaking, although Greek did preca-
riously survive in some communities; and Pontos on the south-
eastern shores of the Black Sea, whose Greek dialect was by
1922 well on the way to detaching itself from the main body of
the language. Early in 1915, the *Entente* allies offered Greece
important, but unspecified, territorial concessions in Asia Minor
in return for the cession of parts of Macedonia to Bulgaria.
Venizelos, the prime minister at the time, was intoxicated by
the vision of doubling yet again the territory of a Greece that had
already doubled in size during the Balkan wars. King
Constantine and his advisers were more pessimistic about the
formidable geographical and military obstacles. When Venizelos
once again became prime minister in 1917, he was quick to align
Greece with the British and French who had engineered his
return to power. In 1919, the victorious allied powers, fearful
of Italian ambitions in the area, gave their blessing to the Greek
occupation of the Smyrna (Izmir) region. In August 1920, the

1919 a substantial Greek force, protected by allied warships, occupied the city. The ostensible purpose was to protect the local Greek population from Turkish reprisals. But, in an ominous presentiment of future trouble, the landings were marked by Greek atrocities, with some 350 Turks being killed or wounded in fighting with Greek troops. Despite the ruthless punishment of the Greek culprits and the arrival a few days later of the Greek high commissioner, Aristeides Stergiadis, an austere disciplinarian with a genuine commitment to the even-handed treatment of Greeks and Turks, the damage had been done. The landings in Smyrna had acted as the catalyst for a revived Turkish nationalism under the leadership of Mustafa Kemal (subsequently Atatürk), who repudiated the authority of the supine Turkish government centred in Istanbul. Before long irregular warfare had broken out between rival Greek and Turkish forces.

In August 1920, more than a year after the Smyrna landings, the Treaty of Sèvres, which contained the terms of the peace settlement with the Ottoman Empire, was signed. The most important provision in the treaty from the Greek perspective was that their administration of the Smyrna region was to continue for a further five years. Turkish sovereignty was to be retained but, after five years, the region could be formally annexed to Greece if the local parliament that was to be created so requested, in which case the League of Nations might require a plebiscite. Venizelos was confident that the requisite majority could be secured through the in-migration of Greeks from other regions of Asia Minor and as a consequence of the higher birthrate of the Anatolian Greeks in comparison with their Turkish neighbours. The treaty was greeted with much

---

Caption for Plate 30 (*cont.*).

Treaty of Sèvres gave formal sanction to the occupation and Venizelos' supporters spoke triumphantly of the emergence of 'the Greece of the two continents [Europe and Asia] and the five seas [Ionian, Aegean, Mediterranean, Marmara and Black]'. But critics of the Anatolian adventure were to be proved right and the campaign was to end in disaster.

31 Refugees crowded on the waterfront at Smyrna on 13 September 1922 after fire had devastated much of the Greek, Armenian and Frankish (European) quarters of the city which the Turks had called *Gâvur Izmir* or 'Infidel Izmir', so large was its non-Muslim population. Only the Turkish and Jewish quarters survived the holocaust. The fire had been started by the Turks after they had retaken the city following the chaotic defeat of the Greek forces occupying Asia Minor. At the outset, the Turkish occupation of the city in the wake of the retreating Greek troops had been relatively orderly. But law and order broke down as Turkish troops sought their revenge, initially against the Armenians. In the ensuing bloodbath, in which some 30,000 Christians perished, Archbishop Chrysostomos of Smyrna was hacked to death after being handed over to a Turkish mob, meeting a martyr's death a century after the execution of the Ecumenical Patriarch Grigorios V. A few minutes after this photograph was taken the heavily overloaded boat on the left capsized. The cutter in the foreground flying the American flag is probably from the USS *Simpson*. Eyewitnesses reported panic-stricken refugees jumping into the water to escape the flames and that their terrified screaming could be heard miles away. In such an ignominious fashion a 2,500-year Greek presence in Asia Minor came to an abrupt end. The elusive vision of the *Megali Idea*, or Great Idea, was to be consumed in the ashes of Smyrna.

enthusiasm in Greece. Venizelos' supporters talked excitedly of his having created a Greece of 'the two continents and the five seas', the two continents being Europe and Asia and the five seas being the Mediterranean, the Aegean, the Ionian, the Sea of Marmara and the Black Sea. But, ominously for Greece, the Treaty of Sèvres was never to be ratified by the Turks and the whole grandiose irredentist edifice in Asia Minor was soon to collapse.

Two months after the signing of the treaty, King Alexander died of blood poisoning caused by a bite from a pet monkey. His death revived the constitutional question and with it all the passions of the 'National Schism' and transformed the elections due in the following month, November, into a contest between Venizelos and the exiled King Constantine, Alexander's father. In these elections, Venizelos, the triumphal architect, or so it seemed, of a 'Greater Greece' was roundly defeated, ignominiously losing his own seat in the process. Anti-Venizelists, for the most part supporters of King Constantine, secured 246 out of 370 seats. Defeat may have come as a surprise to virtually all observers but it was clear that the result reflected war weariness (the country had been on a war footing for the best part of eight years), coupled with feelings of resentment and humiliation at the flagrant meddling in the country's internal affairs by Britain and France and at the vengeful and arbitrary behaviour of some of Venizelos' supporters during his second period in office between 1917 and 1920. During the election campaign, royalists, as protagonists of a 'small but honourable Greece', had criticised the prolongation of the war. But once in power it became apparent that they intended to continue with the campaign in Asia Minor.

Britain, France and Italy voiced their opposition to the king's return, but in a patently rigged plebiscite there were 999,960 votes for the restoration of the monarchy and only 10,383 against. Once returned to power the royalists took their revenge on the Venizelists and the grim cycle of victimising political opponents once more got under way. Politically inspired changes in the command structure of the forces in Asia Minor did nothing to enhance their fighting capabilities. Italy and France found in the royalist restoration a useful pretext for making their peace with Mustafa Kemal and abandoning their own claims to parts of Asia Minor. In April 1921, all the allies declared their strict neutrality, although neither the Italians nor the

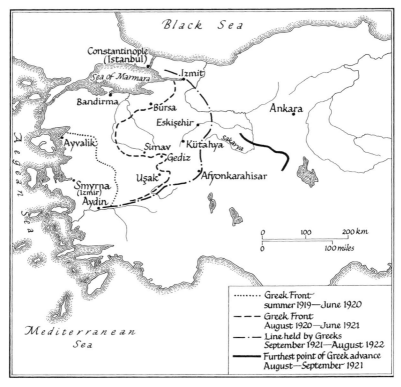

Map 6 Greece in Asia Minor, 1919–22
Source: Michael Llewellyn Smith, *Ionian vision* (1973)

French had qualms about selling arms to the Turkish nationalists. Although they took unwarranted encouragement from the philhellenic statements of the British prime minister, Lloyd George, the Greeks were unable to obtain supplies or to secure loans.

A major offensive launched in March 1921 ground to a halt at the Sakarya river, tantalisingly close to the Kemalist stronghold of Ankara, and leaving dangerously exposed lines of communication. Thereafter the Greek military and political situation steadily deteriorated. In March 1922 the Greeks declared their willingness to accept a British proposal for a compromise peace based on the withdrawal of their forces and the establishment of a League of Nations protectorate over the Greeks of Asia Minor. But the Turks, fully aware that the military tide had turned in their favour, looked to a military reckoning. The end, when it came, was swift and devastating. Mustafa Kemal launched a massive offensive on 26 August which quickly turned into a rout. The Greek forces withdrew to the coast in disarray, evacuating Smyrna on 8 September. The Turkish occupation of the city was accompanied by a massacre of some 30,000 Greek and Armenian Christians. In the great fire that ensued only the Turkish and Jewish quarters survived. 'Infidel Izmir', as the Turks had called Smyrna on account of its huge non-Muslim population, was consumed in the holocaust as panic-stricken refugees sought to escape to the neighbouring Greek islands.

4

Catastrophe and occupation and their consequences 1923–49

The chaotic rout of the Greek forces in Asia Minor at the hands of the Turkish nationalists under Mustafa Kemal (Atatürk) signalled the collapse of the 'Great Idea' and an ignominious end to Greece's 'civilising mission' in the Near East. As the demoralised remnants of the Greek armies, beset by tens of thousands of panic-stricken and destitute refugees, flooded the Aegean islands and the mainland, a group of Venizelist officers seized power. At their head was Colonel Nikolaos Plastiras, who was to remain a major player on the political scene until the 1950s. King Constantine abdicated, briefly to be replaced by his eldest son, who reigned as King George II. A new civilian government was installed but there could be no doubt that effective power lay in the hands of the revolutionary committee. The army, indeed, was to be a critical factor in the political life of the country throughout the inter-war period.

The bitterness and chaos of defeat were compounded by the feeling that Greece had been abandoned in her hour of greatest need by traditional friends. It was perhaps inevitable that there should also be a hunt for domestic scapegoats. Eight politicians and soldiers, including the military commander in Asia Minor, General Hadzianestis, were court-martialled on charges of high treason, although it was clear that there had been no deliberate treachery. This judicial charade culminated in the execution by firing squad of six of the accused. These included Hadzianestis, who had showed signs of being mentally unbalanced, and Dimitrios Gounaris, the former prime minister, who was so ill with typhus that he had to be helped to the place of execution. The 'Trial of the Six', stoking up as it did the already venomous feud between supporters and opponents of Venizelos, was to poison the political climate of the inter-war period.

For a time the revolutionary committee contemplated launching an offensive on the Thracian front where its forces were still in good order. However, it soon became apparent that peace could only come through a negotiated settlement with the new Turkish republic, which looked upon the Greek–Turkish war of 1919–22 as its own war of independence. A peace conference was convened in Lausanne at which the Greek case was put with his customary diplomatic finesse by Venizelos. But he was unable to prevent virtually all the territorial gains of the Treaty of Sèvres from being wiped out. The exchange of populations that formed part of the Lausanne settlement was not an entirely novel solution to Greek–Turkish antagonism, for Venizelos had himself proposed such a measure, albeit on a more limited scale, on the eve of the First World War. The basis of the exchange was religion, rather than language or 'national consciousness'. This had some anomalous consequences, for, just as many of the Orthodox Christians of Asia Minor were Turkish-speaking, so many of the Muslims of Greece, and particularly of Crete, were Greek-speaking. The Greeks of Istanbul and of the islands of Imvros and Tenedos, which command the entrance to the Dardanelles, together with the Ecumenical Patriarchate, the senior patriarchate in the Orthodox world, were exempted from the exchange, as were the Muslim, predominantly Turkish, inhabitants of Greek Thrace.

Despite its fearful consequences in terms of human misery there was probably no realistic alternative to such an uprooting. The events of recent years, the cycle of atrocity and revenge, had destroyed beyond repair the possibility of the peaceful symbiosis of Greek and Turk. Some 1,100,000 Greeks moved to the kingdom, as a consequence of the 'catastrophe', as the Asia Minor disaster came to be known, and of the ensuing exchange. In return some 380,000 Muslims were transferred to Turkey. In addition there were approximately 100,000 Greek refugees from revolutionary Russia and from Bulgaria. Among the incoming refugees there was a disproportionately high ratio of women (and of widows) and of orphans

32 General Georgios Hadzianestis testifying at the court martial of 'The Six' in November 1922. The other defendants can be
seen in the front row with their backs to the camera. The
'catastrophe' of September 1922 had prompted a military
coup. King Constantine I went into exile, briefly to be succeeded
by his eldest son, George II. The new revolutionary committee
court-martialled the last military commander in Asia Minor,
General Hadzianestis, together with seven leading politicians
and military figures, including two prime ministers, Dimitris
Gounaris and Petros Protopapadakis (fourth and first from
the left in the front row), charging them with high treason.
This was an absurd charge, for whatever their failings there
had been no wilful betrayal. The court martial was presided
over by General Othonaios and as he and his fellow officers
had been selected by the revolutionary committee there
was little doubt about the outcome of what was essentially a
judicial farce. At 6.30 in the morning of 28 November General
Othonaios pronounced the death sentence on six of the eight
defendants. By 10.30 this had been carried out. Gounaris,
who half-way through the trial had fallen ill with typhus, had
to be helped to the place of execution, while Hadzianestis
appeared for some time to have been deranged. It was popularly
believed that he thought his legs to be made of glass, which
might snap if he stood up. In a separate trial Prince Andrew
(the father of the Duke of Edinburgh), who had for a time

(of whom there were some 25,000 in a population of approximately 6 million) as a result of the dislocations consequent on war, flight and deportation. Many of the refugees knew only Turkish. If they knew Greek, it was frequently either the dialect of the Pontos region on the southern shores of the Black Sea, which was scarcely intelligible to the inhabitants of the kingdom, or the stilted *katharevousa* (purified) Greek of the schools. They encountered a considerable degree of prejudice on the part of the natives, who derisively referred to the incomers, among other epithets, as *giaourtovaptismenoi*, or 'baptised in yoghourt', a reference to their extensive use of yoghourt in their (noticeably better) cuisine. Likewise many of the Anatolian Greeks from great Ottoman cities such as Smyrna looked down on what they regarded as the provincial ways of the *palaioelladites*, the inhabitants of 'Old' Greece.

The tensions occasioned by the integration of the territories newly acquired in the Balkan wars had been a significant contributory factor to the development of the National Schism. These were to be exacerbated by the massive influx of refugees, with their nostalgia for their *khamenes patrides*, or lost homelands, and it was to be many decades before they were to be brought into the mainstream of society. The enormous practical problems of their resettlement were overseen in a remarkably efficient fashion by a Refugee Settlement Commission, which was chaired by an American and which raised loans (on rather disadvantageous terms) on international markets. The remaining large estates, including those belonging to the monasteries of Mount Athos, were broken up to provide smallholdings. Many of the refugees, however, proved to be a glut on the labour market and were obliged to eke out an impoverished existence on the fringes of the large towns where the run-down refugee quarters retained their distinctive identity and radical political ethos until well after the

---

Caption for Plate 32 (*cont.*).

commanded the Second Army Corps, was tried for insubordination in similarly bizarre circumstances. He was sentenced to banishment and to be stripped of his military rank. The 'Trial of the Six' was to cast a long shadow over the politics of the interwar period and gave something of the quality of a blood feud to the bitter animosity between Venizelists and royalists.

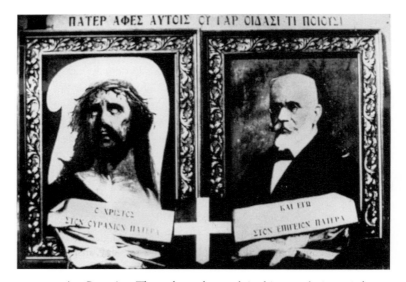

33 As Georgios Theotokas observed in his novel *Argo* (of which an English translation (London 1951) is available), Eleftherios Venizelos was, for one half of Greece, leader, saviour and symbol; for the other he was Satan. These two propaganda postcards reflect such a Manichaean view. The first dates

Second World War. Some of the refugees were able to bring some capital, or at least their entrepreneurial spirit, with them and they injected a new element of dynamism into the economy. The arrival of writers and poets such as Georgios Theotokas and Georgios Seferis and of painters such as Photis Kontoglou were to make a distinctive contribution to the country's cultural life.

The influx of refugees in such numbers and their resettlement principally in the recently acquired lands of 'New' Greece significantly altered the country's ethnic balance. Greeks who had been in a minority in Greek Macedonia in the immediate aftermath of the Balkan wars now became a clear majority. The census of 1928 recorded that almost half the inhabitants of Macedonia were of refugee origin.

Caption for Plate 33 (*cont.*).

from the period of the National Schism during the First World War. Based on the phrenological busts popular in the nineteenth century, and entitled 'THE GREAT BRAIN', it points to the wicked characteristics attributed to Venizelos by his enemies, namely FALSEHOOD, PLUNDER, TREACHERY, HOT AIR, CUNNING, INTRIGUE, DISHONOUR, CONSPIRACY, IMBECILITY, COWARDICE, OBSTINACY, MEGALOMANIA, INSOLENCE. The second was printed following Venizelos' unexpected defeat in the election of November 1920, within months of the Treaty of Sèvres which, on paper at least, represented an astonishing diplomatic triumph. Published as a token of reproof for those who had voted against OUR GREAT LEADER, it was sent by the thousand to Venizelos on his name day by Greeks of Smyrna, the overwhelming majority of whom looked upon him as their liberator. The publisher was arrested for causing disaffection among the troops at the front. The upper text gives Christ's words on the cross: 'Father, forgive them; for they know not what they do.' The text at the foot of the picture of Christ reads 'Christ to the Heavenly Father', that at the foot of the picture of Venizelos 'And I to the Earthly Father'. The card is testimony to the almost religious fervour which charismatic political figures can, to this day, inspire. In the museum attached to the Liberal Club in Athens, which constitutes a kind of shrine to the memory of Venizelos, the bullet-ridden car in which he survived an assassination attempt in 1933, the gold *sphairidia* or ballots cast by his devotees in the election of November 1920, even his half-smoked cigar, are reverently preserved.

At the end of the First World War, Greeks had constituted less than 20 per cent of the population of western Thrace, with its large Muslim element. On the completion of the exchange they made up over 60 per cent.

Greece thus became one of the most ethnically homogeneous countries in the Balkans, even if the issue of her small Muslim (predominantly Turkish), Jewish, Slav Macedonian, Vlach and Albanian minorities was to remain sensitive. What was more, almost all the Greek populations in the Near East were now contained within the boundaries of the Greek state. Apart from the small minorities in Turkey and Albania, both some 100,000 strong and both with rights theoretically protected by treaty, the only other significant Greek populations outside the borders of the state were those of the Dodecanese islands (the Italian 'temporary' occupation of which in 1912 was to last until 1947), numbering some 110,000, and Cyprus some 80 per cent of whose population, totalling 310,000 in the 1920s, was Greek. Cyprus, which had come under British administration in 1878 at the time of the Congress of Berlin, was formally annexed in 1914, when the Ottoman Empire aligned itself with the Central Powers, and became a crown colony in 1925.

The refugees, to the manifest chagrin of the more conservative elements in the indigenous population, were sufficiently numerous and compactly settled to act as the arbiters of political life during the inter-war period. Some among the dispossessed were attracted by the revolutionary doctrines of the recently founded (in 1918) Communist Party of Greece (KKE), a number of whose leaders were of Anatolian origin. But, despite the widespread deprivation, the appeal of communism was to be critically impeded by the Comintern's insistence (between 1924 and 1935) that the Greek party support the idea of a separate Macedonian state, the creation of which would have entailed the detachment of a large area of northern Greece. Few among the newly settled refugees, having had their worlds turned upside-down once, were inclined to repeat the experience.

In their overwhelming majority the refugees remained faithful to Eleftherios Venizelos, the charismatic protagonist of a 'Greater Greece' and their would-be liberator. His irredentist vision had now been shattered but this was explained away by the treachery of domestic reaction and by the machinations of external powers. This

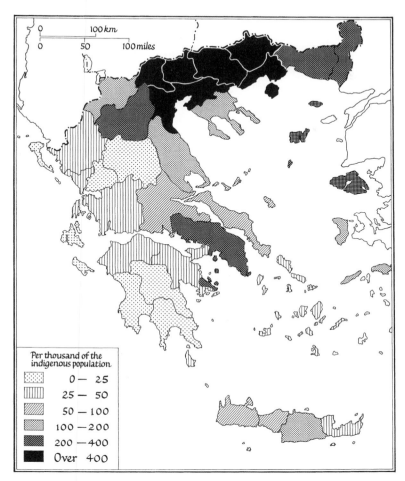

Map 7 The pattern of refugee settlement during the inter-war period

loyalty survived Venizelos' *rapprochement* with Kemal Atatürk in 1930, which was only achieved through substantial Greek concessions over compensation for the huge amount of immovable property left behind in Turkey by the departing refugees. The refugees voted heavily for the abolition of the monarchy in the 1924 referendum which resulted in a 70 per cent (758,472 to 325,322) vote for the republic. Since King Constantine's abdication in September

1922, King George II had been largely ignored and he was obliged to leave Greece in December 1923. His departure followed elections held after an abortive counter-coup directed against Plastiras and his revolutionary committee.

The 1923 elections were for an assembly empowered to revise the constitution. Since they were boycotted by the anti-Venizelist camp, the assembly was overwhelmingly dominated by supporters of Venizelos. These ranged across the political spectrum from conservatives to the moderately socialist. Although the monarchy was abolished in 1924, and Admiral Koundouriotis, a hero of the Balkan wars, was elected president, a republican constitution, providing for a two-chamber parliament, was not formally instituted until 1927. For part of the intervening period the country was ruled by a bombastic military dictatorship, headed by General Pangalos. The dictator threatened war against Turkey and actually invaded Bulgaria, to which Greece was obliged to pay an indemnity by the fledgeling League of Nations. Pangalos' overthrow in 1926 by a military coup, was followed by elections, the first to be held under a system of proportional representation. From the new parliament an 'ecumenical' government was established, so called because it drew its members from both the Venizelist and anti-Venizelist blocs.

When Venizelos became prime minister in 1928 he called new elections under a majority system, inaugurating the practice which has continued until the present day whereby incumbent governments have seldom been able to resist the temptation to manipulate the electoral system to their own advantage. Venizelos' 'electoral engineering' (the 47 per cent of votes cast for his Liberal Party translated into 71 per cent of the seats in parliament) alienated some powerful erstwhile allies. The defection of one of these, General Kondylis, to the anti-Venizelist camp, was to have serious consequences in the longer term for the Venizelists. Venizelos, enjoying the support of the business interest and of the emergent working class during his two previous administrations (1910–15 and 1917–20), had been a powerful force for political and economic modernisation. But this was no longer the case. Now aged sixty-four, his growing conservatism was reflected in the *idionym* law of 1929. Aimed at the communists, whose largest share of the vote in elections to date had been 4 per cent, the law made attempts to undermine the existing social order illegal and was eagerly seized on by subsequent governments to harass opponents.

Venizelos' skills as a statesman were harnessed to a policy of better relations with neighbouring countries. Treaties of friendship were signed with Italy and with the newly created state of Yugoslavia. Italy had exploited Greece's weakness in the aftermath of the 'catastrophe' by reneging on its undertaking to cede the Dodecanese islands to Greece and had briefly occupied Corfu in 1923. Relations with Bulgaria and Albania likewise improved. Venizelos was centrally involved in the preliminaries to the negotiation of the Balkan Pact of 1934, which brought together the 'anti-revisionist' states of the Balkans (Greece, Yugoslavia, Romania and Turkey) in a mutual guarantee of existing frontiers. Undoubtedly Venizelos' greatest achievement in foreign policy during this period was reconciliation with Turkey. This was secured through the Ankara Convention of 1930, although only at the price of considerable concessions on the part of Greece. In the same year Venizelos paid an official visit to Turkey and became the first Greek prime minister to visit the Ecumenical Patriarchate in the Phanar. In his zeal for better relations he went so far as to propose, unsuccessfully, the Turkish president, Kemal Atatürk, for the Nobel peace prize.

These promising achievements in foreign policy took place against the backdrop of the massive slump in the world economy that had been triggered by the Great Crash of 1929. Although Greece was not as badly affected as some of her neighbours, her economy, heavily dependent as it was on 'luxury' agricultural exports such as tobacco, olive oil and currants, and on shipping and migrant remittances, proved vulnerable. In 1933 she was obliged, as in 1893, to default on the interest payments on her substantial foreign loans. Venizelos was ill equipped by temperament and experience to cope with an economic crisis of such magnitude.

Uniquely in the inter-war period, the Venizelos government elected in 1928 served out its full four-year parliamentary term. The elections of 1932, however, were to usher in a period of political instability and growing polarisation that was to culminate, four years later, in the imposition of outright dictatorship. The Liberal Party slumped badly in comparison with 1928 and Venizelos retained only the narrowest of leads over the People's Party. A return

34 Eleftherios Venizelos (1864–1936) dominated political life
during much of the first third of the twentieth century. After
making his mark in the politics of his native Crete, he was projected on to the stage of national politics by the military coup of
1909, becoming prime minister between 1910 and 1915. He first
achieved international prominence as the architect of Greece's
spectacular victories in the Balkan wars of 1912–13. His feud
with King Constantine I during the First World War precipitated
the National Schism which split the country into two rival camps.

to proportional representation had resulted in parliamentary deadlock. But in elections the following year, 1933, held under a majority system, the People's Party, headed by Panayis Tsaldaris, and its allies, secured a comfortable majority over the Venizelists.

This was too much for diehard Venizelists such as Colonel Plastiras, the main protagonist of the 1922 coup. He now sought to achieve through force what his hero, Venizelos, had been unable to achieve through the ballot box. Although the attempted coup of 5/6 March 1933 was a miserable failure and Plastiras was forced into exile, his role in politics was far from ended. The March 1933 coup brought an abrupt end to the period of relative stability that had followed the overthrow of the Pangalos dictatorship in 1926. The passions of the National Schism had now been reawakened in all their old intensity. Whether or not Venizelos had himself been implicated in the plot his opponents suspected the worst. In June 1933 he had a miraculous escape when his car (the bullet-ridden chassis of which is still preserved) was shot up. A bodyguard was killed and his second wife, the hugely rich Helena Schilizzi, was

---

Caption for Plate 34 (*cont.*).

Prime minister once again between 1917 and 1920, he presented his country's case with such flair at the Paris Peace Conference that a British diplomat ranked him and Lenin as the two most important political figures in Europe. Prime minister once more between 1928 and 1932, he was forced into exile in 1935 following an attempted coup by his supporters. Here he is shown in his old age with a grandson. In keeping with the strong dynastic element in Greek politics Venizelos' sons and grandsons entered politics. Other well-known political dynasties in modern times are those of the Rallis and Papandreou families. Both the paternal (Dimitrios Rallis) and maternal (Georgios Theotokis) grandfathers of Georgios Rallis, the New Democracy prime minister in 1980–1, had themselves been prime ministers. Georgios Papandreou was prime minister in 1944 and 1963–5. His son, Andreas, was a minister in his father's second government and, as prime minister between 1981 and 1989, in turn appointed his own son, a deputy representing his grandfather's old constituency, as minister of education. Family connections are all-important in politics, as in so many walks of life in Greece.

35 The wedding of Anna Marcellas (born in Piraeus) and
Nicholas Mouskondis (born in Aghia Marina, Crete) at the
Paradise Café in Salt Lake City's 'Greek Town' in 1921. The
large Greek community in Utah was mainly employed in
the early years of this century in mining and railroad construction. If no church was available, weddings and baptisms would
be held in homes and restaurants. *Xeniteia*, or sojourning in
foreign parts, has long been a fundamental part of the historical
experience of the Greek people and emigration has traditionally
acted as a safety valve for poor economic conditions at home.
Wherever they have settled Greeks have tenaciously sought to
retain their identity through the establishment of churches,
schools, *kapheneia* or coffee shops, and associations based on
their place of origin. They have for the most part maintained
close links with the old country and the existence of a government minister for Greeks abroad is testimony to the interest of
the Greek state in encouraging contact with, and where possible
mobilising the support of, Greeks overseas. In the eighteenth
century Greek communities came into existence in central
Europe, southern Russia, Italy, Holland, France, Egypt, even in
India and, albeit briefly, in New Smyrna in Florida. In the nineteenth century a prosperous Greek community was established
in England, mainly in London, Manchester and Liverpool.

wounded. Now it was the turn of the Venizelists to suspect government involvement in the assassination attempt, one of eleven known plots against Venizelos' life during his long political career. Tsaldaris, the People's Party prime minister, had earlier declared his acceptance of the republican constitution. But pressure for a royalist restoration was mounting. Alarmed at the prospect of purges of republicans in the armed forces, a group of Venizelist officers, this time with the indisputable connivance of Venizelos, launched a further coup in March 1935. Although more broadly based than the 1933 coup this, too, ended in failure. Venizelos joined Plastiras in exile in France. Two of the rebellious officers were executed, while many hundreds of others were drummed out of the army in humiliating circumstances. Civilians of known Venizelist sympathies were likewise purged from public office.

The anti-Venizelists were now to demonstrate no greater respect for constitutional proprieties than had their opponents. The senate, still under Venizelist control, was peremptorily abolished and elections were held in June 1935 with the country still under

---

Caption for Plate 35 (*cont.*).

From the 1890s large-scale emigration, initially predominantly from the Peloponnese, got under way to the United States. It has been estimated that as many as a quarter of all Greek males aged between fifteen and forty sought their fortune in America between 1900 and 1915, many of them intending to return to their home country. During the 1920s, 1930s and 1940s the flow was severely restricted by US legislation but by 1980 over half a million Greeks (not counting those of Greek ethnic origin from areas outside the Greek state) had emigrated to the US. The Greeks constitute the most upwardly mobile immigrant group in America and in Governor Michael Dukakis of Massachusetts, a second-generation immigrant, produced the Democratic candidate for the presidency in 1988. In the period after the Second World War new patterns of emigration to Australia and Canada emerged. Rather over 12 per cent of the population emigrated between 1951 and 1980. Large numbers sought employment as *Gastarbeiter* in Germany. Many of these, unlike those who had emigrated further afield, have returned to Greece to set up small businesses once they had acquired some capital.

36 Constantine Cavafy (1863–1933), perhaps the best known and most translated Greek poet in modern times. He is pictured in his flat in rue Lepsius in Alexandria. His father was a wealthy merchant in Egypt but on his death the family fell on hard times. His widow took the family to England and the young Constantine spoke English as his first language. He subsequently spent three years in Constantinople before settling for good in Alexandria in 1885 at the age of 22. He gained a living as a bureaucrat in the Irrigation Office but his poetry, which he worked and reworked with minute care, was his life.

martial law. The Venizelists' abstention in protest made a People's Party landslide inevitable: 65 per cent of the votes resulted in 96 per cent of the seats in parliament. Although the communists received their highest share of the vote in the inter-war period, almost 10 per cent, the majority system in force ensured that they received no seats. The ultra-royalists, led by Venizelos' erstwhile lieutenant Kondylis, were no longer prepared to pay even lip service to constitutional procedures. In October a group of high-ranking officers demanded of the prime minister, Tsaldaris, that he either engineer an immediate restoration of the monarchy or resign. He chose the latter course and was replaced by Kondylis who, in turn, declared the abolition of the republic. This was followed in short order by a patently farcical plebiscite in favour of a restoration (1,491,992 votes for, 32,454 against).

King George II, who had spent much of his twelve-year exile in England, duly ascended the throne for the second time. Seemingly bent on reconciliation, he appointed a law professor at the University of Athens to head a caretaker government charged with holding fresh elections under a system of proportional representation. As in 1932, these produced deadlock between the two main political camps. In a 300-seat parliament, the People's Party and its royalist allies controlled 143 seats, the Liberal Party (now led by Themistoklis Sophoulis) and its allies 141. This left the communists, hitherto an insignificant force in the political spectrum, holding the balance of power, their 6 per cent share of the vote giving them control of a critical 15 seats.

The two main party leaders, Tsaldaris (People's Party) and Sophoulis (Liberal), struggled to find a way out of the impasse, although their freedom of manoeuvre was restricted by die-hards in

---

Caption for Plate 36 (*cont.*).

The source of much of his inspiration was the Hellenistic world in its decline and the conflict between paganism and Christianity. On being asked by his niece why he did not move from the seedy surroundings of rue Lepsius, he replied that he could think of no better place to live than amid 'these three centres of existence; a brothel, a church for forgiveness and a hospital where you die'.

37 Venizelist army officers on trial for their part in the abortive coup of 1 March 1935. This was the second such attempted coup (the first was in March 1933) launched in the 1930s by army officers who were not prepared to accept the rejection of their hero Eleftherios Venizelos at the polls. Venizelos, who was himself directly implicated in the 1935 coup, was forced into exile in France, where he joined one of his strongest supporters, Colonel Nikolaos Plastiras, a leading protagonist in the 1922 coup and the organiser of the failed 1933 coup. Although only a handful died in the 1935 coup attempt, sixty of those implicated (including Venizelos and Plastiras) were sentenced to death, of whom two were executed, most of the rest having fled abroad. Over a thousand were tried for complicity and a number of convicted officers were publicly stripped of their badges of rank. Some 1,500 army, navy and air force officers were cashiered. Not only did the coup fail but it precipitated what those who were behind it most feared, namely a restoration of the monarchy, following a rigged plebiscite in November 1935. Military intervention has been a recurrent feature of political life. The army forced King Otto to grant a constitution in 1843; it brought Venizelos to power in the aftermath of the Goudi coup of 1909; and it spectacularly misruled Greece between 1967 and 1974. The officer corps, permeated with patronage networks and with close ties to politicians, acted as one of the principal arbiters of political life during the inter-war period, when there were numerous coups, successful and otherwise, and pronunciamentos.

their respective parties. A principal stumbling-block to co-operation was the Liberals' insistence on the reinstatement of the Venizelist officers cashiered in the aftermath of the 1935 coup. Both blocs simultaneously engaged in secret negotiations to gain the support of the communists. In a country where secrets are seldom long kept, news of these contacts leaked out, prompting unrest in an army by now thoroughly purged of republican elements. When the caretaker minister of war, General Papagos, voiced the army's concerns to the king, he was replaced by General Ioannis Metaxas, the leader of the Freethinkers' Party, an ultra-right-wing party even more marginal in terms of electoral support than the communists. On the death of the caretaker prime minister in April, the king appointed Metaxas as his successor, pending a resolution of the political stalemate.

The atmosphere of crisis was exacerbated by widespread labour unrest. As a consequence of the world slump, the market for a major export, tobacco, had been badly hit and a demonstration by striking tobacco workers in Salonica had resulted in the shooting of twelve of the strikers by the police. Metaxas, who made no secret of his contempt for the 'political world', was able to play on the seeming inability of the politicians to compose their differences and on the serious labour troubles to predispose the king to accept his proposals for 'strong' government. The king, having rejected an eleventh-hour deal between the Liberals and the People's Party, acquiesced in Metaxas' suspension on 4 August 1936 of key articles of the constitution on the pretext of thwarting a 24-hour general strike called by the communists for the following day. This was viewed, unconvincingly, by Metaxas as the prelude to a bid for power.

The establishment of the 'Regime of the Fourth of August 1936', as Metaxas liked to style his dictatorship, formed part of the general trend towards royal dictatorships that occurred throughout the Balkans during the late 1930s, as insecurely established parliamentary regimes proved incapable of responding to the stresses occasioned by the slump. Although its critics were to denounce the Metaxas dictatorship as fascist, it altogether lacked the dynamism of German Nazism or Italian fascism. Rather it was an authoritarian, backward-looking and paternalistic dictatorship, overlaid with a patina of quasi-fascist rhetoric and style, owing not a little to Salazar's corporate state in Portugal. Unusually for an ultra-conservative, Metaxas, who was no philistine,

38 General Ioannis Metaxas, the diminutive dictator of Greece
between 1936 and 1941, receiving the fascist salute from members
of a labour battalion and a priest. The tall figure standing behind
him is Kostas Kotzias, the 'minister–governor' of Athens. Metaxas'
dictatorship, which he liked to dignify with the title of the 'Regime
of the Fourth of August 1936', manifested a number of the external
trappings of fascism. In imitation of Hitler's Third Reich Metaxas
elaborated the notion of the 'Third Hellenic Civilisation'. The first
was that of ancient Greece, the second that of medieval Byzantium,
the third being an amalgam of the essentially contradictory values
of both which would enshrine and perpetuate the values of his
regime. He also chose to style himself *Protos Agrotis* ('First
Peasant') and *Protos Ergatis* ('First Worker'). But, although he
shared Hitler and Mussolini's hatred for communism, liberalism
and parliamentarism, his regime lacked the dynamism and radicalism of true fascism and was not racist. The National Youth
Organisation (EON) through which, in the absence of any basis
of popular support, Metaxas sought to institutionalise his power
was but a pale imitation of the Hitler Youth. Although, to a degree,
he imitated the domestic practices of the fascist dictators he
never questioned the British connection, which was strongly
championed by King George II, and in October 1940 he caught
the popular mood in standing up to Mussolini's bullying.
Essentially, Metaxas was an authoritarian paternalist, bent, like

championed the demotic or spoken form of the language. In commissioning the first proper grammar of the demotic language, he characteristically did so in the belief that grammatical rules would help curb what he viewed as the unbridled individualism of the Greeks. In the manner of Greek dictators before and since, Metaxas, indeed, was obsessed with the idea of instilling 'discipline' into his unruly fellow countrymen. Borrowing from Hitler's Third German Reich and with the dictator's customary lack of a sense of proportion, he preached the 'Third Hellenic Civilisation'. This, under his guidance, would somehow synthesise the pagan values of ancient Greece, and particularly those of Sparta, with the Christian values of the medieval empire of Byzantium. Styling himself 'First Peasant', 'First Worker', 'Leader' and 'National Father', his populist, anti-plutocratic rhetoric, although not lacking in sincerity, was seldom matched in practice. He dragooned young people into his National Youth Organisation, which he intended as the vehicle to perpetuate his ideals after his death, and vented his spite on the whole spectrum of the 'political world', reserving a particular loathing for the far left.

[We must subordinate] our appetites, our passions and our overweening egotism before the totality of the national interest . . . then we shall be a people that is truly free. Otherwise, under the false cover of freedom, anarchy and indiscipline will rule over us.

General Ioannis Metaxas (1939)

Although his regime lacked legitimacy or any kind of popular base, Metaxas and his formidably efficient minister for public order, Konstantinos Maniadakis, had little difficulty in neutralising such opposition as existed. The communists, with their discipline and experience of clandestine activity, potentially constituted a greater threat than the bourgeois politicians and their vestigial party organisations. But the far left had a long history of factionalism, and Maniadakis was able to infiltrate and sow discord in the underground communist organisation with remarkable facility. A particularly successful

---

Caption for Plate 38 (*cont.*).

the 'Colonels' some thirty years later, on 'disciplining' what he considered to be the turbulent character of his compatriots.

ploy was to extract, by force if necessary, 'declarations of repentance', in which communists renounced not only their political beliefs but their former comrades. By the standards of twentieth-century totalitarianism, Metaxas' authoritarian methods were not particularly nasty and he did not physically eliminate his opponents. But he was able, through an efficient police network, to instil a climate of fear that helped to neutralise the threat of active opposition.

If Metaxas was able to create a passable simulacrum of the externals of a fascist regime, neither he nor, even less, the king showed any sign of seeking to depart from the traditional orientation towards Britain in foreign policy. Following the pattern elsewhere in south-east Europe, German penetration of the economy grew apace in the second half of the 1930s but in Greece this did not bring in its wake increased political influence. Indeed, Metaxas in 1938 proposed a formal treaty of alliance with Britain, but the latter, fearful of new commitments, did not respond. Nonetheless, Britain and France, in the wake of the Italian occupation of Albania in April 1939, did offer a guarantee of territorial integrity to Greece (and Romania), provided that she chose to resist external aggression.

On the outbreak of the Second World War in September 1939, Metaxas hoped to be able to keep Greece out of the hostilities, while maintaining a benevolent neutrality towards Britain. Mussolini, however, was anxious to demonstrate to his Axis partner, Hitler, that he, too, could win spectacular victories and he picked on Greece as, or so he thought, a soft target. In August 1940 an Italian submarine torpedoed the cruiser *Elli*, with considerable loss of life. Two months later, in the early hours of the morning of 28 October 1940, the Italian minister in Athens delivered a humiliating ultimatum to Metaxas, which was rejected out of hand. Within hours Italian forces crossed the Greek–Albanian frontier and Greece was at war. In standing up to Italian bullying Metaxas captured the national mood and, buoyed up by a great wave of national exaltation, Greek troops were soon on the counter-attack. Within a matter of days they had pushed the invaders back into Albanian territory, for this was not solely a campaign to defend the motherland. It also aimed at the 'liberation' of the large, and partly Greek-inhabited, area of southern Albania that, in Greek eyes, constituted northern Epirus and which, during the brief Greek occupation, was administered as a part of Greece. Korytsa, Aghioi Saranda and Argyrokastro (to use their Greek names) were captured in short order and Valona appeared to be within grasp before extremely severe winter weather set in and with it military deadlock.

Britain, at this stage of the war with no active ally save Greece, supplied limited air support. But Metaxas declined Churchill's offer of troops for fear of provoking Hitler, still hoping to avoid entanglement in the wider war through German mediation between Greece and Italy. When Metaxas died at the end of January 1941 his successor, Alexandros Koryzis, had no such inhibitions. A British expeditionary force, mainly composed of Australian and New Zealand troops, was sent to Greece. But misunderstandings between the Greek and British military authorities critically delayed the concentration of troops on the line of the Aliakmon river in western Macedonia, which afforded the best possibility of stemming the ever more likely German invasion. This was launched on 6 April 1941, with devastating efficiency through Yugoslavia and Bulgaria, by a Hitler who was anxious to secure his Balkan flank in advance of the invasion of the Soviet Union.

The Greek and British forces were rapidly overcome, and in the chaos of defeat the prime minister committed suicide, to be succeeded by Emmanouil Tsouderos, a banker known for his opposition to the Metaxas regime. Three days before the fall of Athens on 23 April, General Tsolakoglou, without government authorisation, negotiated an armistice with the Germans. Much of the British expeditionary force was, however, successfully evacuated and King George II, his government, and some Greek forces were withdrawn to Crete, there to join substantial but ill-equipped British forces in the defence of the island. It was intended to hold Crete as a base from which to launch air raids against the Romanian oil fields which were a vital source of German fuel supplies. Despite the fact that German plans were known as a result of 'Enigma' radio intercepts, the island fell at the end of May after fierce fighting between the defending forces and German airborne troops, the margin of victory being narrow indeed. The king and his government, the symbols of constitutional legitimacy, withdrew to the Middle East together with contingents of the armed forces. In Greece itself a collaborationist government, headed initially by General Tsolakoglou, was established.

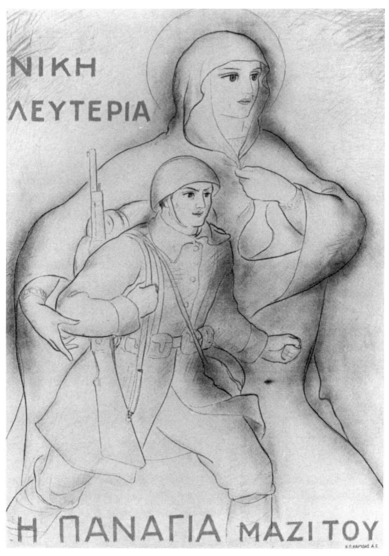

39 'Victory, Freedom, the Panaghia [Virgin Mary] is with him.'
A famous propaganda poster by Georgios Gounaropoulos dating from the period of the Greek–Italian War of 1940–1.
The poster captures the mood of almost religious exaltation
which followed Metaxas' dignified defiance of the ultimatum of
28 October 1940 which demanded that Italy be allowed to

By the beginning of June 1941 the whole of Greece was under a tripartite German, Italian and Bulgarian occupation. The Germans occupied Athens and Salonica, Crete and a number of the Aegean islands, together with the sensitive border with neutral Turkey. The Bulgarians, traditional enemies of the Greeks, were permitted to occupy western Thrace and parts of Macedonia, where they settled Bulgarian migrants and persecuted the Greek population. The Italians controlled the rest of the country. From the outset the Germans, who made little secret of their contempt for their Italian allies, imposed a harsh occupation regime, plundering the country's agricultural resources, such industry as existed, and, in a particularly nasty twist, requiring Greece to pay for the costs of the occupation. An early consequence of these policies was the devastating famine of the winter of 1941/2, which claimed some 100,000 victims.

Food shortages, massive inflation, the black market and the everyday struggle for survival were the major preoccupations of most of the population. But it soon became apparent that defeat and wanton

---

Caption for Plate 39 (*cont.*).

occupy strategic points of Greek territory. This was the culmination of a series of provocations, the most blatant of which was the torpedoing of the cruiser *Elli* as she lay off the island of Tinos, with its miracle-working icon of the Virgin Mary, for the Feast of the Dormition [Assumption] of the Virgin on 15 August. Greek defiance of the Italian ultimatum is marked every year on 28 October by a national holiday, '*Okhi* [No] day'. Within days the Italian invasion forces were repulsed in a crusade for the liberation of what the Greeks term northern Epirus, an area of southern Albania with a sizeable Greek minority. The spectacle of the Greek David worsting the Italian Goliath aroused worldwide admiration and at this stage of the war Greece and Britain were the only two countries actively resisting the Axis powers in Europe. By early December the three major towns of southern Albania – Korytsa, Argyrokastro and Aghioi Saranda – had been captured and the occupied areas were administered as part of the Greek state. Poor communications and bad weather, however, impeded further advance and the troops on the Albanian front were forced to withdraw in disarray at the time of the lightning German invasion of Greece in April 1941.

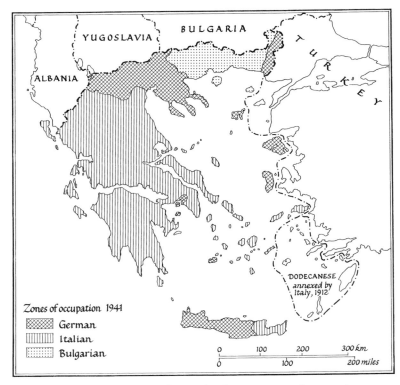

Map 8 The German, Italian and Bulgarian zones of occupation
in 1941

deprivation had by no means blunted the will to resist. As early as 31 May 1941 the Nazi swastika was torn down from the Acropolis in Athens. Isolated acts of resistance were to be given cohesion when the communist party, immediately after the Nazi invasion of the Soviet Union in June 1941, switched from regarding the war as 'imperialist' to urging loyal communists to do all in their power to contribute to the defence of the Soviet motherland. Such assistance could best be rendered from within Greece by resistance to the fascist occupation.

With such an objective in view, the communists moved quickly to establish, in September 1941, the National Liberation Front (EAM). This had two principal aims: the organisation of resistance and a free choice as to the form of government on the eventual liberation of the country. Although leaders of the old political parties rejected the communists' call for co-operation and stood largely aloof from the resistance struggle, some small and insignificant agrarian and social-ist groups were also parties to the establishment of EAM. This was created as the political wing of a mass-based resistance movement, while the National People's Liberation Army (whose Greek acro-nym, ELAS, sounded like the Greek word for Greece) was established as its military arm. EAM was also behind the formation of other organisations such as National Solidarity, which provided relief for the victims of the occupation, and a youth movement known by the initials EPON.

The inability or unwillingness of the traditional 'political world' to offer leadership perpetuated under the occupation the political void that had developed during the Metaxas dictatorship. The commu-nists, a marginal force during the inter-war period, albeit with an experience of clandestine political activity that the bourgeois parties wholly lacked, were quick to fill this vacuum. Through example, discipline and propaganda they were able to offer a vision of a better and more just future that was quite beyond the politicians, whose old antagonisms appeared irrelevant in the misery of the occupation. EAM had a particular appeal to young people and to women, to whom it held out the prospect of emancipation in a society which, in rural areas, was still patriarchal. Although the party leadership kept a firm grip on the leadership of both EAM and ELAS, the great majority of the rank and file were not communists. Moreover, a number of non-communist resistance groups also came into exis-tence, the most important of which was the National Republican Greek League (EDES), whose power base was in north-western Greece. What these groups had in common, besides their determi-nation to resist the Axis occupation, was a strong antipathy towards the exiled King George, whom they blamed for the rigours of the Metaxas dictatorship and the horrors of the ensuing occupation.

The king and the government-in-exile, based first in London and from March 1943 in Cairo, had little contact with occupied Greece and generally took the view that sabotage and resistance could not be justified in the light of the vicious reprisals inflicted on innocent civil-ians. The Germans decreed that for every one of their soldiers killed

40 (a) An old man photographed by Dimitris Kharisiadis in a Piraeus soup kitchen during the terrible famine of the winter of 1941–2. The occupation had been followed by large-scale requisitioning. This had disastrous consequences for a country that had been a wheat importer. German sources recorded that, in December 1941, 300 people a day were dying from starvation in Athens, while annual per capita consumption of bread fell from 179 kilos in 1939 to 40 in 1942. So appalling was the plight of city dwellers that the British government, after some initial hesitation, lifted its blockade and food supplies, imported and administered by the Red Cross, prevented a repetition of the worst of the famine of the first winter of the occupation. Life for the majority remained very harsh and the everyday struggle for existence was exacerbated by astronomical levels of inflation. An *oka* (nearly three pounds) of bread, which cost 10 drachmas at the time of the Italian invasion, had reached 34,000,000 by the time of the German withdrawal in October 1944. The price of cheese increased from 60 drachmas per *oka* to 1,160,000,000 during the same period. Hyperinflation on this scale resulted in the British gold sovereign becoming the effective currency by the end of the occupation. The black market flourished. The extent to which those with money could eat well is strikingly demonstrated by the photograph (b) of an Athenian grocery, *To Agrotikon*, taken by

Caption for Plate 40 (*cont.*).

the *Life* photographer, Dmitri Kessel, in early November 1944. This was a time, shortly after the German withdrawal, when food was still in desperately short supply. American, British, French and German foods were on sale in this well-stocked shop. Many observers drew attention to the stark contrast between the luxuries available to the rich and the deprivations of the mass of the population.

fifty Greeks should be shot, while the destruction of villages in an effort to deter resistance activity was a commonplace. As elsewhere in occupied Europe, the Nazis sought to exterminate the Jewish population. In early 1943, within the space of a few weeks, virtually the whole of the Sephardic Jewish community of Salonica, which, at almost 50,000, constituted approximately one-fifth of the city's

41   Three *andartisses* or women guerrillas photographed in 1944
by Costas Couvaras. Couvaras, a Greek who had studied in
America, had been sent into Greece by the Office of Strategic
Services (OSS), the US equivalent of the British Special Operations
Executive (SOE), to make contact with the leadership of EAM
(National Liberation Front). The woman in the middle is
Melpomene Papaheliou (whose *nom de guerre* was *Thyella* or
'Tempest'). She was subsequently killed in the December 1944
fighting between ELAS and the British. EAM had been founded in
September 1941 on communist initiative and rapidly developed
into much the largest of the resistance movements in occupied
Greece. Estimates of its adherents in 1944 range from 500,000 to
2 million. EAM had a number of offshoots. The most important
of these was its military arm, ELAS (National People's Liberation
Army), which by the German withdrawal in October 1944 numbered some 60,000. Like many of the other protagonists in the
drama of occupied Greece, EAM aspired to postwar power.
Ruthless in its treatment of its domestic opponents, EAM/ELAS
at the same time enjoyed a considerable basis of popular support.
It developed this support by demonstrating a vision of a better
future that proved beyond the capability of the old political
establishment. It strove to improve the educational level of isolated mountain communities; to give the peasants a sense of
political involvement; and, in particular, to improve the status
of women. The first Greek election in which women had a vote
was that organised in April 1944 for a National Council in the
substantial areas of mountain Greece by then under EAM
control.

population, was deported to Auschwitz. Only a handful survived. A community which, in its prime, had been known as *Malkah Israel*, the 'Queen of Israel', was no more.

Armed bands, both communist and non-communist, took to the mountains in the spring and summer of 1942 and the military potential of resistance was demonstrated by the destruction in November 1942 of the Gorgopotamos viaduct, which carried the Salonica–Athens railway line. This, one of the most spectacular achievements of the resistance anywhere in occupied Europe, was achieved by saboteurs parachuted into Greece by the British Special Operations Executive, together with guerrillas drawn both from ELAS and EDES. The subsequent British attempt to co-ordinate resistance activities was to be critically impeded by the official policy of support for the return of the king on liberation, for which there was little enthusiasm in occupied Greece. The British prime minister, Winston Churchill, was particularly wedded to the king's cause, regarding King George as an especially staunch ally during the dark winter of 1940/1, when Greece had been Britain's only active ally in Europe. Almost from the outset there was friction between the communist-dominated and non-communist bands, for most of the protagonists in the drama of the resistance, as elsewhere in occupied Europe, had longer-term political objectives. EAM enjoyed genuine popular support but did not shrink from the use of terror against its opponents in its bid to monopolise resistance activity. Its vastly greater strength was recognised by the 'National Bands' agreement of July 1943. This created a joint general head-quarters in which EAM/ELAS nominees enjoyed a considerable numerical superiority over those of the non-communist resistance and of the British military mission.

The (never strong) prospects for co-operation between the various resistance groups and their would-be British mentors were to be fatally compromised by the failure of a guerrilla delegation to Cairo in August of 1943. The fact that this delegation was able to fly from an improvised landing strip is testimony to the fact that large areas of mountain Greece were by this time under resistance control. There was no meeting of minds between the guerrillas, the British military and political authorities, the king and the government-in-exile. The guerrilla delegation had two basic demands: that they

42 Four young Greek Jews (Alberto/Avraam Nahmias, David
Sion, Isaac Algava standing left to right; the kneeling figure is
unknown) photographed towards the end of February 1943 in
the temporary ghetto established in the Baron Hirsch hospital
compound in Salonica. Not only were Jews obliged to wear the
Star of David but the community was required to make them.
Shortly afterwards the four, with some 46,000 members of the
once flourishing Jewish community in the city, approximately
one-fifth of its entire population, were deported to Auschwitz.

exercise the powers of a number of key ministries (including the interior and justice) in the exile government in those considerable areas of Greece now under their control and that the king undertake not to return until a plebiscite had voted in his favour. Both demands were rejected and the delegation was summarily returned to the mountains, convinced that it was British policy to bring about a restoration of the monarchy irrespective of the wishes of the people.

Shortly after the Cairo fiasco, the tensions within the resistance came to a head, as in October 1943 ELAS attacked EDES, alleging collaboration with the occupation authorities. It was clear that, as in Yugoslavia and Albania, the communists were seeking to ensure that they would be the only organised, armed force in the country when liberation came, in which case they would clearly be well placed to assume control of the levers of power. In the internecine fighting of the winter of 1943/4 the British sought to sustain EDES by cutting off supplies to ELAS. But such a move was of limited effect, for ELAS was able to commandeer much of the weaponry of the Italian forces in Greece, following the Italian armistice of September 1943 and the

---

Caption for Plate 42 (*cont.*).

Almost all of them perished. Of the four in the photograph only David Sion survived. Altogether some 67,000 Greek Jews lost their lives during the Axis occupation, 87 per cent of the total Jewish population of the country. Some Jews were able to escape to Turkey, others fought with the guerrilla *andartes* in the mountains. Still others were protected by Orthodox families and the archbishop of Athens, Damaskinos, and the chief of police, Angelos Evert, did their courageous best to alleviate the plight of Greek Jewry. At the time Salonica was incorporated into the Greek kingdom in 1912 almost half the population of the city was Jewish. Approximately another third were Greeks, the rest of the population being composed of Bulgarians, Turks and others. These Sephardic Jews were the descendants of the Jews expelled from Spain in 1492 who had been offered refuge in the Ottoman Empire. They worshipped in over thirty synagogues in the city and spoke Ladino, or Judaeo-Spanish, essentially fifteenth-century Spanish which they wrote with Hebrew characters. Elsewhere in Greece there were small communities of 'Romaniot' Jews whose roots in the country went back to antiquity.

subsequent surrender of thousands of Italian troops. The German occupation authorities, naturally delighted by the outbreak of civil war within the resistance, created armed 'Security Battalions', under the authority of the quisling government, into which they enticed collaborators and those whose fear of communism outweighed their dislike of the Nazis. Only with difficulty was a truce patched up between the warring resistance groups in February 1944, with EDES being confined to its regional power base of Epirus.

EAM had by no means abandoned its political objectives, however, and soon afterwards announced the establishment of a Political Committee of National Liberation, which would exercise governmental functions in free 'Mountain' Greece. The establishment of the Political Committee constituted a direct challenge to the beleaguered and impotent government-in-exile and sparked off mutinies by EAM sympathisers in the Greek armed forces stationed in Egypt. The mutineers demanded the creation of a government of national unity based on the Political Committee. The mutinies, which were forcibly suppressed by British troops, contributed powerfully to Churchill's mounting obsession with the prospect of a postwar communist take-over in Greece. This was reinforced by the murder by a (probably maverick) ELAS band of Colonel Psaros, the leader of a small, non-communist resistance group, and by the fact that the Red Army was poised to descend on the Balkans. These developments prompted Churchill to contemplate some kind of deal with the Soviet leader, Stalin, whereby British preponderance in postwar Greece would be assured in return for acceptance of Russian hegemony over Romania. The essence of this arrangement was negotiated in May 1944, and despite American reservations, was consolidated in the famous 'percentages' agreement reached by Churchill and Stalin in Moscow in October 1944. This high-level dealing was quite unknown to the protagonists in the Greek drama. As so often in its history the direction of events in Greece was to be determined by the interests of the Great Powers rather than by what was happening on the ground in the country.

Let us settle about our affairs in the Balkans. Your armies are in Roumania and Bulgaria . . . Don't let us get at cross-purposes in small ways. So far as Britain and Russia are concerned, how would it do for you to have ninety per cent predominance in Roumania, for us to have ninety per cent of the say in Greece, and go fifty-fifty about Yugoslavia?

Churchill to Stalin, Moscow, October 1944

One direct consequence of the mutinies was the installation as prime minister of the government-in-exile of Georgios Papandreou, a politician recently escaped from Greece. To the British, he had the great virtue of a Venizelist background allied to a militant anti-communism. Papandreou, under British aegis, now set about constructing a government of national unity at a conference in the Lebanon which was attended by representatives of all the resistance and political forces. The communists were much under-represented in relation to their actual military and political strength and their delegates, on the defensive after the mutinies, were browbeaten into accepting five insignificant ministries for EAM nominees in the new government. Their concessions were, however, soon repudiated back in the mountains by the communist leadership, which demanded key ministries and Papandreou's head as the price of participation in the government.

The deadlock was suddenly broken when, in August, the EAM leadership backed down and agreed to accept the essence of the Lebanon agreement. As this sudden about-face occurred a matter of days after the unexpected arrival in the mountains of a Soviet military mission, it has plausibly been assumed, in the absence of hard evidence, that the mission brought with it advice, which would have been in keeping with Stalin's understanding with Churchill, to moderate its intransigent line. Whether or not this was the case, by accepting a subordinate position in the Papandreou government and by agreeing to place its military forces under British command, together with the much smaller forces of EDES, the communist leadership of EAM, as some leading cadres argued at the time, threw away its best opportunity of seizing power in the confusion of the German withdrawal from Greece in October 1944.

The Papandreou government returned to liberated Athens on 18 October, having delayed its arrival by twenty-four hours to avoid landing on a Tuesday, always of ill omen in the Greek world as the day on which Constantinople had fallen to the Turks. It was accompanied by a small British force which had been established to

43 The members of the Political Committee of National Liberation (PEEA), photographed with Ioakheim, the metropolitan of Kozani and a fervent supporter of EAM. PEEA was established in March 1944 to administer the large areas of mountain Greece controlled by the guerrilla forces of EAM/ELAS. From left to right: Kostas Gavriilidis (agriculture), secretary of the Agrarian Party; Stamatis Khatzibeis (national economy), Left Liberal; Angelos Angelopoulos (economic affairs), professor of economics in the University of Athens; General Manolis Mandakas (army); Georgios Siantos (interior), acting secretary-general of the communist party; Petros Kokkalis (social welfare), professor of medicine in the University of Athens; Alexandros Svolos, president of the committee (external affairs, education and religion, popular enlightenment), professor of constitutional law in the University of Athens; Colonel Evripidis Bakirtzis, vice-president (supply); Ilias Tsirimokos (justice) secretary of the Union of Popular Democracy; Nikolaos Askoutsis (transport), Left Liberal. Of the members of PEEA, only Siantos was an open member of the communist party. But Kokkalis and Mandakas, and possibly also Bakirtzis (the 'Red Colonel'), were covert members and EAM, which was communist-dominated, exercised effective control over the committee. PEEA organised the elections

ensure its return in view of fears of a communist take-over. With the entry of the communist nominees, Papandreou had plausibly been able to portray his cabinet as a true government of national unity. The problems that confronted it, however, were legion. The civil war within the resistance had created a climate of fear and suspicion; the economy had been devastated by the years of occupation; communications were disrupted throughout the country, critically impeding the distribution of relief supplies; the merchant fleet was almost wholly destroyed; food (except to those with access to money) was in desperately short supply; disease (particularly tuberculosis) was rampant, the consequence of years of malnutrition; inflation, which had already reached astronomical proportions during the occupation, was again spiralling out of control (the only money with any value was the British gold sovereign).

As the euphoria of liberation began to fade, practical problems were compounded by political ones. Demands for the punishment of collaborators were not given a high priority by Papandreou (or, indeed, by his British mentors). But one problem loomed above all. This was the demobilisation of the guerrilla armies and their replacement by a regularly constituted national army. Although the ELAS forces, amounting to some 60,000 men (and women) and much the largest single armed formation, were under notional British command, their very existence constituted a potential threat to the authority of the Papandreou government. Agreement appeared to have been reached on this thorny issue, but the left, with some justification, then accused Papandreou of going back on his word and refused to demobilise. In an atmosphere of mounting crisis EAM's nominees resigned from the cabinet at the beginning of December.

Caption for Plate 43 (*cont.*).

for the National Council which met in the village of Kory-schades in Evrytania in May 1944. Although PEEA did not formally put itself forward as an alternative government to the government-in-exile, its very existence constituted a challenge to the government's authority. PEEA's call for a government of national unity and greater co-operation with the left-wing resistance forces precipitated mutinies by elements sympathetic to EAM and PEEA in the Greek forces in the Middle East.

Three days later, on 3 December, EAM organised a mass demonstration, the prelude to a general strike, in the centre of Athens. Ill-disciplined police fired on the demonstrators in Constitution Square in the centre of the city, leaving some fifteen dead.

ELAS units now began attacking police stations and within days there was furious street fighting between ELAS units and British forces in Athens. But ELAS did not deploy its considerable forces outside the capital, and appeared to be bent not so much on an outright seizure of power as on destabilising the Papandreou government. Characteristically obsessed with the Greek crisis, Churchill flew on Christmas Day to Athens, with his foreign secretary, Anthony Eden. His intervention had little immediate result but he was now at last apprised of the need to establish a regency pending a plebiscite on the constitutional issue. With some difficulty, he persuaded King George, who had not yet returned to Greece, to stand down in favour of Archbishop Damaskinos of Athens as regent. Papandreou was replaced as prime minister by the veteran Venizelist, General Plastiras. British troops gradually won the upper hand in the Battle of Athens but only with difficulty, and only after being heavily reinforced from Italy. A ceasefire in mid-January 1945 was followed in mid-February by the Varkiza agreement, which sought a political settlement to the crisis brought about by the communist insurgency.

ELAS undertook to disarm and in return was promised an amnesty for what were termed 'political' crimes. It was also agreed that a plebiscite on the monarchy should be followed by elections, but the passions aroused by the December fighting proved difficult to quench. Ultra-right-wingers, incensed by the murder of some of the hostages taken by ELAS, and with memories of left-wing terror against political opponents during the occupation, now took a brutal and indiscriminate revenge on the left. A succession of weak governments proved unwilling to check the polarisation or incapable of doing so. Towards the end of 1945, as a result of British pressure, a seemingly more stable government was established under Themistoklis Sophoulis, the octogenarian leader of the Liberal Party and political heir of Venizelos.

Sophoulis announced that elections, the first since those of 1936, would be held on 31 March 1946. These were to be followed by a plebiscite, thus reversing the order agreed at Varkiza. The far left protested that fair elections could not possibly be held in the prevailing climate of disorder. The communists, once again under the leadership of Nikos Zakhariadis, who had spent the war in a German concentration camp, decided, after some wavering, to abstain. So, too, did some members of the Sophoulis cabinet. Sophoulis, however, was under strong pressure to persist from a Britain exhausted by the war and anxious to end her onerous Greek commitment. The elections went ahead, observed by an allied mission which contained British, American and French members (the Soviet Union having declined to participate). The abstention of the left, the disarray of the centre and the continuing disorder, particularly in rural areas, contributed to an overwhelming victory (55 per cent of the popular vote) for a right-wing coalition dominated by the People's Party. The foreign observers declared the elections to have been 'on the whole' free and fair and estimated abstentions at a mere 9 per cent of registered voters. This figure was clearly too low but only participation in the elections by the far left could have given a clearer indication of the true level of its support. The communist leadership subsequently conceded that the decision to abstain had been mistaken.

Greece is the only country in Europe in the camp of the victors where fascist collaborators with the occupier, quislings and traitors are once again throttling democracy. The resistance movement is in a state of general terrorist persecution. Hundreds have been murdered and are being murdered. Tens of thousands are in jail. Hundreds of thousands are being persecuted.

Central Committee of the Communist Party of Greece (1945)

The new People's Party government, headed by Dino Tsaldaris, now brought forward the plebiscite on the constitutional issue, originally intended for March 1948, to September 1946. Like the March 1946 election, this was held in anomalous circumstances and on the basis of out-of-date electoral registers, although the turn-out was much larger. The result was a 68 per cent vote for the return of the king, a dubious result, but one which appears to have reflected the view of significant numbers of erstwhile republicans that the return of the king was a lesser evil than the possibility of the establishment of a communist regime. Moderate republicans found

44 Winston Churchill photographed in Athens with Archbishop Damaskinos of Athens on 26 December 1944 during the *Dekemvriana*, the bitter fighting between units of the communist-controlled resistance army ELAS and British troops supporting the government of Georgios Papandreou, which had returned to Greece two months earlier as the Germans withdrew. The very presence of the British prime minister in the Greek capital at this particular juncture is testimony to his growing obsession with political developments in Greece during the later part of the war and to his determination to thwart a communist take-over. This had been reflected in his earlier agreement, finalised in Moscow in October 1944, with the Soviet leader, Joseph Stalin, to trade Russian predominance in Romania and Bulgaria for British predominance in Greece, the famous 'percentages' agreement. To the consternation of his staff, Churchill had embarked upon the hazardous flight to Greece with his foreign secretary, Anthony Eden, on Christmas Day, at a time when the war on the western front was at a critical stage. Despite prolonged meetings with the parties to the conflict Churchill, for all his immense prestige, was unable to bring about a settlement. He did, however, return to London much more aware of the strength of feeling against the return of King George II before the holding of a plebiscite. He also came

themselves ruthlessly squeezed between the extremes of left and right. The elections of March 1946 were a critical turning-point for they represented the last chance of a peaceful evolution from the nightmare of occupation and civil strife. A vengeful right-wing government exacerbated an already polarised political situation. Even before the elections right-wing repression had driven former ELAS partisans back to the mountains. This process now gained momentum, although there was still confusion within the communist leadership as to whether it should strive for power through constitutional or military means.

As the country slid towards outright civil war, the Tsaldaris government claimed, in August 1946, that communist guerrilla bands were being supplied from Yugoslavia and Bulgaria. In October the communists announced the formation of the Democratic Army under the leadership of Markos (Vafiadis), a former ELAS leader, although the communist party itself was not declared an illegal organisation until as late as December 1947. As the situation rapidly deteriorated, the British government effectively relinquished the preponderant influence it had hitherto exercised over the country's affairs. The role of principal external patron was now assumed by a United States that had in the past been highly critical of Britain's Greek entanglement. In March 1947, President Truman prevailed upon the US Congress to grant substantial emergency aid to Greece, as part of a programme of support for 'free peoples' threatened by internal subversion that came to be known as the Truman Doctrine.

It was some time before the effects of US aid were felt and, in the meantime, the Democratic Army, making effective use of guerrilla tactics, scored some notable successes over the regular army. But

---

Caption for Plate 44 (*cont.*).

to admire Archbishop Damaskinos, the senior cleric of the Orthodox Church in Greece, whom he had hitherto dismissed as a 'pestilent priest, a survival from the Middle Ages'. Churchill now prevailed upon King George, whose cause he had hitherto staunchly championed, to appoint Damaskinos as regent pending settlement of the constitutional issue. A ceasefire between ELAS and British forces was arranged on 11 January 1945, two weeks after Churchill's dramatic intervention.

45 A propaganda photograph showing King Paul and
Queen Frederica being carried shoulder high by 'reformed'
ex-communists during a visit to the prison island of Makronisos
during the 1946–9 civil war. By the time King Paul had succeeded
to the throne on the death of his brother George II in 1947, the
civil war, which had its origins in the politics of the wartime
resistance, was at full pitch. Makronisos was notorious for the
harsh treatment of supporters of the communist Democratic
Army and particular efforts were made to extract 'declarations
of repentance' in which communists not only renounced their
beliefs but denounced their former comrades. A British official
observer, with characteristic understatement, found conditions
in the camp to be 'contrary to the British and American concept
of humanity and justice'. The Democratic Army for its part
engaged in forcible recruitment and was no less brutal in its
treatment of dissenters. The Democratic Army could rely on
limited assistance from Greece's communist neighbours to the
north, Yugoslavia, Albania and Bulgaria, but Stalin was wary of
provoking an outright confrontation with the United States,
whose logistical support of the national army was vital to its
eventual victory. Inevitably the savagely fought civil war, besides
seriously retarding the process of postwar reconstruction, created bitter divisions within society which took a generation or
more to heal. During the civil war the army became identified

Markos failed in his attempt to secure the town of Konitsa, near the border with Albania, to act as the capital of the Provisional Democratic Government, whose formation was announced at the end of 1947. The Democratic Army was the beneficiary of substantial logistical and other support from the communist regimes of neighbouring Yugoslavia, Bulgaria and Albania. But this was on nothing like the scale of US economic and military aid which was administered through US missions whose powers were both very considerable and frequently invoked. Gradually the military tide turned. In this process the total command of the air enjoyed by the government forces was vital. The Democratic Army lost a crucial advantage when the communist party leader, Zakhariadis, prevailed over Markos and insisted that the Democratic Army abandon guerrilla tactics and fight as a regular army. Markos was purged and replaced as commander by Zakhariadis.

Under increasing government pressure the Democratic Army more and more relied on forced conscription, of women as well as men, in the areas that it controlled. Children were evacuated from the war zone to the countries of the eastern bloc, according to the communists for their own protection, according to their opponents to be indoctrinated as a new janissary levy. By 1949 as much as 40 per cent of the rank and file of the Democratic Army was composed of Slav Macedonians, a fact which led the communist party once again to advocate the right of self-determination for the Macedonians. This reversion to the unpopular policy of the inter-war period once more laid the communists open to charges of being prepared to cede recently and hard-won territory to traditional foes.

The international situation was also changing to the disadvantage of the Greek communists. Loyal as ever to the heartland of

---

Caption for Plate 45 (*cont.*).

with a visceral anti-communism and its close ties with the monarchy lasted until the imposition of the military dictatorship in 1967. During the postwar period the German-born and strong-willed Queen Frederica proved to be a controversial figure, whose relations with Konstantinos Karamanlis, during his first premiership between 1955 and 1963, were frequently stormy.

46 General James van Fleet cracking eggs with General Alexandros Papagos on Easter Sunday 1949. Described by General Dwight Eisenhower as being 'direct and forceful' if 'definitely *not* the intellectual type', van Fleet was appointed in January 1948 as head of the Joint US Military Advisory and Planning Group whose task was to co-ordinate military assistance to the national army during the civil war. Since the proclamation of the Truman Doctrine in March 1947, huge quantities of US military and economic aid had poured in. This was backed up by military advisers and the creation of a joint Greek–American general staff, although Americans had no combat role. Van Fleet arrived at a low point in the fortunes of the national army. Better equipment, improved training, superior numbers and total command of the air, however, helped to turn the tide. The morale of the national army received a further boost when General (later Marshal) Papagos, a hero of the Albanian campaign of 1940, was appointed commander-in-chief. Like a number of serving officers, Papagos had a record of involvement in politics. He was one of three senior officers whose pronunciamento forced the resignation of the prime minister, Panayis Tsaldaris, in October 1935, preparing the way for the restoration of King George II. Once the civil war had ended he founded his own party, modelling himself on de Gaulle. Favoured by the Americans, he was prime minister between 1952 and his death in 1955.

world communism, they sided with Moscow when Yugoslavia was expelled from the Cominform in 1948. As a consequence the Yugoslavs, preoccupied with the threat from the Soviet Union and its allies, discontinued their aid to the Democratic Army and finally closed the border to the guerrillas in 1949. Even before the split, Stalin had made clear his view that, given British and American naval domination of the Mediterranean, the communist cause in Greece was lost. While he would clearly have welcomed a victory for the Democratic Army, he was not going to risk confrontation with the US in order to secure it, not least perhaps because the Soviet Union was not yet a nuclear power. The Yugoslav 'stab in the back' proved a convenient alibi for the defeat of the Democratic Army but the decisive factor was the massive influx of American military aid in the form of equipment and training. This transformed the regular army into an effective fighting force, whose morale was boosted when, early in January 1949, General (later Marshal) Papagos, the military commander during the Albanian campaign, once again became commander-in-chief. By the late summer of 1949 the remnants of the Democratic Army, defeated in pitched battles on the rugged Grammos and Vitsi ranges, had been forced over the frontier into Albania. The communist leadership in October declared a temporary cessation of hostilities. Despite the fact that the defeated remnants of the Democratic Army were for some years kept on a war footing in their bleak east European and Russian exile the civil war was in reality over.

5

The legacy of the civil war 1950–74

The decade of the 1940s was the darkest in Greece's independent history. The glories of her stand at the time of the Italian and German invasions during the winter of 1940/1 and the heroism of the resistance, both collective and individual, to the barbaric German, Italian and Bulgarian occupation had brought in their wake privations on an unprecedented scale. Moreover, famine, reprisals and wanton material destruction, together with the virtual destruction of Greek Jewry, had been accompanied by internecine strife that was to culminate in outright civil war between 1946 and 1949. The war of independence in the 1820s and the National Schism of the period of the First World War had laid bare profound cleavages in society. But these earlier manifestations of a society divided against itself could not compare with the ferocity of the savagely fought civil war, which was to prolong the agonies of the occupation until the end of the decade. Moreover, the atrocities committed by both sides assumed an added dimension of horror in that they were inflicted by Greek upon Greek. The old quarrel had been between Venizelists and anti-Venizelists, broadly speaking between supporters of the republic and of the monarchy, but this schism had now been overlaid by an even more fundamental division, that between communists and anti-communists.

During the second half of the decade the meagre resources of the enfeebled state were not devoted, as elsewhere in Europe, to repairing the ravages of war and occupation, but rather to the containment of 'the enemy within'. By 1949 government military and security forces numbered approximately a quarter of a million. Much of the American aid that in western Europe was being devoted to economic development was channelled into military objectives. The bourgeois order, although at times gravely threatened, was to survive. But the government's dependence for its political and military survival on external patronage effectively made Greece a client state of the United States. Few major military, economic or, indeed, political decisions could be taken without American approval, testimony to a degree of external penetration that had scarcely existed even when British hegemony was at its height.

The crushing defeat of the communist insurgency, or 'bandit war' as the right insisted on calling it, ensured that, alone of the countries of the Balkans, Greece was to emerge from the travails and dislocations of the Second World War without a communist regime. But post-civil war Greece scarcely constituted a model democracy. The bitterness engendered by the civil war, perhaps inevitably, was to cast a long shadow over the politics of the 1950s and 1960s, much as the passions aroused by the National Schism during the First World War had distorted the whole course of the country's inter-war political development.

It soon became apparent that the primary objective of post-civil war governments was the containment of communism, on both the domestic and international planes, rather than any serious effort to reform or restructure society. Nonetheless, in the immediate aftermath of the civil war, there were hopeful indications that more moderate counsels might prevail. In February 1950, martial law, which had been in force since 1947, was lifted and the following month elections were held under the system of proportional representation that had been used in 1936 and 1946.

A plethora of parties contested the 1950 elections. Tsaldaris' rightwing People's Party, the victor in 1946, narrowly emerged as the largest single party. But three centre parties, each laying claim to the mantle of Venizelism, together mustered more than half of the 250 seats. These were the Liberals, led by Sophocles Venizelos, the son and would-be political heir of Eleftherios Venizelos; the National Progressive Centre Union, under the leadership of General Nikolaos Plastiras, the veteran of the Venizelist coups of 1922 and 1933 and the short-lived prime minister in the aftermath of the December

1944 insurgency; and the Georgios Papandreou Party, headed, not surprisingly by the politician of that name. None of these politicians could be described as sympathetic to the far left. Nonetheless, it was a hopeful sign that a majority of the electorate had voted for parties that were committed in some measure to reconciliation and which had rejected the strident revanchism of the People's Party.

The first post-civil-war governments, centre and centre-right coalitions, were divided as to the degree of leniency to be afforded to the vanquished in the civil war and were of short duration. Two new formations contested the next elections, those of September 1951. The first was the Greek Rally, headed by Marshal Papagos, the commander-in-chief during the later stages of the civil war. He had resigned from the army over which he had exercised unchallenged authority, in circumstances that are still not clear, after falling out with King Paul. The second was the United Democratic Left, which was essentially a front for the outlawed communist party. The Greek Rally displaced the People's Party on the right and won a larger share of the vote than any of the other parties. Significantly, Papagos' share of the separately recorded army vote was noticeably higher than that in the country at large. The result was still inconclusive, however, and another centre coalition was formed. This upset the American ambassador, who publicly threatened a reduction in US aid (of which Greece had been the recipient of almost a billion dollars over the previous five years) unless the electoral system was changed from proportional to majority. Such a move would clearly benefit Papagos who, in the climate of heightened international tension following the outbreak of the Korean war, was regarded by the Americans as the best guarantor of political stability and of a firm line against the left. The politicians protested at such flagrant interference but the change was duly made in time for the elections of November 1952.

These produced a massive victory for the Greek Rally. The majority system translated 49 per cent of the popular vote into 82 per cent of the seats. Now began a period of right-wing rule that was to last until 1963. Although a new constitution afforded guarantees of basic political liberties, these were frequently negated in practice by emergency legislation introduced during the civil war. Law 509 of 1947, for instance, remained in force and provided severe penalties for advocating the overthrow of the existing social order, while the security police, armed with mountainous files on the real or imagined views of the populace, maintained a close watch on those suspected of left-wing sympathies. A key instrument of political control was the requirement for police clearance for those who sought state employment, a passport or even a driving licence. Repressive though these measures were, they were nonetheless mild in comparison with the treatment meted out to 'class enemies' in Greece's northern neighbours. In April 1952 most of the death sentences still outstanding from the civil war were commuted and many of those convicted of political offences were released or had their sentences reduced.

If political reconciliation was not high on the agenda of the Papagos government, progress was made towards economic reconstruction. Tentative attempts that had been considered in the early postwar period to shift the economy away from agriculture towards industry, with the state taking the lead in such a restructuring, were effectively abandoned. But considerable effort was expended in restoring credibility to the currency, which had been fatally undermined by the staggering inflation of the occupation and immediate post-liberation years. The 1953 devaluation, coupled with a tight monetary policy and some loosening of the often cumbersome shackles of state control, boosted private enterprise and ushered in a twenty-year period of remarkable monetary stability and economic growth. This helped to restore confidence in the drachma, although the price of land and housing continued to be quoted in gold sovereigns well into the 1950s.

There continued to be a marked reluctance to invest in anything other than bricks and mortar, and particularly the latter, as apartment blocks constructed of reinforced concrete cut an unattractive swathe through Athens, Salonica and, increasingly, many provincial towns, sometimes giving the impression that the country was one vast building site. It is no accident that one of the world's largest cement factories was located in Volos. Between 1961 and 1980 no less than 65 per cent of investment was in construction, much of it in the form of housing for rapidly growing urban populations. During the civil war some 700,000 persons, some 10 per cent of the population, had been forced to abandon their homes, the beginning of a flight from the countryside to the cities that has been such a notable feature of the postwar period. Between 1951 and 1971 the proportions of the urban and rural populations were reversed, from 38 and 48 per cent respectively to 53 and 35 per cent. The rest were categorised as semi-urban. Between 1961 and 1971 the population of Greater Athens increased by 37 per cent and, during the following decade, by a further 19 per cent. Very high military expenditures acted as a brake on productive investment. With a few notable exceptions, such industrial enterprises as existed tended to be small, family based and concentrated in low technology sectors such as food, drink, textiles and tobacco. The service sector, however, flourished.

The economy continued to be heavily dependent on US aid and on such traditional props of the balance of payments as emigrant remittances and receipts from shipping. The lure of *xeniteia*, or sojourning in foreign parts, continued throughout much of the postwar period, with some 12 per cent of the population emigrating between 1951 and 1980. Until US quota restrictions were lifted in the mid-60s, much of this emigration was to Australia (by the 1970s Melbourne had one of the largest Greek populations of any city in the world), Canada and, from the late 1950s, to Germany where Greek (and still more Turkish) *Gastarbeiter* undertook many of the more menial jobs shunned by the indigenous population. A significant proportion of these 'guest workers' eventually returned home to set up small service sector businesses. The foundations of many postwar Greek shipping fortunes lay in the adroit purchase of US Liberty ships at the war's end and many of the supertankers built in the 1950s and 60s were Greek-owned, even if the bulk of them sailed under flags of convenience. This 'Greek' merchant marine was to emerge as the largest in the world. Before the war, tourism had been a negligible factor in the economy. Rapidly rising standards of living in western Europe, coupled with the development of mass air travel and much improved internal communications, in part a consequence of the civil war, led to tourism reaching 'take-off' stage by the late 1950s, a development that was to have a significant impact on the country's mores and customs as well as on the balance of payments. In time the ravages inflicted by war and civil war on the economy were healed, and even if the fruits of economic recovery were unevenly distributed, nonetheless living standards rose steadily throughout the 1950s and 1960s. Per capita income almost doubled between 1955 and 1963, while prices rose by only 17 per cent.

During the civil war Greece had been a key area of confrontation in the Cold War. This, coupled with the fact that her three neighbours to the north, Albania, Yugoslavia and Bulgaria, had fallen under communist control, was to ensure that she was harnessed to the western defence system. In 1952, Greece and Turkey were admitted to the NATO alliance, though neither country could be described as 'North Atlantic'. Shared perceptions of common external danger had, during the late 1940s, led to good relations between the two countries, which were joined in a formal alliance in 1953 by a Yugoslavia isolated since her 1948 break with Moscow. This improbable Balkan Pact soon disintegrated as relations between Yugoslavia and Russia improved and as those between Greece and Turkey reached crisis proportions following violent riots directed against the Greek minority in Istanbul in September 1955.

The abrupt ending of the brief honeymoon between the two allies guarding NATO's south-east flank had been precipitated by the growing crisis in Cyprus, the last area of substantial Greek population in the region to remain outside the boundaries of the Greek state. Over the years since the island had come under British administration in 1878 (it was formally annexed in 1914 and became a crown colony in 1925) there had been vociferous demands on the part of the Greek community, which constituted 80 per cent of the population, for *enosis*, or union, with the Greek motherland. For as long as Britain had been Greece's external patron successive governments in Athens had given little encouragement to these unionist aspirations. Now that the Americans, who were perceived to be more sympathetic to the Cypriots' desire to be rid of colonial rule, had displaced the British, and now that Britain was busy dismantling her empire, these inhibitions diminished and Prime Minister Papagos was prepared to give some support to Greek Cypriot aspirations.

After Britain had, perversely, appeared to rule out ever yielding sovereignty over the island, General Georgios Grivas, a Cypriot-born Greek army officer, who had led an unsavoury anti-communist organisation (known as 'Chi') during the occupation and its aftermath, unleashed in April 1955 a campaign of civil disobedience backed up with political violence. This was co-ordinated through his National Organisation of Cypriot Fighters (EOKA) and had the tacit connivance of the Archbishop of Cyprus, Makarios III. As a counterweight to Greek Cypriot demands, the British government encouraged Turkey to assert an interest in the dispute. This was the background to the highly destructive riots of September 1955 that were to precipitate a dramatic decline in the Greek community in Istanbul. It was not long before the Turks were to counter Greek calls for *enosis* with their own demands for *taksim*, or partition.

At the height of this growing crisis in Greek–Turkish relations, the ailing Papagos died. King Paul chose Konstantinos Karamanlis as his successor, to the manifest chagrin of more obvious contenders. Although not drawn from the charmed circle of the Athenian political elite, Karamanlis had made his name as a hard-driving minister of public works. This bluff Macedonian was to be a dominant force in politics, whether in or out of office, for the next thirty-five years. After reconstituting the Greek Rally as the National Radical Union, Karamanlis held new elections in February 1956, the first national elections in which women had the vote. An electoral law of truly Byzantine complexity, enacted, as was customary, by the outgoing government, achieved the desired effect of favouring Karamanlis' own party. Although the National Radical Union received a marginally smaller share of the popular vote than the main opposition bloc, it nonetheless secured a clear majority in parliament. The idiosyncrasies of electoral practice by which ruling parties, of whatever hue, felt, and feel, free to manipulate the electoral law to their own advantage were further highlighted in elections held two years later in May 1958, following a short-lived split within the ruling National Radical Union party. On this occasion, despite a substantial fall in his share of the popular vote, Karamanlis' majority in parliament actually increased.

Nonetheless, the right and, indeed, the centre, suffered a severe shock when the United Democratic Left, essentially a cover for the outlawed and exiled communist party, emerged from the 1958 elections as the main opposition party, with almost a quarter of the popular vote. This upsurge in support for the far left could only be partly explained by disarray in the centre. For the United Democratic Left had adroitly exploited widespread resentment at the failure of her NATO allies to support the Greek case over Cyprus. But the result did contribute significantly to breaking the logjam over Cyprus, for both Karamanlis and the United States

administration were worried by the apparent rise in neutralist sentiment. What was more, in the aftermath of the disastrous Suez
adventure in 1956, Britain had belatedly come to realise that her
strategic interests in the eastern Mediterranean could be as well
served by sovereign bases on the island. The possibility of real
progress towards a settlement became apparent when, in the
autumn of the same year, 1958, Archbishop Makarios, then in
exile in Athens, let it be known that he would be prepared to
consider independence for the island as an alternative to *enosis*.

The way was now clear for a resolution of the conflict, provided it
fell short of the union of the island with mainland Greece. Such a deal
was rapidly made early in 1959 at a meeting in Zurich between
Karamanlis and his Turkish counterpart, Adnan Menderes. At a subsequent meeting in London the draft agreement was presented as a *fait
accompli* by the British, Greek and Turkish governments to
Archbishop Makarios and Fazil Kütchük, the leaders of the Greek
and Turkish communities on the island. Makarios signed only with
considerable reluctance, while Grivas was clearly unhappy at the
betrayal of the sacred cause of *enosis*, for which he had fought with
skill and tenacity. The settlement provided that Cyprus would become
an independent republic within the British Commonwealth, with
Britain retaining sovereignty, in perpetuity, over two base areas.
Greece and Turkey were entitled to station small military contingents
on the island and, with Britain, became co-guarantors of the settlement. Makarios' caution was justified, for the new state was lumbered
with a cumbersome and essentially unworkable constitution. This
guaranteed 30 per cent of the seats in parliament and of positions in
government service (40 per cent in the police) to a Turkish minority
which constituted 18 per cent of the total population.

Karamanlis came under fire from the opposition for betraying the
cause of Hellenism in the interests of NATO and the Americans. But
the settlement did afford him respite to turn his attention, which had
been largely preoccupied with Cyprus during his first four years in
office, elsewhere. He succeeded in negotiating in 1961 an association
agreement, the first of its kind, with the European Economic
Community. This envisaged the possibility of full membership by
1984. The terms provided for a phased reduction in tariffs and customs duties, and promised much-needed competition for inefficient

47 'Fraternisation by numbers'. The uneasy state of Greek–
Turkish relations throughout much of Greece's independent
history is reflected in this NATO propaganda photograph (a)
taken on manoeuvres in Greek Thrace in 1953. It shows Turkish

industries that had hitherto sheltered behind high tariff barriers. But it is clear that Karamanlis' motives were as much political as economic: association was perceived at once as a means of anchoring Greece even more firmly to the western alliance and of legitimising her still somewhat uncertain European identity.

So far, Karamanlis' dominance of the domestic political scene had been without serious challenge. But his luck was to change with his decision to call elections in October 1961, somewhat in advance of the normal four-year term. For in the wake of their dismal showing

---

Caption for Plate 47 (*cont.*).

on the right in British-style uniform) and Greek (in American-style uniform) platoons fraternising somewhat hesitantly for the benefit of the cameras. At this time relations between the two countries, newly admitted to the NATO alliance, were at their best during the post-Second World War period. Venizelos' adroit diplomacy had initiated a much improved climate in Greek–Turkish relations during the 1930s although the Greek minority in Istanbul suffered heavily from the imposition of discriminatory taxation during the Second World War. The shared perception of the Soviet threat brought the two countries close together in the late 1940s and early 1950s. But within two years of the taking of this photograph relations deteriorated sharply in the wake of riots inspired by the Turkish government against the Greek community of Istanbul. There were a number of deaths and the damage to property was on a massive scale. Over 4,000 shops, 100 hotels and restaurants and 70 churches were damaged or destroyed. In (b) the Ecumenical Patriarch, Athinagoras, walks bareheaded in the ruins of the church of the *Panaghia Veligradiou*. The riots prompted a process of emigration that was to lead to the virtual extinction of the Greek minority in Turkey by the late 1990s. By contrast the Turkish minority in Greece numbers some 120,000. The 1955 riots were provoked by the demand of the Greek Cypriot majority in Cyprus for union with the mainland. Since 1955 the question of Cyprus has proved a permanent 'apple of discord' between the two countries, with relations reaching their nadir at the time of the Turkish invasion of northern Cyprus in July 1974, when an outright Greek–Turkish war was only narrowly averted. Since then the Turkish occupation of the north of the island and a whole complex of bilateral differences between the two countries have led to an almost permanent state of tension.

in the 1958 election, the centre parties had been welded together to form the Centre Union by the veteran Liberal politician, Georgios Papandreou, who had been scarcely less dismayed than Karamanlis himself by the upsurge in support for the far left.

The new centre alignment, however, ranging as it did from dissident right-wingers with a grudge against Karamanlis to former adherents of the far left, was always prone to the centrifugal tendencies that, in the end, were to tear it apart. Papandreou was able to achieve one of his principal objectives in the 1961 election by cutting the United Democratic Left down to size and pushing it into third place, but he was unable to make much headway against Karamanlis, whose share of the vote increased substantially in comparison with the 1958 result. No sooner had the election results been announced than both the Centre Union and the United Democratic Left denounced them as fraudulent, the result of manipulation and improper pressures by the army, the gendarmerie, the rural security battalions and other 'dark forces'. Certainly there were some extraordinary fluctuations in voting patterns between the 1958 and 1961 elections which could scarcely be explained in terms of the routine ebb and flow of political support.

The opposition parties claimed that the army had implemented a NATO plan, code-named Pericles and designed to deal with threats to internal security, to preserve the right's hold on power. This was never proved (although Colonel Georgios Papadopoulos, the dictator of Greece between 1967 and 1973, did subsequently acknowledge that the army had been involved), nor was Karamanlis' personal responsibility for what Papandreou termed an 'electoral putsch'. The opposition leader, a brilliant orator, promptly launched what he termed an 'unyielding struggle' to nullify the results of the elections. This proved an effective rallying cry that helped give greater coherence to his newly founded Centre Union. It was also useful in harnessing the support of a new generation of recent migrants to the cities (the population of Greater Athens had increased in size between 1951 and 1961 by 35 per cent) who felt excluded from the country's growing prosperity, wanted greater educational opportunities for their children, and were no longer convinced of the need for the battery of repressive legislation dating from the civil war period.

The perception that the Karamanlis government had lost its way was heightened by the murder in May 1963 at a peace rally in Salonica of Grigorios Lambrakis, a United Democratic Left deputy. His assassins, drawn from the sinister underworld of the far right, the 'para-state' as it was known, were subsequently found to have links with senior gendarmerie officials. Karamanlis had also clashed with the palace and, more particularly, with the German-born, strong-willed Queen Frederica, a somewhat ironic development given that it had been King Paul who had unexpectedly plucked Karamanlis from obscurity to succeed Papagos in 1955. Karamanlis resented the special links that had been forged between the armed forces and the palace, whose relative extravagance offended his austere provincial temperament. The last straw in an increasingly fraught relationship was the royal couple's refusal in the summer of 1963 to heed the prime minister's advice to postpone their state visit to London, where they were likely to meet with violent protests by demonstrators seeking the release of imprisoned communists. A man of somewhat authoritarian inclination, Karamanlis had also for some time chafed under a constitution that in his view gave too much power to parliament at the expense of the prime minister.

Karamanlis resigned in exasperation and left the country, returning only to fight elections in November 1963 under a caretaker government concerned to prevent a recurrence of the irregularities of 1961. Georgios Papandreou was able adroitly to exploit the weaknesses of a right that appeared to have lost its self-confidence, while there are indications that two of the principal arbiters of the political scene, the palace and the US embassy, were now prepared to look with favour on a mildly reformist centre government as the best defence against a possible resurgence of the far left such as had occurred in 1958. Papandreou secured a narrow victory over Karamanlis, giving the lie to allegations on the part of its more extreme critics that the right would never voluntarily surrender its grip on power. A chagrined Karamanlis left for France and an exile from which he was not to return for eleven years and then in the most dramatic of circumstances.

The fact that the balance of power in the new parliament was held by the United Democratic Left was, however, unacceptable to a politician who was as suspicious of the far left as he was opposed

48 Archbishop Makarios of Cyprus photographed at a meeting on Rhodes with General Georgios Grivas and Nikos Sampson (centre) in 1959, shortly after agreement had been reached between Britain, Greece and Turkey that Cyprus would be granted independence in 1960. This was a disappointing outcome for all three, and particularly for Grivas. A Cypriot who had served in the Greek army, he had masterminded the campaign of terror and civil disobedience launched in 1955 to bring an end to British colonial rule, dating from 1878, through the union with the Greek state of Cyprus, the last substantial area of Greek population in the Near East to remain outside its boundaries. Makarios reluctantly accepted independence as the only alternative to the partition of Cyprus between Greece and Turkey, whose interest in the island derived from the fact that 18 per cent of the population were Turks. Very much in the Orthodox tradition, Makarios combined the political with the religious leadership of his flock by becoming president of the new Republic of Cyprus. Grivas was never reconciled to the settlement which, until his death in 1974, he sought to undermine. Nikos Sampson, who had recently been released from prison by the British authorities when the photograph was taken, was one of the most ruthless and effective members of Grivas' EOKA (National Organisation of Cypriot Fighters). When President Makarios was briefly deposed in 1974 in a coup launched by the military regime in Athens, Sampson was installed as president of Cyprus. He held office for barely a

to the right and Papandreou soon resigned, forcing a new election three months later in February 1964. His gamble paid off and his Centre Union was rewarded with a 53 per cent share of the vote, a figure only once (narrowly in the exceptional circumstances of 1974) exceeded in the postwar period, and a seemingly unassailable parliamentary majority.

But the high (and perhaps unrealistic) hopes that had been aroused by the Centre Union victory were not to be fulfilled and Papandreou was to survive in office for barely eighteen months. A major new crisis over Cyprus formed a continuous backdrop to his premiership and, as so often in the country's history, the primacy of foreign over domestic policy was critically to impede the implementation of his election promises. Just as he assumed office the elaborate system of power sharing which had been enshrined in the 1960 Cyprus settlement broke down as, sooner or later, it was bound to do. In November 1963, President Makarios, who, very much in keeping with Orthodox tradition, combined the political with the spiritual leadership of his flock, demanded a reduction in the powers that had been granted to the Turkish minority. His proposals, significantly and ominously, were rejected out of hand by the Turkish government on behalf of the Turkish Cypriot minority. At the end of December fierce intercommunal fighting broke out and the threat of direct Turkish intervention in the island loomed large. This was averted in the summer of 1964 only by some very tough talking by the American president, Lyndon Johnson.

* * * *your Parliament and your Constitution. America is an elephant. Cyprus is a flea. Greece is a flea. If those two fleas continue itching the elephant, they may just get whacked by the elephant's trunk, whacked good.
President Lyndon Johnson to the Greek ambassador in Washington (1964)

An uneasy peace was maintained by a UN peace-keeping force, which has maintained a presence on the island ever since, and a

---

Caption for Plate 48 (*cont.*).

week but the imposition of a hardline supporter of union was one of the factors that precipitated the Turkish invasion of 20 July 1974 which resulted in the occupation of almost 40 per cent of the island.

49 *Sailor in a pink background* (1955) by Yannis Tsarouchis (1910–90), painter, stage designer and book illustrator. A student of Photis Kontoglou, his work reflects the same intense preoccupation with Greek tradition.

sizeable proportion of a Turkish population that had hitherto been scattered throughout the island was gathered into enclaves from which Greek Cypriots were excluded. Papandreou made himself highly unpopular with the US administration by rejecting a form of 'double' *enosis*, which envisaged the union of Cyprus with Greece in return for the creation of self-governing Turkish cantons on the island, the establishment of bases controlled by mainland Turkey and the cession to Turkey, as a gesture of goodwill, of the small Greek island of Kastellorizo.

These developments overshadowed much of Papandreou's short premiership but he was able to make a start on his reforming programme. Some, but not all, of those who were still in prison for activities during the civil war were released and the freeze in relations with the eastern bloc countries was partially thawed. Important educational reforms were enacted which, had there been time to implement them, would have gone some way towards modernising an archaic school system and would have placed emphasis on the spoken 'demotic' form of the language at the expense of the purist *katharevousa*. Never one for the detail of economic policy, Papandreou relied heavily for advice on his son, Andreas, who had recently returned after many years spent in the United States as an academic economist. He had become a minister in his father's government, to the manifest chagrin of a number of Centre Union stalwarts who viewed him as a threat to their own chances of eventually leading the party. One of these was Konstantinos Mitsotakis. The rivalry between Mitsotakis and the younger Papandreou was to resurface twenty years later when Mitsotakis in 1984 became leader of the conservative New Democracy party midway through Andreas Papandreou's initial eight-year premiership.

Georgios Papandreou's mildly inflationary economic policies alarmed the country's economic and financial oligarchy for they appeared to threaten the remarkable price stability that had been achieved during the first Karamanlis era (consumer prices had actually fallen in 1962). More ominously, it became apparent that elements in an army schooled to regard itself as the guardian of national values under threat from the communist menace within and without looked upon the Papandreou government as a kind of Trojan horse, threatening to open the country up to dangerous left-wing influences. The particular bugbear of ultra-right-wing elements in the army was Andreas Papandreou, who espoused views which were mild compared with some of his later positions but were noticeably more radical than those of his father. The suspicions of the far right were fuelled by allegations that the younger Papandreou was looked upon as leader by a conspiratorial group within the army, known as *Aspida* (Shield), a vaguely left-wing counterpart of the ultra-right-wing IDEA (Sacred Bond of Greek Officers), which had been founded among the Greek forces in the Middle East during the Second World War.

The older Papandreou had little option but to try to exert full political control over the armed forces but in this he was thwarted by his own defence minister. The latter not only blocked proposed changes in the command structure of the army but refused Papandreou's demand that he resign, even after he had been formally expelled from the Centre Union. The crisis reached a climax in July 1965 when the prime minister sought royal assent to his taking over the ministry of defence in addition to the premiership. The king, Constantine II, had succeeded his father, King Paul, to the throne at the age of twenty-four in March of the previous year, 1964.

The stage was now set for a confrontation between the young, politically inexperienced king and his advisers and the septuagenarian prime minister, whose career in politics extended as far back as the First World War. King Constantine refused Papandreou's request to take over the ministry of defence on the grounds that to do so would be improper when the prime minister's own son was under investigation for his supposed role in the *Aspida* conspiracy. Following an acrimonious, and public, exchange of correspondence, Papandreou offered his resignation, not really expecting it to be accepted. But the king called his bluff and set about implementing a strategy of trying to split the Centre Union. This had always been an uneasy coalition of centrist, radical and conservative elements and, like all the bourgeois parties, lacked any proper structure. After much effort, the king succeeded, against a background of massive demonstrations by Papandreou's supporters, who called the July 1965 events a 'royal putsch' to match Karamanlis' 'electoral putsch' of 1961.

King Constantine may have been acting within his constitutional rights but whether his strategy was politically sensible is another matter. Even if the support of the conservative National Radical Union was enough to give it the slenderest of majorities in parliament, the government formed by defectors from the Centre Union, the 'apostates' as they were bitterly denounced by the party faithful, clearly lacked legitimacy. Constantly under fire from Papandreou, always more at home in opposition than in power, the 'apostate' Stephanopoulos government could clearly do little more than mark time. Moreover, the continuing political turmoil and uncertainty served to feed the paranoia of the extra-parliamentary right and to create a dangerous climate of disillusionment with politicians among the population at large.

Papandreou had consistently argued that new elections offered the only way out of the most serious political crisis to date in the postwar period. Eventually, these were scheduled to take place, under a non-political 'caretaker' government, in May 1967, following agreement between Papandreou and Panayiotis Kanellopoulos, who had succeeded Karamanlis to the leadership of the National Radical Union. But the campaign was overshadowed by demands that Andreas Papandreou's parliamentary immunity be lifted so that he could be charged with complicity in the *Aspida* affair. Wrangling over this issue led to the downfall of the 'caretaker' government and the king, unusually, charged Kanellopoulos with overseeing the elections. But, within a matter of days, on 21 April, a group of relatively junior officers mounted an efficiently executed coup, the purpose of which was to pre-empt an almost certain Centre Union victory at the polls.

There was virtually no resistance to this first overt intervention by the military in the political arena in the postwar period. The king, the politicians from right to left, and, indeed, the highest ranks of the armed forces were all caught off guard. The fragmented nature of the trades unions and the virtual lack of structure in the political parties, combined with the manifest failure of the 'political world' to overcome the crisis of the previous eighteen months, all contributed to the ease with which the army was able to seize power. Ignoring the pleas of his legitimate prime minister, Kanellopoulos, the king afforded a grudging recognition to a nondescript civilian government that served as a front for the troika of two colonels, Georgios Papadopoulos and Nikolaos Makarezos, and a brigadier, Stylianos Pattakos, that had engineered the coup.

The military junta, which chose to dignify itself, ludicrously, as the 'Revolution of 21 April 1967', initially justified its action, in the time-honoured fashion of military dictators and following the precedent established by General Metaxas in 1936, by the need to forestall an imminent communist seizure of power. But no evidence of such communist intrigue was ever produced. Indeed, it was clear that the left was as much caught unawares by the coup as had been the bourgeois parties. Moreover, this very unpreparedness was one of the factors that precipitated the split in the exiled leadership of the communist party the following year (1968) into two factions, one unwaveringly loyal to the Soviet Union, the other (the Communist Party of Greece of the Interior) broadly 'Eurocommunist' in orientation.

Some members of the military regime undoubtedly took seriously its self-proclaimed mission of defending the traditional values of 'Helleno-Christian civilisation' from the western and secular influences consequent on the rapid pace of social and economic change in the postwar period. There were numerous echoes in its ideological propaganda of the authoritarian and paternalistic precepts of the Metaxas regime, even if these were seldom explicitly acknowledged. It soon became clear, however, that the primary motivation of the 'Colonels', as they came to be known, was less elevated. Terrified at the prospect of the return to power of a Centre Union government in which Andreas Papandreou might be expected to have even greater influence, they feared a purge of precisely the ultra-right-wing elements in the armed forces that lay behind the coup. For the most part of provincial and peasant or lower middle-class social background they were resentful of the privileged lifestyle of the traditional political elite, which, as they saw it, played out its elaborate political games in the urban affluence of Athens while they, in the boredom of provincial garrison towns, defended the country's borders from the enemies of the nation, the communists and the Slavs.

Young people of Greece . . . You have enfolded Greece in your breasts and your creed is the meaning of sacrifice, from the time of the 'Come and get them' of Leonidas, later of the 'I shall not give you the City' of Constantine Palaiologos, of the 'No' of Metaxas and, finally, of the 'Halt or I shoot' of 21 April 1967 . . . Today's ceremony is a re-baptism in the well springs of ancestral tradition; an expression of the national belief that the race of the Greeks is the greatest and best under the sun.

Brigadier Stylianos Pattakos (1968)

They could find virtually no political allies from among the old politicians of whom they were so contemptuous. Indeed, the traditional right reciprocated this loathing quite as much as did politicians of the centre and left. In contrast with most previous instances of praetorianism the Colonels did not intervene on behalf of any given *parataxis* or political family, only to withdraw from the political arena once their favoured political clients had been established in office. Rather they took their revenge on the 'political world' across the spectrum from right to left, harbouring, like Metaxas before them, a particular animosity towards communists, real or supposed. Thousands with dossiers indicating left-wing sympathies were sent into internal exile and a number of politicians and other dissidents were imprisoned, exiled or placed under house arrest. Andreas Papandreou was released from prison and allowed to leave the country following intense American pressure. Georgios Papandreou spent much of the time until his death in November 1968 under house arrest and his funeral, attended by as many as half a million Athenians, a fifth of the entire population of the city, was a massive, albeit implicit, indication of the unpopularity of the regime.

Following the failure of an amateurish counter-coup launched by the king in December 1967, the ruling troika of Colonels threw off any pretence at rule through civilian puppets. They set up a regency to replace the king, who had fled into exile. Colonel Papadopoulos now emerged into the limelight as the strong man of the regime, becoming prime minister. A cunning political operator, he subsequently amassed more and more power, taking over, in addition to the premiership, the ministries of foreign affairs, defence, education and government policy, eventually combining these portfolios with the regency. In 1968, in a clear effort to institutionalise the military's grip on power by giving it a permanent and determining say in the governance of the country, a highly authoritarian constitution was introduced and ratified in a fraudulent plebiscite.

The inability of the regime to build up any degree of popular support soon became apparent and its reluctance to countenance elections, even within the restrictive parameters of its own anti-democratic constitution, was confirmation of this. Although a number of small resistance groups came into existence, and an attempt was made to assassinate Papadopoulos in 1968, there was little organised opposition. Many of those who did resist were harshly treated by a brutal and efficient security apparatus. Moreover, the regime, through a policy of profligate borrowing and offering lavish inducements to foreign and domestic investors, was broadly able to sustain, at least until the world oil crisis of 1973, the momentum of economic growth that had developed under the democratic governments of the late 1950s and early 1960s. This inhibited the development of mass opposition.

The regime's brutal, and frequently absurd, ways attracted much hostile comment abroad but, by and large, Greece's partners in the NATO alliance were unwilling to translate rhetorical condemnations, where they could be prevailed upon to make them, into concrete action. Moreover, the American administration, seen by many Greeks as having been instrumental in installing the dictatorship in the first place (although there is no evidence for this), was prepared to offer aid and comfort to a regime that it saw as a bastion of pliant stability in an increasingly volatile eastern Mediterranean. One of the few foreign dignitaries to visit a country which for seven years became something of an international outcast was the US vice-president, Spiro Agnew (born Anagostopoulos), the child of a Greek immigrant father. The junta for its part was careful to avoid giving offence to its US patron and to carry out its NATO commitments faithfully, particularly after a humiliating confrontation with Turkey over Cyprus in the autumn of 1967 soon after the seizure of power. This crisis marked the beginning of a steady deterioration in relations between the military regime and President Makarios that was to culminate in the catastrophe of July 1974, when Turkey invaded Cyprus.

In 1973, serious cracks began to appear in the seemingly stable, if oppressive, façade of the regime. It was no coincidence that in this year the rate of inflation, having been very low for the preceding twenty years, shot up to double figures. Students took the lead in opposing the regime and in March occupied the Law Faculty of the University of Athens. An abortive naval mutiny in May demonstrated that anti-regime pockets had survived within the armed forces, despite repeated purges in the officer corps. Papadopoulos promptly declared King Constantine deposed, accusing him of having been mixed up in the naval mutiny from his exile in Rome, and proclaimed the establishment of a 'presidential parliamentary republic'.

A farcical referendum duly followed in which Papadopoulos, the only candidate, was elected president for an eight-year term. He then called on Spyros Markezinis, a minor politician, to oversee elections, the proposed first stage in the introduction of a 'guided' democracy.

Before these elections could materialise they were overtaken by large-scale student demonstrations, which culminated in the occupation of the Athens Polytechnic in November 1973. This action was brutally suppressed by the army, and the ensuing loss of life resulted in the overthrow of Papadopoulos and his puppet prime minister by even more hardline members of the junta, led by Brigadier Dimitrios Ioannidis, the head of the much-feared military police. Lieutenant-General Phaidon Gizikis was installed as president. The November 1973 changing of the guard within the junta coincided with a deterioration, as sharp as it was sudden, in relations with Turkey. This was occasioned by Turkish claims to the right to prospect for oil in parts of the Aegean Sea claimed by Greece as forming part of her continental shelf. This Turkish interest had been prompted by the discovery of oil in exploitable quantities in the region of the Greek island of Thasos.

Against the background of the dispute in the Aegean, the Ioannidis regime adopted an increasingly menacing line towards Cyprus, seeking to force a reluctant President Makarios to accept Athens as the 'national centre' of Hellenism. When Makarios, in early July 1974, demanded the removal of almost all the mainland Greek officers in the Cyprus National Guard and protested that the junta was trying to destroy the state of Cyprus, Brigadier Ioannidis' mindless response was to launch a coup against the president, who was forced to flee the island. It seems that Ioannidis was desperately seeking to bolster his regime's popularity by bringing about a spectacular nationalist triumph, namely the union of Cyprus with Greece. Fearing precisely that the coup presaged the *enosis* which had been specifically excluded under the terms of the 1960 constitutional settlement, Turkey launched an invasion of the northern part of the island on 20 July.

Both Greece and Turkey mobilised and, for a time, there was the very real possibility of outright war between the two countries. But the Greek mobilisation proved to be a shambles and the military commanders refused to carry out Ioannidis' orders to attack Turkey.

50 The student occupation of the Athens Polytechnic in November 1973. The lettering on the balustrade next to the Greek flag reads 'No to the junta'. The graffiti call for the overthrow of fascism and equate the United States with the Nazis. Student unrest was the first manifestation of large-scale opposition to the military dictatorship established after the Colonels' coup of April 1967. It began with the occupation of the Law Faculty of the University of Athens in March 1973. This was followed by an unsuccessful naval mutiny in May. This, in turn, prompted Colonel Papadopoulos, the leader of the junta, to move towards a 'guided' democracy under the provisions of the authoritarian constitution of 1968. These plans were thwarted by further student occupations of university buildings in Athens and Patras and of the Athens Polytechnic in November. The military authorities became seriously worried at manifestations of public support for the students when a

Lacking any kind of domestic support or legitimacy and with not a friend in sight on the international scene, the Ioannidis regime began to disintegrate, the *coup de grâce* being delivered by the demand of powerful elements within the army for a return to civilian government. A meeting of military leaders and senior members of the old political establishment called on Konstantinos Karamanlis to oversee the dismemberment of the dictatorship and the return to democratic government. Karamanlis returned to Greece from his French exile for the first time in eleven years like some *deus ex machina*, and amid scenes of wild jubilation was sworn in as prime minister at 4 a.m. on 24 July 1974.

Caption for Plate 50 (*cont.*).

clandestine radio began broadcasting appeals for a worker–student alliance to overthrow the junta. On the night of 16/17 November troops and police, spearheaded by tanks, put an end to the occupation. The exact casualty figures have never been established, but there appear to have been at least twelve deaths, many more injuries and still more arrests. Although the students were crushed by overwhelming force, their action helped precipitate the overthrow of Papadopoulos. This had already been planned by hardliners headed by Brigadier Ioannidis, the commander of the hated military police, who disapproved of the hesitant steps in the direction of greater liberalisation. After Papadopoulos' overthrow power effectively lay with the firebrand Ioannidis, whose coup against Archbishop Makarios in Cyprus in July 1974 brought about the downfall of the dictatorship.

6

The consolidation of democracy and the populist decade 1974–90

In July 1974 Karamanlis was pitchforked into a crisis which was to test his political skills to the full. The mindless chauvinism of the military had provoked the Turkish invasion of Cyprus, brought Greece and Turkey to the brink of war, and precipitated an unprecedented collapse in civil authority. Yet the resources at the prime minister's disposal were minimal in the face of a military power structure which for more than seven years had been without effective restraint or challenge. It still contained significant elements that were disinclined to make way for politicians for whom they had professed nothing but contempt. But the manifest bankruptcy of the junta and its demonstrable unpopularity, together with the huge upsurge in support for Karamanlis, coupled with his own steady hand, were to ensure a remarkably smooth transition from military rule to a pluralist democracy. For the next seven years, the political system functioned more effectively than at any time previously. That Karamanlis was balancing on a delicate tightrope was demonstrated by the fact that for several weeks following his return he slept on board a yacht, watched over by a destroyer.

Karamanlis' overriding priority was to defuse the risk of war with Turkey, never a realistic option given the imbalance between the two countries' armed forces and the shambles of the mobilisation ordered by Brigadier Ioannidis in the twilight hours of the military dictatorship. In mid-August the Turkish army, following the breakdown of peace talks in Geneva, fanned out from its initial beachhead in northern Cyprus. It established a zone of occupation, delimited by the Attila line extending from Morphou in the west to Famagusta in the east, that covered nearly 40 per cent of the island. Despite this, Karamanlis made it clear that he rejected a military solution to the crisis. He could, moreover, expect little support from notional allies. The United States was convulsed by President Nixon's resignation under the threat of impeachment and Dr Henry Kissinger, the secretary of state, who had been inclined to dismiss President Makarios as the 'Castro' of the eastern Mediterranean, was slow to react to the crisis. Britain, whose colonial policies had created the Cyprus problem and who, with Greece and Turkey, was a guarantor of the 1960 constitutional settlement, effectively washed her hands of the imbroglio.

On Cyprus itself, the trauma of the invasion, the flight of 185,000 Greek refugees to the south of the island, coupled with perceptions that the US had 'tilted' towards Turkey, prompted violent demonstrations in which the US ambassador was shot dead. In Greece, Karamanlis was quick to respond to an upsurge in anti-American sentiment, occasioned as much by the benign tolerance extended to the military regime by successive US administrations as by the failure to exercise restraint over Turkey, by calling into question the future of the US bases and by withdrawing Greece from the military wing of the NATO alliance.

During the seven-year dictatorship the politicians had maintained a united front in their opposition to the junta that was all the more remarkable in the light of the polarised political climate of the pre-coup years. Communists, as under the pre-war Metaxas dictatorship, had borne the brunt of the repression. Shared experiences of opposition and persecution had blunted animosities dating from the period of the civil war. Karamanlis reflected this climate of greater tolerance by moving quickly to legalise the communist party. It had been outlawed in 1947, and since the end of the civil war in 1949 had maintained both a precarious underground presence within Greece, sheltering behind the façade of the United Democratic Left, and a factionalised existence among the many thousands of political refugees living in frequently grim exile in the countries of eastern Europe and the Soviet Union. The conflict between a Stalinist old guard and reformists had, in the wake of the Warsaw Pact invasion of Czechoslovakia in 1968, erupted in an open split. The dissident reformists, who were to espouse broadly 'Eurocommunist' policies, styled themselves the Communist Party of the Interior, a title reflecting the view that the exiled leadership of the party had lost touch with changing political and social realities within the country. The mainstream communist party was nevertheless to retain the loyalties of the great bulk of those on the far left of the political spectrum.

There was a certain irony in the fact that it was Karamanlis, a scourge of the communists in the pre-coup period, who now sought to incorporate the far left within the political system. But his willingness to legalise the communists was symptomatic of a more general leftward swing among the electorate at large. The experience of the dictatorship and of the Cyprus disaster had dented confidence in the anti-communist, pro-American and pro-NATO shibboleths of the 1950s and 1960s. Although there was no doubting the wide basis of popular support enjoyed by Karamanlis in cleansing the Augean stables left by the junta, he soon made it clear that he wanted to legitimise his power, which so far he had exercised by the grace and favour of a section of the army, by holding elections.

These took place in mid-November 1974, a mere four months after the collapse of the dictatorship. They were contested, for the first time in the postwar period, by parties which ranged across the whole of the political spectrum from the authoritarian right to the communists. There was never much doubt that Karamanlis' New Democracy party (essentially a reconstituted version of the pre-coup National Radical Union) would sweep the board. It duly did so with a virtually unprecedented 54 per cent share of the poll. This translated into a massive majority of 219 out of 300 seats in parliament. The electorate had clearly voted for a safe pair of hands at the helm and had been impressed by the implicit slogan of 'Karamanlis or the tanks'. What was more surprising was the collapse of the Centre Union, the only pre-coup party to run under its old colours. Its share of the vote slumped from 53 per cent in the elections of 1964, the last to be held before the 1967 coup, to 21 per cent.

A portent of things to come was the respectable showing of Andreas Papandreou's Panhellenic Socialist Movement (PASOK), a new political formation unlike either New Democracy or the Centre Union. The kernel of PASOK comprised members of the Panhellenic

Liberation Movement (PAK), the rather ineffective anti-junta resistance group directed from abroad by Papandreou, and another left-of-centre resistance group, Democratic Defence, many of whose members were soon to rebel against Papandreou's authoritarian leadership. PASOK's performance (14 per cent) in the 1974 election was a considerable achievement, given that Papandreou had no pre-existing organisation on which to base his new party. Clearly a sizeable number of voters had been attracted by his harnessing of nationalism to the rhetoric of socialism and by his slogan of 'National Independence, Popular Sovereignty, Social Liberation and Democratic Structures'.

The election was followed a month later by a referendum on the future of the monarchy. King Constantine had unwisely not returned to Greece on the fall of the junta. Living in Britain, he was able to put his case in a series of television broadcasts. The centre and left parties actively campaigned against his return but Karamanlis maintained an attitude of studied neutrality. Had he thrown his great authority behind a restoration then it is likely that the vote would have gone in the king's favour. Clearly, however, the wounds from Karamanlis' clashes with the palace in the early 1960s had not healed. Only 30 per cent of the electorate, mainly concentrated in the traditional royalist heartland of the Peloponnese, voted for the monarchy.

This referendum was certainly the fairest of the six to be held on the issue of monarchy versus republic during the course of the twentieth century, and the 70 to 30 split in favour of the republic replicated almost exactly the result in the only other plebiscite to be held under reasonable conditions, that of 1924. Since 1974 the issue of the monarchy has effectively been dead apart from brief flurries of excitement, as when the deposed king was allowed back to Greece for a few hours to attend his mother's funeral in the family burial ground at Tatoi in February 1981; as when, in 1988, Konstantinos Mitsotakis, the leader of the New Democracy party, publicly questioned the 'fairness' (he used the English word) of the 1974 plebiscite; or as when, during the political impasse of 1989, Constantine expressed his willingness to return should the people want him to.

Within the remarkably short space of five months Karamanlis had not only legitimised his authority through honest elections but had, through the referendum, resolved, permanently as it seemed, the debate over the monarchy. This was an institution which had been a source of friction ever since it had been imposed as the price of independence by the Protecting Powers. For a period of thirty years after the National Schism of the First World War, it had been a source of chronic political instability. Karamanlis was now able to use his massive parliamentary majority to promulgate, in 1975, a new constitution. It incorporated many of his ideas about the need to redress the balance in favour of the executive at the expense of the legislature. But the considerable powers vouchsafed to the president under the new constitution were in practice never exercised either by the first elected president, Konstantinos Tsatsos (1975–80), an academic philosopher and conservative politician, or by Karamanlis himself when, in 1980, to no one's great surprise, he relinquished the premiership for the presidency.

In the early months after the *metapolitefsi*, the transition from dictatorship to democracy in the summer of 1974, Karamanlis had to steer a delicate course. On the one hand he had to be seen to respond to the demands – which were particularly insistent on the part of the students whose resistance to the dictatorship had been instrumental in its destabilisation – for the severe punishment of the tyrants, and the *apohountopoiisi* or 'de-juntification' of the entire state apparatus of the appointees of, and collaborators with, the military regime. On the other hand, indiscriminate revenge could easily have provoked a backlash on the part of junta sympathisers still firmly entrenched in the armed forces. That these represented a real danger is indicated by the uncovering in February 1975 of a plot, whose true dimensions were, for obvious reasons, played down at the time. This aimed at the overthrow of both Karamanlis and Makarios (who had been restored to the presidency of Cyprus in December 1974). With this threat in mind Karamanlis entrusted the key post of minister of defence to Evangelos Averoff, whose impeccably conservative and anti-communist credentials were calculated to reassure hardline elements in the armed forces.

During the course of 1975 a number of trials, whose public impact was the greater for being televised, were held of those with primary responsibility for establishing the dictatorship, for the widespread ill-treatment and torture of dissidents, and for the brutal suppression of the student occupation of the Athens Polytechnic in November

1973. Those found guilty were given long prison sentences. They included Brigadier Ioannidis, the former head of the much-feared military police, who received a seven-fold life sentence for his involvement in the Polytechnic killings. The original troika behind the coup, Colonels Papadopoulos and Makarezos and Brigadier Pattakos, were sentenced to death. The haste with which the government commuted these death sentences to life imprisonment suggests that Karamanlis was alert to the dangers inherent in any repetition of the executions of politicians and military leaders that had followed the Asia Minor disaster in 1922 and which had fatally poisoned inter-war political life. The fact that the principal military conspirators remained in gaol in some cases until their deaths indicates nonetheless that the sentences were intended to give a salutary warning to others minded to subvert democratic institutions. In other spheres, the more notorious of the collaborators with the junta were removed and the purges, in deference to student pressure, were particularly pronounced in the universities.

The process of democratic consolidation was played out against a background of continuing tension with Turkey. Although the immediate crisis of the summer of 1974 had been defused, the underlying antagonism remained. To the original dispute that had flared up in 1973 over the delineation of the respective continental shelves of Greece and Turkey in the Aegean (and hence their rights to any oil that might be found there) was added a whole complex of issues deriving from the 1974 crisis. In the wake of the Turkish invasion of Cyprus, Greece had heavily fortified her Aegean islands, many of which lie only a few miles off the Turkish coast. Turkey argued that this was in contravention of the treaties of Lausanne (1923) and Paris (1946), which in formally recognising Greek sovereignty over the islands had provided for them to be demilitarised. Greece contested the continuing validity of these provisions in the light of the 1936 Montreux convention, arguing that, in any case, no sovereign state could relinquish its right to self-defence.

There were disputes, too, over air traffic control in the Aegean, with Turkey challenging the existing status quo; over Greece's theoretical right (not so far exercised and not a likely prospect) to extend the limit of her coastal waters from six to the more usual twelve miles, a move which, in the Turkish view, would transform the

Map 9 The Aegean dispute
Source: Andrew Wilson, *The Aegean dispute* (1979)

Aegean into a Greek lake and constitute a *casus belli*; and over the treatment of their respective minority populations. The continuing Turkish occupation of northern Cyprus further poisoned relations between the two NATO allies, although Karamanlis always insisted that Cyprus was not strictly a problem in bilateral relations. Impatient outsiders who thought Greek fears of Turkish aggression exaggerated failed to take into account the extent to which the burden of the past and the remembrance of past wrongs, real or imagined, influenced mutual perceptions. Moreover, the emergence of *détente* between the super-powers lessened the fears that Greece and Turkey had of their communist neighbours, and removed what had been a powerful force making for good relations between the two countries in the late 1940s and early 1950s, namely the fear that if they did not hang together they would hang separately.

The potential for the simmering crisis in Greek–Turkish relations to flare up at any time was demonstrated in the summer of 1976 when the Turkish government sent a survey ship, the *Sismik I*, to carry out soundings in disputed waters. Andreas Papandreou, the leader of PASOK, called for the sinking of the *Sismik*, an action that would undoubtedly have precipitated war. Karamanlis, for his part, preferred recourse to the UN Security Council and the International Court of Justice at The Hague. But neither body was able to contribute constructively to a resolution of the conflict.

What gave a particular edge to the Aegean dispute was the hope of finding oil beneath the sea bed, for both countries had few indigenous sources of energy and both had been particularly badly hit by the energy crisis of the early 1970s. Commercial quantities of oil had been found off the island of Thasos, but, at its peak, oil production from this field has never exceeded 5 per cent of Greece's total consumption. It remains to be seen whether the Aegean sea bed will yield the hoped-for oil reserves. Greek perceptions of the Turkish threat have had serious economic consequences, for enhanced spending on the armed forces has consumed as much as one-fifth of budget expenditures, even if it has had the incidental advantage of giving the officer corps a genuine sense of mission and of diverting it from political activity. Massive expenditures on military hardware meant that the infrastructural reforms, e.g. in education and health care, that demanded urgent attention received a low priority. The economic inheritance of the junta was unpromising. The momentum of the pre-coup period had been maintained during the early years of the dictatorship but it had been sustained only by profligate borrowing and excessive generosity to foreign investors. By the last years of the junta inflation, the scourge of the 1940s which had been largely contained through the prudent monetary policies of the 1950s and 1960s, once again became a major problem. For a government ostensibly wedded to the free enterprise system, New

Democracy displayed a curious penchant for taking banks and other enterprises into state ownership, adding to the very large numbers of those employed, directly or indirectly, by the state.

But relatively few of Karamanlis' energies could be diverted to coping with matters of domestic policy, a fact that was to have serious consequences for the future fortunes of the right. Throughout his six-year premiership his sights were to be firmly concentrated on matters of foreign policy. His overriding priority was the accelerated accession of Greece to the European Community. The 1961 treaty of association had provided for the possibility of accession in 1984. But Karamanlis was determined to speed up this process, seeing in membership of the Community compensation for the deterioration in relations with Greece's traditional patron, the United States, safeguards for her newly re-established democratic institutions, and protection against the Turkish threat. It was significant that relatively little emphasis was placed on the potential economic benefits of membership, although these in the event were to prove real enough. An unspoken assumption underlying the enthusiasm of many Greeks for Europe was that membership would somehow place the seal of legitimation on their country's somewhat uncertain European identity: after all they habitually spoke of travelling to Europe as though Greece did not form part of the same cultural entity.

The European Commission in Brussels had some doubts as to whether the economy (and the inflated and cumbersome bureaucracy) was yet ready to withstand the competitive rigours of the Common Market. But Karamanlis skilfully exploited feelings of guilt at Europe's inertia during the dictatorship, and the existing members were soon falling over themselves to ease the path to entry of the country which they liked to hail as the fount of European civilisation. Karamanlis' persistence paid off when, in May 1979, the treaty providing for full membership of the Community as of 1 January 1981 was signed in the Zappeion building in Athens. But when, the following month, the ratification of the treaty was debated in parliament both PASOK and the communist party boycotted the proceedings.

Another important dimension to foreign policy during the Karamanlis era – and here he was following through policies initiated by the Colonels – was the 'opening' to the Balkans, a region in which Karamanlis travelled widely. Although there had been some signs of a thaw in relations with Greece's communist neighbours in the early 1960s, relations in the aftermath of the civil war had been generally, and inevitably, bad, with the partial exception of those with Yugoslavia, with which Greece had a short-lived treaty of alliance in the mid-50s. Clearly, one purpose of these initiatives was to win support for the Greek case over the Aegean and Cyprus. Although there was a noticeable improvement in bilateral relations, little emerged in concrete terms from the Balkan summit held in Athens in 1976 under Karamanlis' aegis.

The primacy of foreign policy concerns over domestic issues characteristic of so much of the country's independent history was reflected in the decision to hold elections in 1977, a year earlier than the constitutionally prescribed term. The results demonstrated Karamanlis to have been to a degree the victim of his own success in restoring the country's political equilibrium. While in 1974 there had been a widespread perception that only he stood between democracy and dictatorship, in 1977 there were no such constraints on voting behaviour. New Democracy's share of the vote fell by 12 percentage points from 54 to 42. Under the prevailing system of 'reinforced' proportional representation this was more than enough to give the party a comfortable working majority in parliament (172 out of 300 seats). But the result gave a clear warning that the party could not indefinitely rely on Karamanlis' personal charisma and authority to retain its hold on power.

The surprise of the 1977 election was the virtual doubling in the vote for Papandreou's PASOK, from 14 per cent in 1974 to 25 in 1977, a swing achieved largely at the expense of the Union of the Democratic Centre (the Centre Union of 1974). This, lacking the internal discipline of either New Democracy or PASOK, rapidly disintegrated into warring factions. PASOK, with sixty seats in parliament, was now the official opposition. Part of New Democracy's decline was clearly explained by the drift of some of its 1974 supporters to the far-right National Camp, a motley grouping of royalists, supporters of the dictatorship for whose imprisoned leaders it demanded an amnesty, and of those who regarded Karamanlis, improbably, as too much of a socialist. The emergence of this group testified to the success of Karamanlis' efforts to define without ambiguity the borders between the democratic and authoritarian right, borders that had been distinctly blurred in the 1950s and 60s. On the far left, the communists secured 9 per cent of the vote and the communists 'of the Interior', now in alliance with some small left-wing groups, 3 per cent.

PASOK's achievement, for a party founded as recently as 1974, was impressive. Clearly the advocacy of nationalism, and, in particular, of an uncompromising policy towards Turkey, combined with socialist rhetoric, albeit a rhetoric now shorn of the radical 'Third World' liberationist sloganeering of the early years, had struck a responsive chord with a significant segment of the electorate. More important, perhaps, than rhetoric was organisation. PASOK was the first party outside the far left to develop a nationwide, if not necessarily very democratic, organisational structure. Its dramatic emergence as the official opposition served notice on New Democracy that it, too, must modernise, organise and match PASOK's ideological appeal if the right was to maintain its almost unbroken grip on power in the postwar period.

Greece belongs to the West.

Konstantinos Karamanlis

Greece belongs to the Greeks.

Andreas Papandreou

Karamanlis proved incapable of doing this. Although successful in distancing his party from the authoritarian elements that had blemished its image in the 1950s and 60s and in making New Democracy's commitment to a genuinely pluralist political system transparent, his efforts to modernise and democratise the party structure and develop a credible ideological basis were less certain. His espousal, at the first party congress of New Democracy in 1979 (PASOK's first full congress was not held until 1984), of a policy of 'radical liberalism' merely confused his supporters. Provision was, however, made for the election of his successor by the New Democracy parliamentary group, a bold innovation for a bourgeois party. Much of Karamanlis' time continued to be taken up with foreign affairs, and in particular with negotiating the final terms of entry into the EC. An inconclusive summit meeting in 1978 with Bülent Ecevit, the

Turkish prime minister, led to some improvement in the climate of bilateral relations but none of the fundamental differences dividing the two countries came anywhere near to solution.

Once his overriding objective of membership of the EC had been assured, Karamanlis, as had been widely expected, elevated himself to the presidency in May 1980, at the end of Konstantinos Tsatsos' five-year term, securing just three more votes in parliament than the constitutional minimum of 180. In a closely fought contest for the now vacant leadership of New Democracy, Georgios Rallis, a dark-horse candidate whose paternal and maternal grandfathers had both held the premiership, secured a narrow victory over his more conservative rival, Evangelos Averoff. Rallis' conviction that Karamanlis should have soldiered on until the next election, due in October 1981, proved well founded, for under his decent but lacklustre leadership, New Democracy, deprived of Karamanlis' charismatic presence, relapsed into the factionalism and clientelism that he had striven to reform. This further weakened the party's ability to fend off the challenge posed by Papandreou. Karamanlis' elevation to the presidency was to benefit PASOK in another, and more significant, way. The fact that the presidency was now occupied by a strong and charismatic personality, of impeccably conservative credentials, and armed with considerable reserve powers under the 1975 constitution, was a reassurance to wavering voters attracted, on the one hand, by the heady mix of nationalism, populist demagogy and socialist rhetoric on offer from Papandreou but, on the other, fearful that things might get out of control under a radical PASOK government.

Papandreou himself was alert to the need to reassure voters broadly in the centre of the political spectrum who might be tempted to switch from New Democracy to PASOK. If there had been a perceptible moderation in PASOK's policies before the 1977 election, this process became even more pronounced during the period between those of 1977 and 1981. Cynics dubbed this the 'era of the tie', during which Papandreou abandoned his roll-neck sweater for a more respectable collar and tie. Not only was the early insistence that PASOK was a class-based Marxist party tacitly abandoned, but even the emphasis on socialism was played down, a sensible avoidance of giving hostages to fortune in a society where some 60 per cent

of the economically active population were working on their own
account and only some 40 per cent were wage and salary earners.
Papandreou offered the 'average' Greek, the owner of a house, a shop
and a car, and perhaps more importantly those who aspired to such a
status, the assurance that a PASOK victory at the polls posed no kind
of threat. In claiming to represent the interests of the 'non-privileged'
against those of the 'privileged', he defined the latter as the handful of
families that constituted the financial and economic oligarchy, ever
ready to sell out their country to foreign interests.

Similar reassurance was given that a PASOK victory would not
lead to any dramatic switch in foreign policy orientations. Gone were
the days when the EC was denounced as a capitalist club, a front for
the multinationals seeking to exploit countries such as Greece that
were on the capitalist periphery. Now the demand was for a referendum on membership of the Community. This was never in fact a
realistic prospect, for the calling of a referendum was a presidential
prerogative, and Karamanlis, having invested so much of his personal prestige in securing entry, was scarcely likely to sanction a
referendum if there was any chance of the vote going against
Europe. Likewise the early calls for a precipitate withdrawal from
the NATO alliance were abandoned. Now withdrawal was stated to
be a strategic objective, contingent on the international configuration
of power. The future of the US bases was similarly to be a matter for
negotiation rather than precipitate closure. A further note of reassurance to wavering centrists was the addition to the PASOK ticket of
Georgios Mavros, briefly the standard bearer of the traditional
centre in the post-coup period.

If Papandreou had been careful to retain his freedom of manoeuvre
over issues such as these, he nonetheless held out the prospect of
radical social transformation, coupled with a determination to
break the cycle of dependence that had characterised the country's
history as a notionally sovereign state. His programme, spelt out in
elaborate detail in the 'Contract with the People', ranged from an
undertaking to ensure the 'objective' teaching of history to the elimination of the *nefos*, or smog, that blanketed Athens for much of the
year. All these promises were summed up in PASOK's catch-all
slogan of *Allagi*. This was scarcely a novel one in the Greek political
context, but 'Change' was clearly something that younger voters in

particular hankered after, given the right's domination during the postwar period.

A tired-looking New Democracy, under the worthy but uncharismatic leadership of Rallis, proved quite incapable of responding to the challenge posed by PASOK. It, too, had to appeal to the floating voters of the centre if it were to have any chance of clinging on to power. Yet at the same time it had to try to woo back into the fold those disgruntled ultra-right-wingers who, in 1977, had defected to the National Camp. This was to prove an impossible balancing act. Enormous resources were expended in the campaign, which was the most expensive to date in the country's electoral history. PASOK enjoyed a major advantage in that the newspapers supporting it had almost twice the circulation of the pro-New Democracy press. As the day of the election approached press coverage became ever more polarised, and a curious note of religious imagery emerged, with Andreas Papandreou's entry into Patras being compared to Christ's entry into Jerusalem on Palm Sunday. When the 'Holy Day' of the election, as another pro-PASOK newspaper put it, came in October 1981, PASOK achieved the astonishing feat of once again virtually doubling its share of the vote from 25 per cent in 1977 (14 per cent in 1974) to 48 per cent, which gave it control of 172 seats in the 300-seat parliament. By contrast New Democracy's share of the vote slumped from 42 to 36 per cent, with the communist vote at 11 per cent remaining almost static.

Although in its early years there had been a tendency to regard PASOK as the voice of rural protest, the distribution of its vote in 1981 was remarkably even between urban and rural areas and between men and women. PASOK's 'short march' to power since its foundation in 1974 was a remarkable testimony to Andreas Papandreou's political charisma, to his ability to articulate the aspirations, and more particularly, perhaps, the frustrations and prejudices of a very sizeable proportion of the electorate, especially in the younger age groups, in a period of rapid economic and social change. In particular he spoke to the condition of the hundreds of thousands who had migrated to the towns in the postwar period and who faced a hard struggle in making ends meet in an era of high inflation, in a deteriorating physical environment and with inadequate educational, welfare and health provision. In blaming their problems, in populist fashion, on the sinister machinations of external and domestic reaction he had clearly struck a responsive chord. His was a challenge and an appeal which cut across class differences and to which politicians on the right, bereft of the leadership of their one charismatic leader, Karamanlis, proved incapable of responding. New Democracy could only offer more of the same and while it was true that overall standards of living had risen markedly during the period of the right's hegemony, the new prosperity had been unevenly distributed. Many had felt excluded from the fruits of the country's increasing prosperity and the emergence of a consumer society, and formed a natural constituency for PASOK.

The smoothness of the transfer of power from the right to the centre left was testimony, or so it appeared, to a growing maturity in the political system and to the genuine commitment of the post-coup right to pluralist democracy. It could also be argued that in 1981 the evolution of the political system reverted to the course on which it had been set in the mid-1960s and from which it had been rudely diverted by the military coup of 1967. Whether or not this was the case, Papandreou had certainly aroused high expectations. He sought to dampen these by arguing, with some justification, that the profligate economic policies of the outgoing New Democracy government and the underlying structural weaknesses of the economy circumscribed his freedom of manoeuvre and that he would need two full four-year terms in office to carry out his ambitious programme.

He was able, however, quickly to signal a shift in the style of government by implementing a number of reforms, most of which carried no economic cost and many of which were long overdue. His policy of 'national reconciliation' encompassed the official recognition of the resistance to Axis occupation during the Second World War; the granting of permission to return to communists who had fled to the eastern bloc countries at the end of the civil war (the fact that this concession was limited to those of Greek ethnic origin, however, excluded the large numbers of Slav Macedonians who had constituted a near majority of the communist Democratic Army during the closing stages of the civil war); and an end to ceremonies commemorating the victory of the national army over the communists in the civil war.

The *monotoniko*, or single accent system, was adopted, drastically simplifying the system of accents employed in the written language. Civil marriage was introduced, against stiff opposition from the Church, as was divorce by consent. Adultery was removed from the catalogue of criminal offences, and the dowry system was, in theory at least, abolished. Some real progress was made in amending family law and in improving the position of women, even if the representation of women in the PASOK parliamentary group was not significantly greater than that in New Democracy. Reforms were introduced which were intended to democratise the universities, whose structure was modelled on German prototypes, by increasing the power of junior staff and students against a hitherto all-powerful professoriate. In practice these tended to compound an already chaotic situation and to add a further dimension of politicisation. Efforts were made to boost cultural life in the provinces. These were paralleled by attempts to bring about administrative decentralisation and to break the stranglehold over the country's administration exercised from Athens. These met with little success, however, as local administrative bodies had no means of raising revenue. The various measures, however, combined with worsening pollution and a general deterioration in the quality of life in the capital (the *nefos*, or smog, did not, as promised, disappear along with the right), did result in a slight, but discernible, tendency for a reversal of the seemingly inexorable process of migration from the provinces to the major urban areas. A national health service was introduced, in the face of fierce opposition from the medical profession. The building of clinics and hospitals (and cultural centres) in the rural areas helped strengthen the tendency that became ever more marked during the initial eight years of PASOK rule for support for the party to hold up better in rural than in urban areas. Although Greece had more doctors per head of population than any other country in the EC, those who could afford it (including the prime minister himself when he developed serious heart problems) still tended to seek medical treatment abroad.

Although many of these measures were low cost, any hope of creating a modern welfare state, one of PASOK's objectives, hinged critically on putting the economy on a sounder footing, and in particular on improving productivity. PASOK, once in power, was quick to

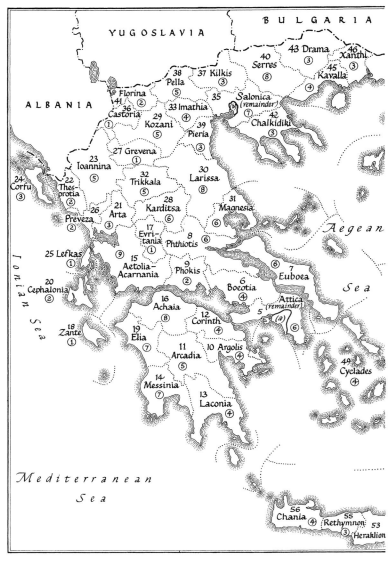

Map 10 Electoral and administrative districts
Source: Howard Penniman, *Greece at the polls* (1981)

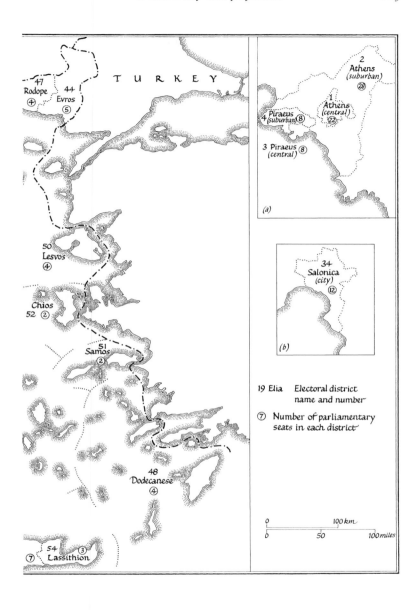

T U R K E Y

47
Rodope
④

44
Evros
⑤

2
Athens
(suburban)
㉘

1
Athens
(central)
㉒

4 Piraeus
(suburban) ⑧

3 Piraeus
(central) ⑧

(a)

50
Lesvos
④

Chios
52 ②

51
Samos
②

34
Salonica
(city)
⑫

(b)

19 Elia   Electoral district
           name and number

⑦   Number of parliamentary
    seats in each district

48
Dodecanese
④

54
⑦   ③
Lassithion

0   100 km
0   50   100 miles

51 Andreas Papandreou being sworn in as prime minister in
October 1981 by Archbishop Serapheim of Athens in the
presence of President Konstantinos Karamanlis. Charismatic
leaders have played a pivotal role in the political system, with
Karamanlis and Papandreou dominating the political scene
during the second half of the twentieth century much as
Kharilaos Trikoupis and Theodoros Deliyannis dominated the
politics of the later nineteenth century. Karamanlis, a
conservative, was prime minister between 1955 and 1963 and
1974–80, president between 1980 and 1985 and was re-elected
for a further five-year term in 1990. Papandreou, a populist
socialist, was prime minister between 1981 and 1989, and 1993
and 1996. The most formidable test of Karamanlis' political
skills came in 1974 when he was charged with overturning the
disastrous legacy of the military dictatorship which misruled
Greece between 1967 and 1974. The best measure of his success

raise wages and salaries in the already bloated state sector inherited from the right. The promised indexation of wages and salaries, however, one of the party's most attractive promises in a country which had for many years experienced double-digit inflation, soon gave way to policies of harsh pay restraint and to the circumscription of the right to strike of those in the state sector.

In opposition PASOK had promised a decentralised socialism based on the 'socialisation' of key sectors of the country's economic life and on self-management. Socialisation differed from mere nationalisation (and even under the right a sizeable proportion of the economy had come under direct or indirect state control) in that it envisaged a high degree of worker participation. A somewhat elusive concept in theory, it proved even more elusive in practice. Most of the candidates for socialisation tended to be drawn from the so-called 'problematic' companies, already heavily indebted to the largely state-controlled banks. Far from bringing with it any noticeable improvement in productivity, socialisation all too often merely provided opportunities to dispense patronage through padding the payroll.

If the changes wrought by PASOK in matters of domestic policy were more in style than in substance, this was equally true in matters of foreign policy. There was no substantive breach in traditional foreign policy orientations. PASOK's rhetoric in opposition about withdrawal from the NATO alliance and the EC and the closure

Caption for Plate 51 (*cont.*).

was the peaceful handover of power in 1981 by the right to the first socialist government in the country's history. This was led by Andreas Papandreou. Papandreou was 74 when he won the 1993 election and Karamanlis 83 when re-elected president in 1990. Advanced age has never been an obstacle to political ambition in Greece. Themistoklis Sophoulis was aged 88 when he died in office as prime minister in 1948, while the prime minister of the all-party government that emerged from the second election in 1989, Xenophon Zolotas, was 85. The three party leaders at the time, Konstantinos Mitsotakis of the conservative New Democracy, Andreas Papandreou of the socialist PASOK and Kharilaos Florakis of the communist Alliance were all in their seventies.

of the American bases was not matched in practice. Papandreou's early demand, once in power, for a NATO guarantee of the border with Turkey met with no response and was tacitly dropped. Greece refused to participate in a number of NATO exercises in the eastern Mediterranean in protest against repeated Turkish infringements of her airspace in the Aegean and against Turkey's demand that the island of Lemnos be demilitarised under the terms of the 1923 Treaty of Lausanne. But outright withdrawal from the alliance was never to prove an issue.

With regard to membership of the European Community the initial demand for a referendum on the principle of membership was tacitly abandoned, although Greece did go through the motions of trying to renegotiate the terms of accession, achieving some concessions in the process. But at the 1984 PASOK congress Papandreou explicitly declared that withdrawal from the EC would have deleterious consequences for the economy. As the years passed it became increasingly clear that Greece was a significant beneficiary of EC agricultural subsidies, and observers attributed PASOK's relatively greater strength in rural areas in the 1985 and 1989 elections in part to the effects of such subventions. The US bases in Greece, established in the 1950s on the basis of a number of bilateral agreements, also survived PASOK. Indeed, a new agreement was reached in 1983 which provided for the four bases to continue in operation for a five-year period until 1988. At the time the agreement was signed there was confusion as to whether the agreement would 'terminate' in 1988 or whether it was merely 'terminable', upon either party giving the appropriate notice. As the 1988 deadline approached there were protracted and tortuous negotiations for the renewal of the agreement. These eventually resulted in a significant diminution of the American military presence in Greece.

If the promise of a radical reorientation of the country's external relations which characterised PASOK's rhetoric in opposition did not materialise, there was nonetheless a definite change in the style in which the country's foreign policy was conducted. In keeping with the promised adoption of a 'nationally proud' stance, in contrast with the purported subservience of PASOK's conservative predecessors, the PASOK government was noisily out of step with Greece's NATO and EC partners on a number of issues. Papandreou championed the concept of a nuclear-free zone in the Balkans, and urged delay in NATO plans for the establishment of cruise and Pershing missiles in Europe to give further time for disarmament negotiations. Greece also spectacularly broke ranks with the European Community in several respects. Papandreou's refusal to join in sanctions against the military regime in Poland following the establishment of martial law was combined with a benign attitude towards General Jaruzelski's military dictatorship. Papandreou was the first western leader to break Poland's isolation by making an official visit in 1984.

The most flamboyant example of breaking ranks with European partners occurred during Greece's presidency of the EC in the second half of 1983. The foreign minister, Yannis Haralambopoulos, was able to stifle criticism when the Soviet Union shot down a Korean Airlines 747 airliner. PASOK's championing of radical causes world-wide was symbolised by the presence at the 1984 party congress of Hortensia Allende, the widow of Salvador Allende of Chile, and of representatives of the Nicaraguan Sandinistas. Papandreou was outspoken, too, in his criticism of the 1982 Israeli invasion of Lebanon and in his support for Yasser Arafat and the Palestine Liberation Organisation. Relations with the US were further strained by allegations that the PASOK government was prepared to turn a blind eye to the activities of Arab terrorist groups in Athens and by its failure to stamp out a home-grown terrorist group, 'November 17', whose numerous victims included American officials, as well as prominent Greek businessmen and politicians.

The poor state of relations with Turkey continued to dominate external relations and to be the determining factor in defence policies under PASOK just as it had been during the seven years of conservative rule following the downfall of the military junta in 1974. While in opposition, Papandreou had been a fierce critic of his right-wing predecessors, accusing them of a willingness to negotiate away the country's sovereign rights in the Aegean. He had argued that negotiations with Turkey were essentially pointless because there was nothing to negotiate over. Moreover, it was noteworthy that whereas, in the run-up to the 1981 election, there had been a moderation in PASOK's line over a number of foreign policy issues, there had been no such relaxation in the intransigent stance over Turkey.

This had been symbolised by Papandreou's call to sink the Turkish survey ship *Sismik* in 1976. In 1982 he signalled the priority he gave to confrontation with Turkey by visiting Cyprus, the first-ever visit to the island by a ruling Greek prime minister. In November 1983 the already poor state of relations with Turkey took a sharp turn for the worse when the Turkish Cypriot assembly unilaterally declared an independent 'Turkish Republic of Northern Cyprus'. This was formally recognised, however, only by Turkey.

Four months later, in March 1984, a renewed crisis broke out following allegations that Turkish warships on exercise had fired salvoes in the direction of a Greek destroyer observing from Greek territorial waters. Greece placed her armed forces on alert and recalled her ambassador in Ankara for consultations. This particular crisis blew over but the underlying seriousness of the situation was emphasised by the promulgation, at the end of 1984, of a new defence doctrine, whereby the main threat to the country's territorial integrity was declared to come not from the Warsaw Pact but from Greece's NATO ally, Turkey.

In December 1986 an incident between Greek and Turkish border patrols on the Evros river resulted in the deaths of three soldiers, two Turkish and one Greek. This was followed three months later, in March 1987, by the most serious crisis in relations between the two countries since the 1976 *Sismik* crisis. For a brief time it threatened outright war. As in 1976, the 1987 flare-up hinged on proposed Turkish exploration for oil in disputed Aegean waters. The armed forces of both countries were placed on alert and Papandreou declared that all necessary measures would be taken to safeguard the country's sovereign rights. Holding NATO, and in particular the United States, to be responsible for the crisis, Papandreou took the unprecedented step of ordering the suspension of communications facilities at the American base at Nea Makri and of dispatching his foreign minister to Sofia to discuss the crisis with the Bulgarian communist leader, Todor Zhivkov. In a calculated snub, the ambassadors of Warsaw Pact countries in Athens were briefed before their NATO counterparts. The confrontation was only defused when the Turkish prime minister, Turgut Özal, stated that the Turkish survey ship would operate only in Turkish territorial waters, while Greece likewise undertook to refrain from drilling in disputed waters.

The March 1987 crisis had once again demonstrated the explosive potential of the Aegean dispute and the intractability of differences which were as much rooted in deeply embedded historical memories as in current realities. Less than a year later, however, there occurred what was hailed at the time as an historic breakthrough in relations between the two countries. The Davos agreement of January 1988, the 'no war agreement' as it was characteristically called by PASOK, followed a meeting in Switzerland between Papandreou and his Turkish counterpart, Özal. With a view to inaugurating a much-improved climate in bilateral relations the two leaders agreed to establish a 'hot line' between Athens and Ankara, undertook to meet at least once a year and to visit each other's countries. They called for an intensification of contacts at all levels, with particular emphasis on tourism and cultural exchanges. Joint committees were established to work towards closer political and economic relations.

In the early months after Davos the *rapprochement* appeared to be developing a considerable momentum. The Turkish government rescinded a 1964 decree restricting the property rights of Greek nationals in Turkey, while Greece reciprocated by lifting objections to reactivating the 1964 association agreement between Ankara and the EC which had been frozen since the 1980 military coup in Turkey. The lifting of visa requirements for Greek nationals led to an enormous increase in the numbers of Greeks visiting Turkey. Reciprocal visits by the Greek and Turkish foreign ministers were followed by the official visit of Özal to Athens, the first such visit by a Turkish prime minister for thirty-six years.

It was not long, however, before the old strains were to surface. Greece made repeated protests at Turkish violations of her airspace and by the end of 1988 there were clear signs that the vaunted 'spirit of Davos' was flagging. In a public contretemps in November, Turkey contested Greece's claim that the only issue outstanding between the two countries was the delineation of their respective continental shelves in the Aegean, maintaining that the extent of Greece's airspace, the militarisation of the Aegean islands and the status of the Turkish minority in western Thrace were also in contention. Further strains in the relationship developed during the first election campaign of 1989, when Greece complained that the Turkish government was giving open encouragement to particular candidates

campaigning among the Turkish minority. The election of two independent Turkish deputies went against existing precedent whereby
candidates drawn from the Turkish minority campaigned on the
tickets of established parties. The political stalemate that developed
in 1989 inhibited further initiatives in the field of Greek–Turkish
relations.

After the 1981 elections the conservative opposition had been
quick to draw attention to the gulf between PASOK's aspirations
and its achievements, dubbing what PASOK had termed its 'rendezvous with history' as a rendezvous with reality. It seized on the
opportunity afforded by the elections to the European parliament
in 1984 to demand that they be fought not on specifically European
issues but 'over the whole syllabus'. But the results gave no credence
to New Democracy's hopes of pushing PASOK into second place,
although its share of the vote did increase by 7 per cent while
PASOK's declined by a similar amount in relation to the 1981
national elections. New Democracy's failure to make significant
inroads into PASOK's support in 1984 led to the resignation of its
leader, the 75-year-old Evangelos Averoff, who had led the party
since Georgios Rallis' resignation after the 1981 defeat. His traditional conservatism had proved no match for the charismatic appeal
of Papandreou.

If the 1984 European election had been fought in a polarised
political atmosphere then the temperature was further raised by the
election of Konstantinos Mitsotakis as leader of New Democracy in
succession to Averoff. Mitsotakis, whose political antecedents lay in
the centre, had been one of Papandreou's principal rivals for the
future leadership of his father's Centre Union government and
had been prominent among the so-called 'apostates' whose defection
had brought down the government in the great political crisis of July
1965. Political memories in Greece are long, and, on Mitsotakis'
assumption of the New Democracy leadership, Papandreou roundly
accused him of being a traitor, who had betrayed his father and
who bore a major responsibility both for the ensuing seven-year
military dictatorship and for the invasion of Cyprus. The mutual
antipathy between the two men was to have serious consequences in
the political stalemate that emerged from the two deadlocked elections of 1989.

The electoral campaign for the national election due in 1985 effectively got under way with the 1984 European election. In its 1981 election manifesto PASOK had promised to introduce a system of simple proportional representation, which the far left, the most obvious beneficiary of such a move, had long demanded. But PASOK could not resist the temptation to follow the example of its right-wing predecessors and manipulate the electoral law to its own advantage. It therefore adopted a system that was designed to ensure that a party with a small plurality of the vote could nonetheless secure a working majority in parliament. Not surprisingly, New Democracy was happy to lend its support, although the communists were loud in their condemnation of what they saw as a cosy deal stitched up between the two main parties. Before the elections could take place, however, the country was to be convulsed by a major constitutional crisis. This arose from the fact that Karamanlis' five-year term of office as president came to an end in March 1985. It was generally assumed that he would be a candidate for a second term, despite the fact that he was now seventy-eight. The support of New Democracy could be taken for granted, while Papandreou on a number of occasions had praised Karamanlis' handling of the presidency and had stated that he would be happy to see him continue in office.

In early March, New Democracy duly announced its support for Karamanlis' candidature. PASOK was widely expected to follow suit when Papandreou announced, to his manifestly surprised but clearly enthusiastic supporters, that PASOK's candidate would be not Karamanlis but Khristos Sartzetakis. More than twenty years younger and a judge of the Supreme Court, Sartzetakis had won fame in the early 1960s as the young examining magistrate who had brought to justice the murderers of the left-wing deputy Grigorios Lambrakis in 1963. Papandreou further raised the political temperature by declaring his intention to amend the 1975 constitution so as to weaken the prerogatives reserved to the president. The fact that these had not so far been deployed, either by Karamanlis or by his predecessor Konstantinos Tsatsos, did not preclude, so he argued, their being used by a politically motivated president to thwart the will of an elected parliament.

Why Papandreou should have launched initiatives that were likely to hinder his chances of re-election was not clear, although they

52 In 1797, Rigas Velestinlis, the proto-martyr of Greek independence, declared in his constitution for a revived Greek empire that 'he who speaks modern or ancient Greek, even if he lives in the Antipodes . . . is a Greek and a citizen'. He could have had little idea that within 200 years a Greek population of over 300,000 would have established itself in Australia. By the 1980s Melbourne had become one of the largest centres of Greek population in the world. The photograph shows the Australian prime minister, Bob Hawke, like any street-wise Labour politician anxious to maintain good contacts with ethnic communities, attending the Greek festival in Coburg, a suburb of Melbourne, in 1988. On his right is Bishop

proved popular with the party rank and file and reflected his criticism at the time of the 1975 constitution as totalitarian. They certainly strengthened his claim that PASOK was a radical party that was not beholden to the establishment. Karamanlis himself, stung by this unexpected turn of events, forthwith resigned, a few days before his term of office ended. The battle was now joined to secure the election of PASOK's nominee for the presidency. This was by no means a foregone conclusion for PASOK controlled fewer than the minimum 180 parliamentary votes stipulated in the 1975 constitution. It could, however, be certain of the support of the thirteen communist deputies who had little reason to look with favour on an old and determined political enemy.

It was only on the third round of voting that the election of Sartzetakis was achieved with the precise constitutional minimum of 180 votes. The effective casting vote was that of the (PASOK) president of parliament, who had become acting president of the country on Karamanlis' resignation. New Democracy, claiming that this rendered his vote invalid and objecting to the pressures placed on PASOK deputies to ensure that they did not break ranks, boycotted the swearing-in of Sartzetakis as president. The way was now clear for PASOK to introduce its constitutional amendments, which were enacted in the next parliament and which duly enhanced the powers of the prime minister in relation to those of the president.

Given this background of constitutional crisis it is not surprising that the elections of 1985 should have been fought in a highly

---

Caption for Plate 52 (*cont.*).

Ezekiel of Melbourne and on his left Stelios Papathemelis, the PASOK minister for northern Greece, together with his New Democracy predecessor, Nikolaos Martis. Their presence in Australia on a bipartisan basis not only reflects the fact that many of the postwar migrants came from Greek Macedonia but also concern at the activities in Australia of a vociferous Slav Macedonian community which claims that much of northern Greece forms part of a Slav 'Aegean Macedonia'. Wherever Greek communities have established themselves overseas they have tended to carry with them not only their domestic political divisions but also the national rivalries of their homeland.

polarised atmosphere. A senior PASOK minister set the tone when, in a much-quoted phrase, he described the election as not being about 'oranges and tomatoes' but as being 'a confrontation between two worlds'. These two worlds, Papandreou explained, were the light of the sun (PASOK's logo is a rather mystifying green sun) and the forces of darkness and subservience (New Democracy). He painted a grim picture of an unregenerate right plotting its revenge against the country's progressive forces by reviving the battery of repressive measures that had been used to harass the left in the 1950s, a stark picture that moved even the communists to protest that the right of the 1980s was a different creature from that of the 1950s. Mitsotakis was no less apocalyptic in arguing that the election represented the last chance of preserving pluralist political institutions and of preventing an inexorable slide towards an authoritarian one-party state. His advocacy of 'neo-liberal' economic policies and the cutting down to size of the state sector, however, had a limited appeal in a country in which the state, either directly or indirectly, was such a major employer.

At 46 per cent, PASOK's share of the vote in the June 1985 election was only marginally (2 per cent) down on its performance in 1981, a not inconsiderable achievement given the inevitable wear and tear of office. New Democracy was able to increase its share of the vote by 5 points to 41 per cent. The poor state of the economy did not figure very largely in the campaign, but with the election out of the way, PASOK was forced to introduce a tough austerity programme. It aimed to reduce the country's enormous external and internal deficits by discouraging imports, cutting public expenditure and increasing government revenues. These measures, which were backed up by a massive emergency loan from the EC, prompted a number of major strikes by public-sector employees and this mounting unrest was reflected in the significant opposition gains in the municipal elections of October 1986. These resulted in the election of New Democracy mayors in the three main urban areas, Athens, Salonica and Piraeus.

Against the background of a steadily deteriorating economic situation, the PASOK government in its second term lacked the reformist impetus of the early years and there were significant indications of internal dissension within a party tightly controlled by Papandreou himself. Nonetheless, New Democracy under Mitsotakis' leadership seemed incapable of offering a convincing alternative, while (with the exception of the numerically insignificant Communist Party of the Interior) the far left showed few signs of being able to break out of the political ghetto to which it had been confined by the civil war and its aftermath. When, therefore, the Davos agreement of January 1988 appeared (for a time at least) to hold out the promise of a breakthrough in Greek–Turkish relations, Papandreou looked set for an unprecedented third term.

In the summer of 1988, however, there was a dramatic change in the fortunes of Papandreou and hence of PASOK. In August he suddenly departed for medical treatment in London, where he remained in hospital or convalescing for two months. There was a continuous stream of ministerial visitors to his hospital bed in London, while Papandreou's failure formally to delegate power to a deputy led to opposition gibes of 'government by fax' and of the creation of a power vacuum. Confusion existed as to the seriousness of his condition and matters were further complicated by the announcement from Harefield Hospital that the 69-year-old prime minister was seeking a divorce from his American wife of thirty-seven years, Margaret, herself a figure of some political standing, in order to marry a 34-year-old Olympic Airways stewardess who had latterly become an influential figure in the prime minister's entourage. Papandreou's public appearances in the company of Dimitra Liani provoked massive press publicity and led to bitter exchanges with his family.

After successful surgery, Papandreou returned to Greece. What was intended as a triumphal return, however, was overshadowed by the unfolding of a financial scandal with strong political overtones and on a monumental scale without precedent in the country's history. This centred on the activities of George Koskotas, a Greek-American who had built up, in mysterious circumstances, a huge banking and publishing empire. Soon after Papandreou returned, Koskotas, under 24-hour police surveillance, pending charges of embezzlement, illegal currency transactions and forgery, escaped to the United States. A shortfall equivalent to at least $132,000,000 was discovered in the books of his Bank of Crete. Revelations and allegations in connection with this and other scandals flew fast and furious in a notoriously uninhibited press.

It was alleged that state corporations had been encouraged to deposit their cash reserves with the Bank of Crete at artificially low rates of interest, the difference between the low rates and market rates being siphoned off. There were claims that PASOK functionaries had blocked investigation of the frauds, and that one had been paid off with a diaper box stuffed with 5,000-drachma notes. There were further allegations of illegal commissions in the so-called 'purchase of the century' (the acquisition of sixty French Mirage and forty American F-16 fighters); of irregularities in sales by the state-owned armaments industry; and of frauds at the expense of the EC. It was also alleged that the prime minister had authorised the bugging of the telephones of political enemies and friends, including those of Ms Liani.

Amid an almost daily litany of new allegations of scandal, some ministers were dismissed, others resigned, and still others were reshuffled. In a bid to boost his party's flagging morale, Papandreou claimed that his problems resulted from the activities of unspecified 'foreign centres of destabilisation'. This was a charge which he repeated when Koskotas, fighting attempts at extradition, alleged in a widely publicised interview in *Time* magazine that Papandreou was directly implicated in the scandals. The opposition parties were unanimous in demanding immediate elections as the only way out of the impasse. Papandreou, however, having easily survived a vote of confidence in parliament in December 1988 and another in March 1989, continued to ride out the storm until the end of his second four-year term. Realising that PASOK's share of the vote was bound to fall, one of his last acts in government was to introduce a more purely proportional electoral system, calculated to make it as difficult as possible for New Democracy to obtain a working majority without a substantially increased share of the popular vote.

This time-honoured manoeuvre had the desired effect for, despite a 44 per cent share of the vote, New Democracy secured only 144 seats, seven short of an overall majority, in the elections of June 1989 (PASOK's 46 per cent share of the vote in 1985 had produced a clear working majority of 11 seats). Notwithstanding the prime minister's personal and medical problems, and the mounting tally of scandals, PASOK recorded a 39 per cent share of the vote. In the circumstances this was impressive and translated into 125 seats. This left the 'Alliance of the Left and of Progress', consisting of the communist party and the Greek Left (formerly the Communist Party of the Interior), with 13 per cent of the vote and 28 seats, holding the balance of power. Ten days of hectic horse-trading ensued as President Sartzetakis entrusted the mandate to the three party leaders in turn, beginning with Mitsotakis as the leader of the largest single party.

In ordinary circumstances a PASOK/Alliance coalition against the right might have appeared the logical outcome. But the circumstances were far from ordinary. After Mitsotakis had failed to put together a viable majority, the mandate passed to Papandreou. He was willing to offer a number of ministries to the communists, but, not surprisingly, was not prepared to meet their principal demand that he step down as prime minister. It was then the turn of the leader of the Alliance, Kharilaos Florakis, a 75-year-old communist veteran of the wartime resistance (as was Mitsotakis) and the ensuing civil war who had spent eighteen years in exile or gaol. Florakis likewise had no success and returned the mandate to the president.

It looked as though new elections would have to be called, in which case there would have been no possibility of pressing charges against those PASOK cadres accused of implication in the scandals. At the eleventh hour, however, agreement was reached between Mitsotakis and Florakis to form a government of limited duration, consisting principally of New Democracy politicians with some communist nominees. In a curious echo of the demand of the resistance delegates in Cairo in 1943, communists now held the key portfolios of the interior and of justice. Mitsotakis, while remaining party leader, stood aside for Tzannis Tzannetakis, a New Democracy deputy and former naval officer widely respected for his opposition to the military dictatorship, to become prime minister. The new coalition professed a single objective, namely 'catharsis', the bringing to justice of those implicated in the scandals of the later years of the PASOK government, following which new elections would be held. Given the gulf that existed between the two parties over a whole range of issues, any longer-term co-operation was clearly out of the question. But the short-term coalition worked surprisingly well and the direct involvement of the communists alongside conservatives in government could truly be said to symbolise the healing of the wounds opened up by the civil war forty years previously. The process of reconciliation was further hastened when at least part of the huge volume of files kept by the security police was burned, to the chagrin of some historians. It was noteworthy, however, that it appeared to be the older generation that was more disposed to reconciliation. Substantial elements in the communist youth movement, for instance, remained stubbornly opposed to a deal which they regarded as a sell-out to the hated right. They had found it difficult to reconcile themselves to the somewhat hesitant reception by the orthodox communists of the doctrines of *glasnost* and *perestroika*. There was a certain irony in the fact that communists entered government for the first time in Greece just as communism as a political creed was being massively rejected throughout eastern Europe.

Once the process of 'catharsis', in the form of the establishment of parliamentary commissions to investigate the scandals, was firmly under way, further elections were called for 5 November 1989. The campaign, the second in five months, was a low-key affair, with a brief flurry of excitement arising from the adherence to the New Democracy ticket of Mikis Theodorakis, the maverick left-wing composer. The elections were held under the same system of proportional representation as those in June for the government had pledged not to tinker with the electoral law. They produced a similarly inconclusive result. New Democracy's marginally increased share of the vote (46 per cent as opposed to 44) gave it 148 seats, tantalisingly just three short of an overall parliamentary majority. The real surprise of the election, however, was that PASOK, in the face of allegations of corruption in the highest ranks of the party, was actually able to increase its share of the vote from 39 to 41 per cent, a tribute, if one were needed, to the ability of Andreas Papandreou to inspire fierce loyalty in equal measure with impassioned loathing. Its share of seats increased from 125 to 128. Conversely, the share of the vote secured by the left-wing Alliance fell from 13 to 11 per cent, its seats from 28 to 21. It appeared that whatever votes New Democracy had been able to attract from PASOK had been more than compensated for by defections on the part of Alliance supporters unhappy with their party's temporary accommodation with the right following the June election. Three independents were also elected: one broadly aligned with PASOK, one Green and one member of the Turkish minority.

Mitsotakis, the New Democracy leader, was quick to point out that, even if he had no overall majority, he had achieved a higher percentage of the popular vote than any other ruling politician in western Europe, and that, had the 1985 electoral law been in force, then New Democracy would have secured a clear working majority. Papandreou, for his part, maintained that PASOK had achieved the largest share of the vote of any socialist party in Europe and that the combined level of support for PASOK and the Alliance demonstrated a clear majority for the 'progressive' forces in the country. Once again President Sartzetakis consulted with the party leaders to see whether a coalition enjoying a parliamentary majority could be stitched together, failing which new elections would have to be held.

Each party in turn received an exploratory mandate to form a government, but, after complex negotiations, no possible coalition emerged. A third election within the space of little more than six months seemed inevitable. Faced with this unappealing prospect, however, agreement was reached at the eleventh hour to form an all-party government under a non-political figure, Xenophon Zolotas, a former governor of the Bank of Greece. The fact that Zolotas was eighty-five and that the three party leaders were all in their seventies provided further confirmation that age in itself has never been an obstacle to political advancement in Greece. Agreement was reached that this 'ecumenical' government 'of national necessity' would remain in office until April 1990, when new elections were almost certain if agreement could not be reached on a successor to President Sartzetakis when his five-year term expired in March 1990. Eight ministries were allotted to New Democracy, seven to PASOK and three to the Alliance. Key ministries such as foreign affairs, defence and the national economy were administered on a cross-party basis and arrangements were made for the three party leaders, Mitsotakis, Papandreou and Florakis, to meet regularly to monitor the government's progress.

Elections, the third in less than a year, were duly held in April 1990, again under the same electoral system. New Democracy's marginal increase in its share of the vote to 47 per cent gave it 150 seats, precisely one-half of the total in parliament. PASOK's share fell back to a still respectable 39 per cent (123 seats). It was clear that PASOK's adroit exploitation of its powers of patronage over the preceding eight years had given it a substantial and loyal clientele of some 40 per cent of the electorate. The Alliance's vote fell marginally to 10 per cent (19 seats). The commitment of the one seat that went to Democratic Renewal, a conservative splinter party, was enough to ensure New Democracy a narrow majority in parliament. A month after the elections Konstantinos Karamanlis was elected president for a second five-year term. Thus the era of PASOK, for the time being, came to an end. Mitsotakis, during the course of the three campaigns of 1989/90, had made no secret of the fact that the economic situation facing the country was dire and that the 'neo-liberal' policies which he advocated afforded no easy options in bringing under control huge public-sector deficits and confronting the massive burden of external loans. It was clearly going to be difficult to impose his austerity measures with a bare majority in parliament.

7

Balkan turmoil and political modernisation: Greece in the 1990s

The dramatic circumstances in which the first PASOK era had ended in 1989 prompted the former president, Konstantinos Karamanlis, to declare, with characteristic bluntness, that he felt at times as if he were living in an 'enormous madhouse'. The ensuing turmoil and the holding of three elections within less than a year served to distract attention from the momentous changes that were concurrently taking place in the countries on Greece's northern borders, Albania, Yugoslavia and Bulgaria, all of which had been under communist rule since the end of the Second World War. The end of the communist era in the Balkans inevitably had major implications for Greece, although successive governments were slow to appreciate this and a unique opportunity for Greece, the only politically stable and relatively prosperous country in the peninsula, to exert a positive influence in the region was largely missed.

The gradual thaw in the hitherto rigidly Stalinist policies of the Albanian regime focused attention on what was at once geographically the closest, yet until recently much the most politically isolated, area of Greek settlement outside the borders of the Greek state. Claimed by the Greek authorities to number over 300,000 (the official Albanian figure was 60,000), the Greek minority in southern Albania was for the most part compactly settled in what in Greece is termed 'northern Epirus', an area adjoining the Albanian–Greek border. The sudden exodus of thousands of ethnic Greeks at the beginning of 1991 gave rise to fears that the Albanian government was putting pressure on members of the minority to leave,

53 'As you set out for Ithaca': a Norwegian back-packer waits for an island ferry. As late as the mid-1950s, a writer well acquainted with the country could observe that 'were Greece less remote, there would be no more perfect place for the English

and prompted the Greek government to urge that they remain in Albania in the expectation of better times to come. Like all Albanians, members of the Greek minority had suffered severe repression during the communist era and cross-border family visits had been out of the question. Although basic linguistic, educational and cultural rights were conceded there had been attempts to disperse the minority and pressure had been applied to its members to adopt authentically 'Illyrian' names. Orthodox Christian Albanians, like their Muslim and Catholic compatriots, had been subject to a prohibition against all forms of religious activity. A hopeful precedent was that, at Christmas 1990, members of the Greek minority were able openly to attend religious services for the first time since 1967.

Caption for Plate 53 (*cont.*).

tourist'. At that time travel to Greece was rather difficult and costly. But, within a matter of a few years, rapidly rising living standards in western Europe together with cheap air travel transformed Greece into one of the leading tourist destinations in Europe. Within forty years the number of tourists underwent a near-fiftyfold increase. In 1958 there were just over a quarter of a million visitors. By 1998 the figure was almost 11,000,000, that is to say roughly one foreign visitor for every native inhabitant of the country. Whereas earlier visitors had primarily been attracted to Greece by its archaeological heritage, most visitors in the second half of the twentieth century were more interested in the sea and the sun. By the mid-1990s, the tourist industry employed almost 10 per cent of the labour force and generated foreign exchange earnings of US$4 billion. Many of the visitors, however, came on low-cost package tours and spending per head did not keep pace with inflation. More recently governments have sought to improve facilities in the hope of attracting more affluent tourists. The massive tourist influx contributed significantly to the country's growing prosperity but was by no means an unmixed blessing. In many of the most popular tourist destinations such as the islands of Corfu and Rhodes the coastline has been disfigured by unimaginative hotel developments, not to mention the large number of private houses built in breach of planning regulations. Greece's natural beauty comes under further threat from ever-present litter and from the fires which each year consume tens of thousands of acres of forest land.

During the 1990s large numbers of Albanians who were not ethnic Greeks likewise crossed the frontier, mostly illegally, and found work in poorly paid jobs, without social security benefits, as did immigrants from elsewhere in eastern Europe. The Albanians were periodically rounded up and shipped back across the frontier. By the middle of the decade there were as many as half a million foreigners working in Greece, most of them without work permits. In the popular view they were often held responsible for rising crime rates.

The Albanian Greeks undertook what, in the early months at least, was a hazardous trek across a border that throughout the postwar period had been hermetically sealed. In Greece they joined another influx of ethnic Greek refugees, an unusual phenomenon in a country historically associated much more with emigration (the great influx of the early 1920s apart) rather than immigration. This consisted of Greeks from the former Soviet Union, another hitherto largely submerged minority. According to the last Soviet census, that of 1989, these numbered some 356,000, a figure that probably understated the true figure. Most of them were the descendants of Greeks from Pontos. During the nineteenth and early twentieth centuries, these had migrated, often in the wake of the recurrent wars between the Russian and Ottoman empires, to the more welcoming Caucasus and northern shores of the Black Sea where they came under the rule of their Orthodox co-religionists, the Russians.

During the early years of the Soviet regime the Greeks had enjoyed a considerable degree of cultural autonomy and had been able to publish freely in their Pontic Greek dialect, which was barely intelligible to those in Greece. But they had the misfortune to be deemed by Stalin to be one of the 'disloyal' national minorities. Their intellectual leadership was decimated and most of them were deported to the inhospitable wastes of the central Asian republics. With the ending of the civil war in Greece in 1949, another sizeable number of Greeks, this time communist refugees who had fled behind the Iron Curtain, was settled in Tashkent, in Uzbekistan. This new wave of political exiles were faced with the problem, which they successfully overcame, of maintaining their ethnic identity and that of their children without being able to rely on the Church which played such a significant role in preserving a sense of Greekness in other diaspora communities.

On the death of Stalin, the deportees, as opposed to the communist refugees, had been able to return to their original places of residence in Georgia, Abkhazia and elsewhere, although they were often unable to recover their confiscated properties. Ethnic Greeks in the Soviet Union were to emerge from obscurity as a result of the general increase in ethnic awareness that was one of the major consequences of President Mikhail Gorbachev's policy of *glasnost*. The mayor of Moscow in the early 1990s, Gavriil Popov, was one of these former Soviet Greeks. There was something of a revival in Greek culture and education and even heady but unrealistic talk of establishing an autonomous Greek region in southern Russia. In the chaos that followed the collapse of the Soviet Empire, however, the Greeks were a tiny minority and many felt themselves to be threatened by the new assertiveness of the larger ethnic groups among whom they lived. These fears, coupled with the desire to better their economic status, prompted substantial numbers to take the path of emigration. By no means all of these immigrants retained their ancestral language (the Greeks of Tsalka in Georgia, for instance, were, paradoxically, Turkish-speaking). When Georgia invaded Abkhazia in the summer of 1992, the Greek population of the region was caught up in the war and a considerable number of ethnic Greeks were evacuated from the Abkhazian capital, Sukhum, by the Greek government in 'Operation Golden Fleece'. On arrival in Greece many of the former Soviet Greeks, to their manifest dissatisfaction, were settled in the sensitive and remote region of western Thrace, close to the border with Turkey and far from the bright lights of Athens and Thessaloniki.

The repatriation of Albanian and former Soviet Greeks to Greece, a 'homeland' of which they could have had only the vaguest idea, coincided with renewed sensitivity within Greece about her own minorities. By Balkan standards Greece's minorities are negligible in size, for the educational system has proved to be a powerful instrument for the 'hellenisation' of populations of non-Greek ethnic origin as these were incorporated into the Greek state in the course of its gradual expansion. A significant, if submerged, religious (but certainly not ethnic) minority is constituted by the Old Calendarists. Calling themselves 'True Orthodox Christians', these had refused to accept the adoption by the state and Church of Greece of the

Gregorian calendar in 1923/4. They have their own parallel religious hierarchy, including monasteries and nunneries, and comprise as much as 5 per cent of the population. There is a small Catholic minority, centred principally on the Aegean islands of Syros and Tinos, and a tiny Protestant community, largely composed of the descendants of those converted in Asia Minor in the nineteenth century by American Protestant missionaries. The overwhelming majority of Greece's once substantial Jewish community was exterminated by the Nazis but small communities survive in Athens, Thessaloniki and a few provincial towns.

There is only one officially recognised minority, the 'Muslim' minority of western Thrace. The authorities, invoking the terminology of the Treaty of Lausanne, insist on calling this a Muslim and not a Turkish minority. It is clear, however, that by the 1990s the majority of its members had come to regard themselves as ethnic Turks. Muslims in Greece (including a handful in the Dodecanese) number some 120,000. By contrast, the Greek minority in Turkey, in Istanbul and on the islands of Imvros and Tenedos, straddling the entrance to the Dardanelles, has dwindled to the point of extinction. Whereas in the 1950s the minority numbered over 100,000, there were at the beginning of the 1990s some 3,000 ethnic Greeks in Turkey and by the end of the decade scarcely 2,000. Given the Turkish government's insistence that the Ecumenical Patriarch, the spiritual leader of the world's Orthodox Christians, be a Turkish citizen it is difficult to see how such a small community can long sustain the Ecumenical Patriarchate. A particular complaint of the Greek minority in Turkey is about the refusal of the Turkish authorities to allow the Halki theological seminary, which they had closed down in 1971, to re-open. The only hope for the survival of the Ecumenical Patriarchate, whose origins extend as far back as the sixth century, and indeed of the tiny Greek community as a whole, would appear to lie in the distant prospect of Turkish membership of the EU, when EU norms with regard to minority rights would have to be respected.

There were also complaints of discrimination against the Muslims of Greece: over the right to elect their religious leaders; over property ownership; and over their entitlement to call themselves Turks. When, in 1991, a US State Department report alleged that the country's Muslims were subject to economic and social discrimination there was a strong reaction in Greece. The Mitsotakis government of the early 1990s did, however, institute measures to improve the lot of the minority. In general the treatment of their respective ethnic minorities by Greece and Turkey hinged critically on the overall state of relations between the two countries.

A similar furore ensued when the same State Department report appeared to recognise the existence of a small Slav Macedonian minority in Greece. There certainly are Slav-speakers in northern Greece, although their numbers are difficult to quantify. Many of the younger generation, for instance, have only a passive knowledge of their parents' Slavic idiom. A very small number of these Slavophones identify with the inhabitants of what was known as the Federal Yugoslav Republic of Macedonia, until she declared her independence in 1991 as the Republic of Macedonia. With the break-up of Yugoslavia, propaganda emanating from Skopje, the capital of the new state, complained of the ill-treatment of Slav-speakers in what was termed 'Aegean Macedonia', i.e. a sizeable area of northern Greece including Thessaloniki, and called for open borders and for what was mystifyingly termed the 'spiritual unifica-tion' of Macedonia. Greeks resented the adoption of the sixteen-pointed Star of Vergina, which had been found in what is widely regarded as being the tomb of Philip of Macedon in Vergina, as the national emblem of the new republic and complained that articles in the Macedonian constitution implied territorial ambitions at Greece's expense. The fundamental objection was to the very name 'Macedonia'. In the Greek view, the name could only legitimately be used of her own northern province of Macedonia and Antonis Samaras, foreign minister in the Mitsotakis government, repeatedly stated that Greece would never recognise a state calling itself Macedonia. Andreas Papandreou in opposition proclaimed that even to talk to the Macedonian political leadership was tantamount to recognition. Enormous demonstrations called for the boycott of Macedonia and the dispute was conducted with particular vigour in Australia and Canada which had large numbers of migrants from Greek Macedonia, some of them Slav-speakers, and a much smaller number from the 'Former Yugoslav Republic of Macedonia (FYROM)', under which title the newly independent state was provi-sionally admitted to the United Nations pending resolution of the dispute over its name. Further alarm was caused by the alacrity with which Bulgaria and Turkey accorded recognition to the new state. Fears began to be expressed of an 'Islamic arc' on Greece's northern borders stretching from Albania in the west to Turkey in the east, for a large majority of Albanians were Muslims, there was a substantial Muslim Albanian minority in Macedonia, and a sizeable Turkish minority in Bulgaria.

Greece's EU partners were puzzled as to why such a small, impoverished and landlocked mini-state as FYROM, with serious minority problems, could be perceived as a threat to a country such as Greece, with a stable political system, a relatively strong economy, well-equipped armed forces and membership of both NATO and the EU. Greek government propaganda was focused on demonstrating that Macedonia as a geographical entity had been 'Greek for 4,000 years' and on seeking to prove Greece's prior claim to the region by reference to the glories of the era of Philip of Macedon and Alexander the Great, to whom, somewhat improbably, Slav Macedonian nationalists also laid claim. As a result there was little understanding outside Greece that the fears of most Greeks over the issue were prompted much more by events that had occurred within living memory than in remote antiquity. Large numbers of refugees from Asia Minor and elsewhere had been resettled in Greek Macedonia in the 1920s. There were many living in northern Greece in the 1990s who had parents, grandparents or great-grandparents whose lives had been turned upside down in the process. This rendered them acutely sensitive to any suggestion of claims against Greece's territorial integrity.

Moreover, during the Second World War, western Thrace and a part of Greek Macedonia had been subject to harsh Bulgarian occupation. Greeks had been massacred and 'ethnically cleansed' from the region and Bulgarians settled in their place. Moreover, as recently as 1949, the Greek Communist Party, under increasing pressure during the civil war and needing the support of the Slav-speakers from northern Greece who by that time comprised almost half of the combat strength of the Democratic Army, had called for self-determination for the Slav Macedonians. Such a declaration seemed to point to the creation of a much enlarged Macedonia, which would combine territory which had been partitioned between Greece, Serbia and Bulgaria in 1913, a plan which President Tito of

Yugoslavia certainly favoured in the late 1940s. Had such a 'Greater Macedonia' come into being then it would necessarily have entailed giving up territory so recently and so hardly acquired by Greece during the Balkan wars. Konstantinos Karamanlis, whose second presidency ended in 1995, had been born in Macedonia in 1907 when the region still formed part of the Ottoman Empire. During his (admittedly long) lifetime the region had been convulsed by the bloody Balkan wars of 1912–13; by the savagery of the occupation during the Second World War; and by the internecine strife of the ensuing civil war. It was these recent horrors that underlaid Greek sensitivities over the Macedonian question rather than arcane disputes about the ancient past of the region. As it was, Greece's inept handling of the Macedonian issue at the international level and her expensive but misdirected propaganda campaign caused the loss of much international credibility and goodwill.

The Macedonian controversy was played out against the background of the increasingly bloody conflict in Bosnia which followed the disintegration of the Yugoslav Federation. At a popular level in Greece there was a considerable degree of sympathy for Serbia as the country's oldest ally and a nearby (and once neighbouring) country against which Greece had never fought and which had been an ally in both world wars. Greece's first alliance with another state had been contracted with Serbia in 1867. The Serbs were a fellow Orthodox people and, much as did the Greeks, looked upon themselves as a 'brotherless' people. Indeed, the Ecumenical Patriarch, Vartholomaios, in the course of a visit to Belgrade declared that it was the duty of all Orthodox Christians to rally in support of the Serbs in the conflict in former Yugoslavia. Some observers went so far as to speak of the emergence of an 'Orthodox axis' in the Balkans that would bring together Greece, Serbia, Bulgaria and Romania. But Greek support for the Serbs was expressed at the level of rhetoric, and government policies, whichever party was in power, offered little in the way of practical assistance to the Serbs.

It was against this background of Balkan turbulence that the Mitsotakis government of 1990–3 struggled to address the economic legacy of the profligate Papandreou years. Prices of public utilities were increased, as were duties on petrol, alcohol and the rate of value added tax. Such measures were inevitably unpopular, as were Mitsotakis' proposals for the privatisation of the hugely indebted

54 'Give us back our marbles': Prince Charles and the Greek minister of culture on the Acropolis in Athens in November 1998. If a pilgrimage to the Acropolis, the most obvious symbol of Greece's ancient glories, is high on the itinerary of every official visitor to Greece, this particular visit had a special resonance. For Greece has a long-standing claim for the return of the marbles removed from the Parthenon at the beginning of the nineteenth century by Thomas Bruce, seventh Earl of Elgin, while serving as British ambassador to the Ottoman Porte in Constantinople, and subsequently housed in the British Museum. In *Childe Harold* Byron denounced Elgin's activities as 'the last poor plunder from a bleeding land'. The controversy over the return of the 'Elgin' marbles had been revived not long before Charles' visit by the renewal of allegations that they had been damaged by aggressive cleaning while in the Museum's custody. The minister of culture, Evangelos Venizelos (seen here on the left) expressed the hope that the prince's visit would be a symbolic first step towards the return of the marbles, while the mayor of Athens, Dimitris Avramopoulos, in making Charles an honorary citizen of Athens, urged him to resolve the question on the day that he became king. Characteristically, US President Bill Clinton when he visited the Acropolis a year later, in 1999, in the midst of an otherwise stormy visit to Greece delighted his hosts by calling for the return of the marbles.

and overmanned 'problematic' companies. His austerity measures, dubbed 'Balkan Thatcherism' by his political opponents, were bitterly criticised by the opposition, and even the conservative president, Konstantinos Karamanlis, was moved to protest that the burdens of retrenchment were not being shared equitably. Moreover, when Mitsotakis launched an ill-conceived proposal to sell off thirty-five islets in the Bay of Argolis and in the Saronic gulf it had to be abandoned in the face of opposition from within his own party and amid rumours of interest on the part of a Turkish multi-millionaire in purchasing one of the islets.

In March 1991 the most important of a series of trials arising out of the Bank of Crete scandal got under way. Five former PASOK ministers, including Andreas Papandreou (who refused to attend the court) were indicted. The principal defendant was Agamemnon Koutsogiorgas who, as minister of justice and deputy prime minister, had been one of Papandreou's closest associates. He was accused of taking a $1,300,000 bribe in return for legislation protecting George Koskotas, the former owner of the Bank of Crete, but he died of a heart attack before a verdict could be reached. Papandreou was eventually acquitted. Two former cabinet ministers were sentenced to terms of imprisonment for their involvement in the scandals of the late 1980s.

In July of 1992, in a rare display of near unanimity between the two main parties, Greece's accession to the Maastricht treaty, a significant milestone on the way to a 'deeper' European union, was ratified by a massive majority (286 out of 300 deputies) in parliament. Greece was expected to benefit by an additional 2,000 million ecus

---

Caption for Plate 54 (*cont.*).

The Prince of Wales' visit was a rare official visit to Greece by a member of the British royal family which has close family ties with the former king of Greece. Prince Philip, the Duke of Edinburgh, is the son of Prince Andrew of Greece, ex-King Constantine's great uncle. When Prince Charles married Lady Diana Spencer in 1981, the president of Greece, Konstantinos Karamanlis, declined to attend the wedding because Constantine, in exile since 1967, had been invited as 'King of the Hellenes'.

over a five-year period. Perhaps of greater significance was Greece's concurrent admission to full membership of the Western European Union. Although both main political parties were enthusiastic about the principles enshrined in the Maastricht treaty, the prospects for Greek participation in the European monetary union which it envisaged appeared at the time remote, for not only was Greece the poorest member of the Community but her inflation record, budget deficit and level of interest rates were higher than those of any of her partners.

In a bid to shore up his perilously small parliamentary majority, Mitsotakis distributed government posts to as many as a third of New Democracy deputies. This did not prevent internal dissension within the party. In October 1991, for instance, Miltiades Evert, a potential rival to Mitsotakis, was forced out of his post as minister to the prime minister. A much more serious crisis within the party was precipitated by Mitsotakis' dismissal in 1992 of his young foreign minister, Antonis Samaras, who had consistently taken an intransigent line over the recognition of Macedonia. In June 1993, Samaras founded his own party, Political Spring. When he was able to persuade three New Democracy deputies to defect this left the Mitsotakis government without a majority and provoked bitter charges of 'apostasy'.

Elections were called in October 1993, some fifteen months in advance of the normal term. A mud-slinging election ensued. Although himself well into his seventies, Mitsotakis played, if only by implication, on his relative vigour in contrast with Papandreou's demonstrable frailty and, *inter alia*, hinted that the return of PASOK would increase the likelihood of Greece becoming embroiled in a wider Balkan conflict. He also sought to play on fears of Papandreou's past radicalism. For his part, Papandreou was bitterly critical of the austerity measures introduced by the Mitsotakis government and, in particular, of its programme of privatisation. He also accused Mitsotakis of weakness over the Macedonian issue. Nonetheless, he distanced himself from the radicalism of the 1970s and early 1980s and now sought to project PASOK as a social democratic party on the European model.

The campaign lacked some of the rumbustiousness of previous contests, while the size of PASOK's victory caught most observers by surprise. Papandreou swept back to power with a share of the vote only marginally smaller than that achieved in his great triumph of 1981. Moreover, although PASOK's share of the vote, at 47 per cent was virtually identical with that achieved by New Democracy in 1990, it received a healthy working majority of 20 (170 seats) whereas the Mitsotakis government, with 150 seats, exactly half the number of seats in parliament, had always been vulnerable to defections. Mitsotakis' 1990 revision of the electoral law had back-fired against the interests of his own party, whose 39 per cent share of the vote gave it 111 seats in the new parliament. Samaras' Political Spring, with a 5 per cent share of the vote, secured 10 seats, pushing the Communist Party of Greece, with 5 per cent of the vote and 9 seats, into fourth place. The communists were now led by Aleka Papariga who, on succeeding Kharilaos Florakis in 1991 as general-secretary, had, in her early forties, become the country's first woman party leader. In the wake of defeat, Mitsotakis was replaced as leader of New Democracy by Miltiades Evert, a persistent critic of Mitsotakis and a populist, who had acquired the nickname of 'the bulldozer' during an energetic term as mayor of Athens. In the new PASOK government Papandreou's son, Giorgos, was placed in charge of the affairs of overseas Greeks and the ever-growing influ-ence of Papandreou's third wife, Dimitra Liani, was manifest in her appointment as head of the prime minister's private office. Here she controlled access to the prime minister, whose capacity for sustained effort was increasingly in question.

The return to power of Papandreou clearly occasioned alarm among Greece's EU partners. Worried by the prospect of Greece's presidency of the EU during the first half of 1994 they moved rapidly to open diplomatic relations with the new Macedonian state. They were followed soon afterwards by the United States. These moves prompted an explosion of anger, which included a massive rally outside the US consulate-general in Thessaloniki. In February 1994, Papandreou raised the temperature even further by announcing a blockade of Macedonia, from which only medicines and food were exempted. The EU Commission complained to the European Court of Justice that the embargo was in contravention of community law. Perhaps the lowest point in the entire Macedonian imbroglio was reached in January 1995 when the foreign minister, Karolos

Papoulias, did not attend the ceremony to commemorate the fiftieth anniversary of the liberation of Auschwitz concentration camp, where the greater part of Greek Jewry had perished. This was because the Macedonian flag was to be flown alongside those of the other countries whose nationals had been sent to their deaths in the camp.

Likewise Greek relations with Albania continued to be troubled, reaching their nadir in the post-communist period when, in February 1994, a Greek-speaking band attacked an Albanian army unit near the border, killing two conscripts. This incident led to Albanian allegations, subsequently retracted, of Greek government involvement. It was the catalyst for a serious deterioration in relations between the two countries, with Athens continuing to complain of discrimination against members of the Greek minority in southern Albania and of restrictions placed on the religious freedom of Orthodox Christians. This war of words culminated in the arrest by the Albanian authorities in May of six members of Omonoia, the main Greek minority organisation in Albania. At their subsequent trial, five of the six received prison sentences of between six and eight years for treasonable advocacy of the secession of 'Northern Epirus' to Greece and the illegal possession of weapons. A number of Greek journalists covering the trial were expelled. Greece responded with a mass round-up and deportation of thousands of illegal Albanian immigrants. In turn Albania claimed that her diplomats in Greece were being harassed.

In 1995, however, partly as a result of US pressure, Greece's relations with both Macedonia and Albania underwent a significant improvement. Greece had been encouraged by the recommendation of the advocate-general of the European Court of Justice that the case against Greece over the embargo against Macedonia be dropped as lying outside the court's competence. In the autumn of 1995 there was discernible movement in the long-standing dispute between Athens and Skopje. Following protracted negotiations and a meeting of the foreign ministers of the two countries in New York, an 'interim accord' was signed whereby Macedonia agreed to cease using the Star of Vergina as the national emblem and affirmed that her constitution did not imply territorial claims against Greece. Although no decision was reached on the name issue Greece agreed to lift the blockade.

There was also improvement in relations with Albania. Following the release early in 1995 of the imprisoned members of Omonoia, the Greek foreign minister visited Tirana and agreement was reached on the establishment of joint committees to discuss problematic issues such as the treatment of the Greek minority and the status of the many tens of thousands of Albanians working illegally in Greece. That unsolved problems remained, however, was indicated by the rejection by the Albanian foreign minister of Greek demands for the establishment of a number of private Greek schools in Albania made during the course of his visit to Greece at the beginning of September 1995.

If relations with Macedonia and Albania underwent improvement, those with Turkey remained difficult. The better climate resulting from the Davos agreement of 1988 proved to be one of the many false dawns in the history of Greek–Turkish relations. There were repeated Turkish violations of the ten-mile airspace claimed by Greece: these rose from some 240 recorded intrusions in 1991 to 700 in 1995. Relations became particularly fraught when, in mid-November 1994, the 1982 UN Convention on the Law of the Sea, of which Greece was a signatory, was due to come into effect. This gave rise to Turkish fears that Greece would extend her territorial waters from six to the customary twelve miles, thereby, given the multiplicity of Greece's islands, placing the greater part of the Aegean under Greek control. As the Turks saw it, the Aegean would in effect become a Greek lake and the Turkish parliament made it clear that any such extension would be regarded as a *casus belli* and be met by force. For their part the Greek authorities made it clear that they reserved the right to make such an extension in the future.

Relations between Athens and Ankara were placed under further strain when, in December 1994, Greece vetoed proposals for a customs union between the European Union and Turkey although the veto was subsequently withdrawn. Matters took a turn for the worse when the Greek parliament proclaimed 19 May as a day of remembrance for what was termed the genocide of tens of thousands of Pontic Greeks during the First World War and its aftermath. In July 1994 a Turkish diplomat was murdered in Athens by the shadowy and elusive '17 November' far-left terrorist group, which over a period of over twenty years had engaged in assassinations and terrorist attacks with impunity. In February 1995, two Greek Mirage F-1 fighters intercepted four Turkish F-16 fighters, which Greece claimed had breached her airspace. One of the Turkish planes subsequently crashed off the island of Rhodes, although the pilot ejected safely. In May of the same year, a supposedly private visit to western Thrace by a junior Turkish government minister provoked a number of incidents. In the course of the visit, the minister claimed that ethnic Turks in Greece suffered discrimination and described the 1923 Treaty of Lausanne, which spoke of a Muslim rather than a Turkish minority, as outdated. Papandreou declared the minister's remarks unacceptable and his car was stoned by Greek, Cypriot, Armenian and Kurdish demonstrators.

Although Papandreou had been a harsh critic of Mitsotakis' austerity measures, during his third term as prime minister, with a view to preparing the way for European monetary union, he gave his blessing to policies to cut Greece's massive indebtedness; to curtail public-sector deficits; and to bring inflation under control. These measures, which essentially continued a process started by Mitsotakis, had some effect. By early 1995, for instance, the annual rate of inflation had fallen below 10 per cent for the first time in twenty years. In the same year exchange control regulations were lifted to bring Greece into line with her European partners. When the PASOK government in November 1994 declared its intention to privatise 25 per cent of OTE, the national telecommunications concern, strong opposition was expressed by the trade union movement and a group of deputies on the left wing of the ruling party. Measures to bring farmers within the tax system prompted an angry response in rural areas and, in March 1995, the minister of public order, Stelios Papathemelis, resigned in protest against pressure to use force against farmers who had blocked road and rail communications between the north and south of the country for some ten days. Such was the level of discontent on the left of the party that Dimitris Tsovolas, a leading populist, defected from PASOK to form the Democratic Socialist Movement, which claimed to enshrine the radical socialist aspirations of the early years of PASOK.

Certainly there was little sign of the radical rhetoric (which was seldom matched in practice) of earlier Papandreou administrations. Manifestly frail, the prime minister was capable of working for only a few hours a day. Power was increasingly concentrated in the hands of Ms Liani and a small camarilla of cronies. Disaffection began to mount within the ruling PASOK party, occasioned by the prime minister's failure to address the succession question and by the increasingly overt political ambitions of his wife. Papandreou's building of a lavish villa, dubbed the 'pink palace', in Ekali, an expensive northern suburb of Athens, was the occasion of cynical gossip. This was only fuelled by the prime minister's claim that the villa had been funded with interest-free loans from members of his cabinet. The political climate was further muddied late in 1994 when, in retaliation for the indictment of Papandreou in connection with the Koskotas scandals, Mitsotakis was charged with receiving bribes in connection with the sale of a huge state-owned cement company to an Italian firm. For good measure he was also accused of authorising the phone-tapping of political opponents and with the illegal acquisition of antiquities. The charges were subsequently dropped.

In March 1995, Greece acquired a new president when the 88-year-old Konstantinos Karamanlis stood down shortly before the end of his second five-year term. He was replaced by Kostis Stephanopoulos, an uncharismatic but widely respected lawyer. Formerly a deputy in New Democracy, in whose governments he had held ministerial office, Stephanopoulos had formed a tiny right-wing splinter party, Democratic Renewal, in 1985. He was nominated for the presidency by Antonis Samaras' small right-wing Political Spring party, with whose support and, crucially, that of PASOK, he was elected president in the third round of voting in parliament, with 181 votes out of 300, one more than the constitutional minimum. New Democracy's nominee was Athanasios Tsaldaris, a former speaker of parliament.

During the summer of 1995 rumblings of discontent within the ruling PASOK party provoked by Papandreou's manifest lack of grip on affairs of state came into the open. In September, Kostas Simitis, a prominent 'moderniser' and a leading contender for the future leadership of PASOK, resigned and joined in the growing demands for the prime minister to step down. By this stage Papandreou, visibly in very poor health, was reported to be incapable of working more than two hours a day. In September, he had been forced to abandon celebrations held on the island of Patmos to mark the 1,900th anniversary of the composition of the Book of Revelation by St John the Divine, one of the religious pilgrimages on which Ms Liani was fond of taking her husband. The government's dignity was scarcely enhanced by the repeated publication in the popular press of lewd photographs of Ms Liani taken before her association with Papandreou.

Towards the end of November 1995, Papandreou was taken to hospital suffering from pneumonia, compounded by kidney failure. Attached to a life support machine, for long periods he was unable to breathe without the assistance of a respirator. The mass media kept a round-the-clock vigil at the hospital and reported on his medical condition in minute detail. As foreign specialists were called in to advise on his treatment all but close family members were kept from the prime minister's hospital room. It was reported that Dimitra Liani was invoking the assistance of holy oil, miracle-working icons and astrologers in her efforts to bring about her husband's recovery. Outside the hospital, enthusiastic supporters even offered their organs for transplantation.

With the government of the country more or less paralysed, its day-to-day running was temporarily assumed by Akis Tsokhatzopoulos, the minister of the interior, public order and decentralisation and a prominent figure on the populist wing of PASOK. The prime minister declined to indicate that he was prepared to resign and resolutely refused to say on whom he wished the mantle of succession to fall. This uncertainty inevitably prompted feverish speculation as to who might succeed to the leadership should Papandreou, as appeared to be increasingly likely, fail to make a sufficient recovery to enable him to resume the reins of office. The opposition demanded that the succession question be addressed, as did elements within PASOK itself, including Papandreou's own son, Giorgos, the minister of education, who said that his father should step down 'for the good of the country'. Eventually, in mid-January 1996, after seven weeks during which he had clung to power while near death, Papandreou was prevailed upon to resign as prime minister, although he retained the leadership of the party. His unwillingness to resign earlier, and the distasteful media circus occasioned by his hospitalization, made for an undignified and dispiriting end to an extraordinary political career. Six months later, at the age of seventy-seven, he was dead.

With the ending of the Karamanlis presidency in 1995 (he died in 1998 at the age of ninety-one) and the resignation of Papandreou in 1996 the era of the 'dinosaurs', as the Greeks none too affectionately dubbed their traditionally gerontocratic ruling caste, effectively came to an end. Between them Karamanlis and Papandreou had dominated the politics of the second half of the twentieth century, much in the way that the austere Kharilaos Trikoupos and the demagogic Theodoros Deliyannis had dominated the politics of the last third of the nineteenth century. Their own personal charisma had been essential to the success of the parties with which they were associated. Some observers, for instance, had expressed doubt as to whether PASOK would long survive the death of its founder, Andreas Papandreou. The ending of the Karamanlis/Papandreou era also reflected the political demise of those who had lived through the formative years of the Second World War whose consequences had been so traumatic for Greece. Whereas in other European countries, such as France or Yugoslavia, participation in the wartime resistance had been a key to postwar political preferment this had not been the case in Greece. The new generation who now came to the fore had scarcely been born at the time of the occupation. Their political experience, moreover, derived in the main from the period after the *metapolitefsi*, the political changes consequent on the downfall of the Colonels' dictatorship in 1974. This was particularly true of Kostas Karamanlis, who in 1997 was elected leader of New Democracy in succession to Miltiades Evert. At the age of forty-one he was the youngest-ever leader of a major political party in Greece. The fact, however, that he was the nephew of the founder of New Democracy, Konstantinos Karamanlis, indicated that traditional political mores with their emphasis on family connections had by no means been superseded.

The battle for the soul of PASOK and thereby for its prospects of long-term survival had in effect already got under way before Papandreou's resignation albeit in a somewhat coded fashion. It now commenced in earnest and the 'moderniser' Simitis was able to see off a challenge by three PASOK traditionalists to emerge as prime minister. At the age of sixty Simitis was relatively young by the standards of Greek politics. He had not emerged from the semi-hereditary *politikos kosmos*, the traditional political caste, and, in turn, had kept his family out of politics. His lifestyle was modest indeed when contrasted with that of the Papandreou of the 'pink palace' era. But he altogether lacked Papandreou's personal charisma. His preferred style was not the rabble-rousing oratory of his predecessor but more the boring monologue of the academic, technocratic milieu from which he had emerged. He was noticeably ill at ease in his dealings with the press.

Simitis had scarcely taken over the reins of government than his leadership was put to severe test in the most serious crisis in Greek–Turkish relations since the Turkish invasion of northern Cyprus in 1974. The confrontation, which brought the two countries to the brink of war, had its origins in the grounding in late December 1995 of a Turkish ship on the tiny rocky islet of Imia (Turkish Kardak), situated between the Greek island of Kalymnos and the Turkish mainland. Initially, the Turkish ship refused the assistance of Greek salvage vessels on the ground that Imia was a Turkish island, whereupon the mayor of Kalymnos sent a party, which included a priest, to raise the Greek flag over the islet. In return, a strongly nationalist Turkish newspaper despatched journalists and a photographer by helicopter to tear down the Greek flag and run up the Turkish. The press in both countries inflamed public opinion and from initially somewhat farcical beginnings there developed a potentially extremely serious confrontation. A squad of Greek commandos landed on the disputed islet and ran up the Greek flag in place of the Turkish, while Turkish commandos landed on an adjacent islet. The affair reached a climax at the end of January 1996, as combat-ready warships of the two countries circled the islets in a menacing fashion. An armed clash appeared a distinct possibility.

The crisis was defused only through the direct intervention of US President Clinton. American pressure was instrumental in persuading both sides to withdraw from the islets. Such a withdrawal was perceived in Greece as a national humiliation, and Simitis, barely installed in the prime minister's office, was subjected to fierce domestic criticism. The chief of the defence staff, Admiral Khristos Lymberis, was dismissed. Anti-American sentiment, never far beneath the surface in Greece despite the fact that so many Greeks have relatives in the US, was resurgent and focused in particular on Assistant US Secretary of State Richard Holbrooke, who was deemed to have

55 a and b Despite their common membership of the NATO alliance, relations between Greece and Turkey have remained uneasy. In January 1996, the two countries came close to war in a dispute about sovereignty over the barren islet of Imia (Turkish Kardak) lying a few miles off the Turkish coast. After the mayor of Kalymnos, the nearest inhabited island, had sent a party, which included a priest, to run up the Greek flag, a Turkish newspaper flew in journalists by helicopter to tear down the Greek flag and run up the Turkish flag instead (photograph a). As public opinion became inflamed, both countries despatched warships and commandos to the islet, and only through the personal intervention of the US president, Bill Clinton, was an extremely threatening confrontation defused. The Turkish government continued to insist that there were still 'grey areas' in the Aegean over which sovereignty had not been definitively established. In 1999, however, there was a dramatic improvement in relations between the two countries. When both were afflicted by earthquakes the response of the public in each country to the problems of the other was immediate and generous. 'Earthquake diplomacy', as it came to be known, prompted many expressions of friendship and increased co-operation in a number of fields even if little headway was made in finding a solution to the substantive problems that divided the two countries. But at least serious efforts were being made to

Caption for Plate 55 (*cont.*).

understand each other's viewpoints and perspectives on the history of the region. In photograph (b) a Turkish teacher tells his pupils about the destructive anti-Greek riots of 1955 in Istanbul, known in Turkish as the Altı-Yedi Eylül Olayları favoured Turkey during the confrontation. In early February Simitis refused to accept a visit from Holbrooke. Greek anger was likewise directed at her European partners who were held to have been insufficiently supportive in the crisis. Subsequently Greece made strenuous, and seemingly effective, efforts to persuade the Europeans of the validity of her claim to sovereignty over the contested islets.

What was particularly ominous about the Imia crisis was that it hinged not on the delineation of the continental shelf, the extent of territorial waters or airspace, air traffic control or the fortification of the islands but, for the first time since the Aegean dispute had erupted more than twenty years earlier, on the question of claims to territory. Tension was further heightened by subsequent Turkish questioning of Greek sovereignty over the island of Gavdos to the south of Crete and by suggestions from Ankara that there remained 'grey areas' in the Aegean over which sovereignty had never been definitively established. In the course of a television interview in May 1997 President Süleyman Demirel of Turkey raised hackles in Greece by declaring that sovereignty over as many as 130 islands in the Aegean was debatable. Greeks had reason to believe that Turkey was mounting a challenge to the long-established status quo in the Aegean.

One casualty of the Imia crisis was the abandonment by the US of a commitment to give a high priority in 1996 to a resolution of the long-running Cyprus dispute. This had been exacerbated by the decision of the EU to open negotiations for the accession of Cyprus before there had been a solution to the division of the island that

---

Caption for Plate 55 (*cont.*).

(The events of 6/7 September) and in Greek as the Septemvriana (The September events) (see pp. 147–8). The poster about which he is talking was part of an exhibition to mark the 130th anniversary of the foundation of the municipality of Beyoğlu (Pera) in Istanbul. It shows a tank deployed in İstiklâl Caddesi (formerly the Grande Rue de Pera) to bring an end to the mob violence. By the time of this exhibition, in late 2000, the Greek community of Istanbul, once heavily concentrated in Beyoğlu or Pera and still sizeable in 1955, had dwindled to the verge of extinction.

dated back to 1974. In response, the governments of Turkey and of the 'Turkish Republic of Northern Cyprus' had made it clear that if the Republic of Cyprus were to enter the EU before there had been a political settlement then Turkish-occupied Northern Cyprus would in effect be annexed by Turkey, thus putting an end to any hope of the re-unification of the island. A series of incidents, leading to five deaths (four of Greek Cypriots, one of a Turkish Cypriot), on the UN-patrolled ceasefire line in the summer of 1996, further raised the temperature. In particular, the brutal and televised killing of two Greek Cypriot cousins in protests marking the anniversary of the Turkish invasion of 1974 was followed by a period of sabre rattling by Greece and Turkey. When, towards the end of 1996, the Cypriot government announced that it was to purchase Russian S-300 surface-to-air missiles, the Turkish government threatened to destroy the missile sites once they were installed, claiming that they were capable of striking Turkish territory. The implications of such an increase in tension and of such explicit threats were very serious for Greece. For, under the terms of the 'unified defence doctrine' agreed by Papandreou and President Clerides of Cyprus in 1993, Greece was committed to go to the aid of Cyprus in the event of any conflict on the island. When the deputy foreign minister, Khristos Rozakis, suggested a moratorium on Greek and Turkish military flights in the Aegean as a means of reducing tension the ensuing uproar resulted in his resignation.

The Imia crisis and the tense situation on Cyprus lay behind the announcement in November 1996 that Greece was to embark on a ten-year programme of modernisation of her armed forces at a cost of 4 trillion drachmas ($US16,800 million). This enormous sum was to be spent on new warships, submarines, fighters, helicopters and air defence systems. At 4.6 per cent of GDP, the defence budget was proportionately the highest of any NATO country. Greece's NATO allies from time to time expressed alarm at the arms race that had developed between Greece and Turkey. This did not stop them, and particularly the US government, from encouraging the sale of state-of-the-art military technology to both Greece and Turkey in the knowledge that if this were ever to be deployed it was much more likely to be used by the two NATO allies against each other rather than against a third country.

The death of Papandreou in June 1996, which was the occasion of a massive funeral, had necessitated an election for the leadership of PASOK, for Papandreou, to the manifest discomfiture of Simitis, had retained the party leadership on stepping down as prime minister. Simitis, who had made it clear that he would resign as prime minister if he did not become party leader, was duly elected to the post at the party congress held at the end of June. Having beaten off a strong challenge from Akis Tsokhatzopoulos, the principal flag-bearer for the old populist PASOK and one of those who had been particularly close to Papandreou, Simitis sought to bolster his authority through a general election.

In the course of an uncharacteristically low-key campaign, Simitis played on his image as a technocrat and distanced himself from the populism and demagogy of his predecessor. He espoused a moderate line in foreign policy and made no attempt to conceal the fact that difficult decisions lay ahead if the economy was to be brought into line with the Maastricht criteria. Evert, the New Democracy leader, for his part distanced himself from the 'neo-liberal' policies espoused by Mitsotakis between 1990 and 1993 and pledged ND to scrap the tax and welfare reforms to which PASOK, under Simitis' sober leadership, was now committed. He also criticised the prime minister for not taking a tougher line at the time of the Imia crisis. For the first time in a Greek election, televised debates assumed greater importance than mass rallies as the principal means of trying to win over voters.

In the election of September 1996 'New PASOK', as some termed PASOK under Simitis' leadership, secured 162 of the 300 seats in contention. This gave Simitis a useful working majority and reinforced his position both in the party and in the country at large, although PASOK's overall share of the vote at 41 per cent was the lowest secured by a winning party since 1977. New Democracy, with 38 per cent of the vote, won 108 seats. If there was an element of surprise in the outcome it lay in the relative success of the left-wing parties which between them won 15 per cent of the vote and 30 seats. The failure of the right-wing Political Spring to be represented in parliament reflected the degree to which the passions aroused by the Macedonian issue in the early 1990s had diminished by the middle of the decade. If political charisma was in short supply in 'New PASOK' following the death of Papandreou, another key element of the 'old' politics, clientelism, continued to flourish. Moreover, for all his emphasis on modernisation, Simitis was hesitant in taking on the unions that were so powerful in state-owned monoliths such as Olympic Airways or in seeking to reform a pension system of Byzantine complexity.

On succeeding Papandreou as prime minister, Simitis had made it clear that the overriding objective of government economic policies was to enable Greece to join the single European currency by 2001, two years after the target date of most of her European partners. This was certainly an ambitious aim but, in the wake of the election, he could argue that the electorate had endorsed, if scarcely overwhelmingly, the tough measures implied by such policies. Inevitably these met with resistance and serious unrest erupted at the end of 1996. Protesting farmers interrupted road and rail communications between the north and south of the country for over three weeks. Public service workers joined the fray, including policemen and diplomats, the latter complaining about the level of their hospitality allowances in overseas postings. Despite damage to the economy estimated at $100 million, the Simitis government refused to capitulate to the strikers' demands and the strikes were called off shortly before Christmas. Public-sector strikes and demonstrations, however, continued to be a feature of 'New PASOK' rule. Among the disaffected were schoolteachers, their pupils, policemen and, above all, farmers, who bitterly opposed attempts to bring them into the tax system. Tough measures were also introduced, with variable results, to ensure that middle-class professionals, and particularly doctors and lawyers, made a proportionate contribution to the tax system. There were complaints about the heavy-handed behaviour of the tax 'Rambos' in a society where tax obligations had hitherto tended to be viewed as optional.

Efforts to make more competitive or to privatise parts or all of such state-owned enterprises as Olympic Airways and the Ionian and Popular Bank met with stiff resistance from powerfully entrenched unions, anxious to protect job security. A prolonged strike by employees of the Ionian and Popular Bank resulted in physical violence being deployed against its governor. Repeated go-slows at Olympic Airways played into the hands of the small, aggressive, privately owned airlines that were now allowed to challenge the monopoly hitherto enjoyed by Olympic. Attempts to introduce reforms into an educational system whose inadequacies had forced parents to resort to private education or the ubiquitous *phrontistiria*, after-hours 'cramming' establishments, led to prolonged sit-ins by pupils. The high premium placed by parents on securing educational qualifications, which were seen, rather optimistically, as a guarantee of a secure job, coupled with fierce competition to enter under-funded and over-crowded universities, led many Greek students to study abroad. By the late 1990s, for instance, there were some 30,000 Greek students studying in Britain alone. The costs incurred by this resort to education abroad were a severe drain on the balance of payments. The measures of retrenchment imposed by Simitis's government met with opposition not only in the country at large but within his own party. When, in 1998, eleven PASOK deputies openly criticised Simitis' policies he called for a vote of confidence in parliament, threatening to expel the dissidents if they refused to back him, which they duly did. The unpopularity of the government's measures was demonstrated by the strong showing of the opposition New Democracy party in the municipal elections held in October 1998.

A new development in the 1990s was the attempt by successive governments to mobilise the worldwide Greek diaspora in an effort to promote the country's *ethnika zitimata* or 'national questions'. Many of Greek descent, particularly in the US with its old-established Greek community, but increasingly also in communities of more recent origin such as those in Australia and Canada, had reached positions of power and influence, both economic and political, in their adopted countries. Indeed, observers frequently drew attention to the way in which Greek emigrants found an outlet for their talents, capacity for hard work and entrepreneurial skills in the countries of the diaspora that was often denied them in their homeland, where having the right connections was of critical importance. Great pride was derived from the fact that the (albeit unsuccessful) Democratic Party challenger for the US presidency in 1988, Mike Dukakis, previously a successful governor of Massachusetts, was a second-generation Greek-American, as also from the fact that during the early years of the Clinton administration one of the president's key advisers was George Stephanopoulos, the Greek-American son of an Orthodox priest. The attempt to capitalise on the success outside Greece of those of Greek ancestry found expression in placing a junior minister in the ministry of foreign affairs in charge of 'Overseas Hellenism' and in the establishment of the World Council of Hellenes.

Greeks of the diaspora, settled in some 141 countries, were held to number 7 million although it is not clear how this figure was arrived at or what criteria were used to define Greek ethnicity, while the population of the homeland, according to the 1991 census, amounted to some 10.25 million. At the first convention of the World Council of Hellenes, the minister of culture, Evangelos Venizelos, declared that although Greece might be a small country she had all the characteristics of a 'cultural super-power'. Not all those attending the convention were enamoured of the politicking that accompanied the creation of the World Council. Nonetheless, it was able to raise money to help impoverished Greek communities in the former Soviet Union and to facilitate communication between diaspora communities and the homeland and with each other. Mass communications, and particularly the growth of cheap air travel, made such efforts more feasible and some of Greek descent moved from the diaspora to a Greece whose level of prosperity was far removed from the poverty that had impelled their forebears to follow the path of *xeniteia*, or sojourning in foreign parts.

In 1997 there occurred one of the periodic false dawns that appeared to herald an improvement in relations with Turkey; the chief of the Turkish general staff made a surprise visit to the 25 March national day reception at the Greek embassy in Ankara. This was clearly intended as a gesture of goodwill, and also perhaps, given the political power wielded by the military in Turkey, as a coded warning to Turkish politicians that the armed forces were less enthusiastic about confrontation with Greece than demagogic politicians and sensation-seeking journalists and more aware of the devastating consequences of any outbreak of hostilities. A month later, both countries agreed to set up committees of 'wise men' to help make suggestions for a resolution of the Aegean conflict. This was followed by the signing in July, following pressure from the US, at a NATO summit meeting in Madrid of a 'convergence of views' agreement. This committed the two countries to respect each other's sovereign rights in the Aegean and, with the Imia/Kardak crisis clearly in mind, to renounce the use of force to settle their quarrels. The solemnly affirmed commitment to 'peace, security and the continuous development of good neighbourly relations' lasted barely three months, however, before the Greek government declared the Madrid agreement void. This followed a very serious incident at a time when, under the terms of the Greece–Cyprus common defence policy, units of the Greek armed forces were taking part in manoeuvres on Cyprus. Greece claimed that the aircraft carrying the defence minister to and from the island had been intercepted by Turkish warplanes, which, contrary to existing agreements, were fully armed. For her part Turkey claimed that a Greek warship had tried to ram a Turkish submarine and, moreover, that Greece was giving assistance to Kurdish separatists. Relations were scarcely improved when EU leaders, meeting in Luxembourg, took the decision that Turkey was not to be regarded as a candidate for the next round of EU enlargement, while pressing ahead with accession negotiations with Cyprus although there had still been no political settlement on the island. Turkey's wounded feelings were not assuaged by Simitis' subsequent declaration that Greece did not seek to exclude Turkey from EU membership, provided she played by the EU's rules, particularly in matters concerning human rights.

There was further tension in the Greek–Turkish relationship in the summer of 1998 when Greece despatched four F-16 fighters and two C-130 transports to the airbase at Paphos in Cyprus. This had been named after Andreas Papandreou and Greece had earlier declared that any attack on it would promote immediate retaliation. In response Turkey sent six F-16s to the Gecitkale airbase in the north of the island, near Famagusta. So serious was the situation that the US government diverted an aircraft-carrier to the vicinity of the island. This dangerous game of tit for tat between Greece and Turkey was conducted against the background of the declared intention of the government of Cyprus to deploy Russian-manufactured S-300 missiles on the island and of the Turkish threat to destroy these by force if necessary. The Turkish government refused to countenance a Greek proposal that the island be demilitarised. After stormy negotiations between Simitis and the president of Cyprus, Glafcos Clerides, the Cypriot government accepted Athens' proposal that the missiles should instead be deployed on the island of Crete, well out of range of the Turkish mainland. Even so, the Turkish government protested strongly at this decision.

Early in 1999 relations between Greece and Turkey were once again plunged into crisis. The occasion was the spiriting into Greece in February of Abdullah Ocalan, the leader of the Kurdish Workers' Party (PKK), long a thorn in the side of successive Turkish governments. Ocalan, as a result of Turkish pressure, had been dislodged from his Syrian refuge and had fled to Moscow before seeking asylum in Italy. Despite the sympathy that existed in Greece for the Kurdish struggle, the Greek government, not wishing to add the Kurdish issue to the long list of bilateral differences with Turkey, made it clear that it was not prepared to offer asylum to Ocalan. Nonetheless, the PKK leader was clandestinely flown into Greece in a private plane by a retired army officer, who took advantage of lax security at Athens airport. Forced to leave the country and equipped with a Cypriot passport, Ocalan ended up being sheltered in the Greek embassy in Nairobi while apparently on his way to a more permanent refuge in the Seychelles. The clumsy performance of the Greek security agents placed in charge of the operation contributed to the Kenyan authorities getting wind of his presence in Nairobi. When Ocalan was induced to leave the embassy in the belief that he was to board a plane for Amsterdam he was abducted by Turkish secret policemen and flown in triumph to Istanbul and a show trial. His capture led to large-scale protests by members of the Kurdish diaspora who directed their wrath against Greek diplomatic missions, over twenty of which were occupied, including the Greek embassy in London. The Ankara government accused Athens not only of harbouring Ocalan but of giving active support to PKK militants in the form of military training in Greece. The Ocalan fiasco was widely perceived as a major humiliation in Greece and raised questions as to the degree to which the Simitis government had been in control of events. Three ministers (interior, public order and foreign affairs) were forced to resign. The latter, Theodoros Pangalos, had been a bitter critic of Turkish policies.

Soon after the Ocalan affair, Greece was caught up in NATO's air bombardment of Serbia in retaliation for President Slobodan Milosevic's oppression of the Kosovo Albanians. Opinion polls in

Greece consistently demonstrated levels of opposition to the bombing campaign that were far higher than those recorded in any other member of the NATO alliance. Some polls indicated almost 100 per cent opposition to the war. NATO ground troops making their way via Greece to Macedonia for deployment in Kosovo encountered demonstrations and minor harassment. The Simitis government, on the other hand, while demonstrating a degree of unease over developments and studiously declining to commit Greece to a combat role, demonstrated solidarity with her NATO partners and did not openly rock the boat. Popular opposition to the Kosovo war and, in particular, to the bombing of civilian targets in Serbia, arose partly from feelings of solidarity with the Serbs and partly from a strong current of anti-Americanism that was never far from the surface.

This anti-Americanism manifested itself to such an extent that President Clinton was forced on security grounds to curtail a planned three-day visit to Athens in November 1999 to a mere twenty hours. Violent demonstrations preceded the visit, which was characterised by extraordinary security measures. Despite the fact that opinion polls demonstrated that 60 per cent of Greeks were opposed to it, the visit itself, although the occasion of widespread protest, went off without major incident. Clinton, by publicly apologising for US support of the junta that misruled Greece between 1967 and 1974 and by expressing, during a visit to the Acropolis, sympathy with Greek aspirations for the return of the 'Elgin' marbles from the British Museum, went out of his way to assuage Greek sensibilities.

Relations between Greece and Turkey in the immediate aftermath of the Ocalan affair were extremely tense. But it soon became clear that the new foreign minister, Giorgos Papandreou, was not going to continue his predecessor Pangalos' confrontational style. The latter had described Turkey as a country that trampled human dignity and human rights underfoot. Papandreou, by contrast, publicly stated that he had no objection if members of the country's Muslim minority chose to call themselves Turks, and not, as they were officially designated, Muslims, a declaration that was heavily criticised, not least within his own party. There was good co-operation between the two countries in handling refugees during the Kosovo crisis. The Kosovo war, indeed, helped to bring the two countries together as both felt that, despite their obvious and direct interest in Balkan affairs, they had been excluded from the inner circles of the NATO decision-making process.

The principal catalyst for a dramatically improved climate, at least at the level of rhetoric, in relations between Greece and Turkey was the devastating earthquake, measuring 7.4 on the Richter scale, of 17 August 1999 that caused thousands of casualties and widespread destruction in north-western Turkey. Among Greeks there was an immediate and massive upsurge of popular sympathy for their stricken neighbours, which was rapidly translated into a number of concrete initiatives to bring relief to the devastated areas. Such was the speed of the response that Greek rescue teams were assisting in the search for survivors on the very evening of the disaster. Turkish politicians, the press and, indeed, members of the public were quick to express their gratitude. On 7 September, Greece was herself afflicted by an earthquake, whose epicentre was located slightly to the north of Athens and which measured 5.9 on the Richter scale. Although not of the magnitude of the Turkish earthquake, it was nonetheless serious: 143 deaths were reported, 100,000 were left homeless and some 22 buildings, including factories built without planning permission, were totally destroyed. According to a preliminary survey of 100,000 damaged buildings, 60 per cent were deemed to be habitable, 32 per cent to be in need of repair, while 8 per cent were fit only for demolition.

Turkish rescue teams were no less prompt in their response to the earthquake in Athens. Thus was set in train the phenomenon that soon came to be known as 'earthquake diplomacy'. Giorgos Papandreou declared that he wanted Greece to be the 'locomotive' that would pull Turkey into Europe, while his Turkish counterpart, Ismail Cem, with whom Papandreou had struck up a good working relationship, referred to what he termed an explosion of affection and expectation on both sides of the Aegean. In January 2000, Papandreou paid the first official visit to Turkey undertaken by a Greek foreign minister for thirty-eight years and laid a wreath at the mausoleum in Ankara of Kemal Atatürk, the man responsible for driving the Greeks from Asia Minor in 1922. The following month, Cem said that more had been done to promote good relations between the two countries during the previous six months than in the past forty years. Certainly a number of initiatives were launched to improve co-operation over non-contentious issues such as tourism and technological and economic development, while the decision at the Helsinki EU summit in December 1999 to accord Turkey candidate status with respect to entry into the EU was welcomed in Greece. There was little sign, however, of substantive progress towards a resolution of the Cyprus problem, a perpetual apple of discord between the two countries, or of their numerous bilateral differences. It had been widely expected, for instance, that the Turkish authorities would give permission for the re-opening of the Halki theological seminary in Istanbul during the course of President Clinton's visit to Turkey immediately prior to his visit to Greece in November 1999. But even this modest concession was not forthcoming. Moreover, there were few signs of any let-up in the crippling arms race that had developed between the two countries.

On the domestic front elections were held in April 2000. In terms of policy, not a great deal separated the two main parties, for both were strong proponents of Greek adherence to European monetary union and were in general agreement as to how this might best be achieved. Both sought to capture the vital middle ground in the political spectrum. The election therefore essentially hinged on perceptions as to which party was best equipped to implement such a policy. Opinion polls conducted during the election were inconclusive and the result was one of the closest in the country's electoral history. The result hung in the balance for several hours and, indeed, some New Democracy supporters (not to mention TV analysts of the exit polls) interpreted the early results as heralding a victory for their party. In the event, however, PASOK scraped home with a 1 per cent lead (representing some 70,000 votes) over New Democracy in terms of the popular vote. The electoral system translated this into 158 seats in parliament for PASOK and 125 for New Democracy. The KKE with 5 per cent of the vote secured 11 seats and the Coalition of the Left, representing radicals and former communists, with 3 per cent secured 6 seats. The electorate had preferred, if only narrowly, the boring competence of Simitis, whose nickname was the 'book-keeper', over Karamanlis who remained something of an unknown quantity and who had never held government office. Theodoros Pangalos who had been forced out of the government as a consequence of the Ocalan affair, returned to the cabinet as minister of culture and promptly declared that his major priority was the return of the 'Elgin' marbles. The return of the Parthenon marbles to Greece had been the subject of a personal crusade by Melina Mercouri, the actress who had been minister of culture in the first Papandreou administration.

Shortly after the election, Greece reacted angrily to a US State Department report that ranked Greece as second only to Columbia in anti-American terrorist attacks in 1999 and revealed that the US spent more on security for its diplomats in Athens than in any other capital city in the world. A month later, the '17 November' group, one of the last surviving Marxist-Leninist terrorist organisations in Europe, claimed its twenty-second victim, the British military attaché. '17 November' declared that the killing was in retaliation for the British government's prominent role in the Kosovo war. The impunity with which such assassinations were carried out raised questions as to the ability of the authorities to ensure security at the Olympic games due to be held in Athens in 2004.

The Simitis government's commitment to political, economic and social modernisation was not in doubt. The kinds of obstacles that it faced, however, were strikingly illustrated by the way in which, in the summer of 2000, the issue of whether identity cards, compulsory for all citizens, should give the religious affiliation of the holder gave rise to fierce emotions and massive demonstrations. The practice was held to discriminate against those not of the Orthodox faith which was the religion (at least nominally) of some 95 per cent of the population. When the government announced plans to bring Greek practice into line with that of her European partners by no longer listing religion, the strongly nationalist Archbishop Khristodoulos of Athens, proclaiming that 'our inspiration comes largely from the East and not the West', protested that the move was an attack on the very fundamentals of Greek identity. One factor giving rise to the resurgence of nationalism was the continued growth in illegal immigration. By the year 2000 there were an estimated 700,000 immigrants, most of them illegal, in a population of some 10.25 million.

As Greece entered the third millennium, a quarter of a century (and nine national elections) after the downfall of the Colonels' dictatorship in 1974, the country's democratic institutions were clearly firmly rooted. The difficult transition from an authoritarian military dictatorship to an authentically pluralistic democracy had been accomplished in a remarkably orderly (and bloodless) fashion, even if the people of Cyprus continue to pay a very high price for the follies of the junta in the form of a divided island. In retrospect the Colonels' regime, the only dictatorship to be established in non-communist Europe in the post-Second World War period, seems oddly anachronistic, a throw-back to the inter-war period when the military had acted as the self-appointed arbiters of political life. In the wake of the *metapolitefsi*, the political change of 1974, the spectre of military dictatorship of the kind that had blighted Greece between 1967 and 1974 appeared to have been firmly exorcised. Colonel Papadopoulos, who had masterminded the 1967 coup, died in June 1999, having spent a quarter of a century in custody for his role in subverting the country's democratic institutions, a rare instance of a military usurper paying a heavy price for his presumption at the hands of the civilian politicians whom he had unceremoniously ousted from power. The incorporation of the Communist Party of Greece into the political process after 1974, in contrast to its previous illegality, contributed powerfully to the healing of the bitter legacy of the 1946–9 civil war, as did the formation of the brief New Democracy/KKE coalition of 1989. At the same time it was clear that the right had managed to rid itself of its authoritarian, anti-democratic elements and, indeed, during the grim years of the dictatorship, had given ample evidence of its commitment to democratic values. The peaceful handover of power in October 1981 from a right that had dominated the politics of the postwar period to a radical government that styled itself as socialist, even if its socialism was of an idiosyncratic kind, appeared to indicate a new maturity in the political system. The year 1981, indeed, appeared at the time something of an *annus mirabilis*, for within the space of a few months Greece both became the tenth member of the European Community and voted into power the first 'socialist' government in her history. Socialism, however, was to prove elusive in an economy that was so heavily weighted towards the service sector, in which such a high proportion of the working population was engaged

56 The Orthodox Church Militant. Demonstrators in Athens, waving Greek flags and the double-headed eagle of the Byzantine Empire, while protesting in the summer of 2000 against the removal of religious affiliation from the identity cards which are compulsory for all citizens. In comparison with her Balkan neighbours Greece's minority populations are very small, with

on its own account, and in which the 'black' economy accounted for perhaps as much as 40 per cent of all economic activity.

The successful campaign for accelerated membership of the European Community, which was achieved in part as a consequence of Europe's collective guilt at its supine attitude during the seven-year dictatorship, can be seen as having set the seal on the country's hitherto somewhat uncertain identity as a European, or even, in defiance of the logic of geography and still more of history, a west European country. While Greece certainly hoped for, and in the event gained, significant economic benefits from her membership of the Community, it is clear that the driving force behind her application had been a political, even psychological one. Although Greeks might still talk of travelling to Europe as though their country was not properly a part of it, it is difficult now to gainsay her European credentials.

Caption for Plate 56 (*cont.*).

over 95 per cent of the population adhering, at least nominally, to the Orthodox faith. The largest minority, and the only one to enjoy formal recognition, is the Muslim, settled in western Thrace and consisting of Turks, Pomaks (Slav-speaking Muslims) and gypsies. There are also small Jewish, Catholic, Protestant and Armenian communities, together with a small number of Albanian, Slav and Vlach (a form of Romanian) speakers. In the 1990s Greece's small minority populations became something of a political issue. When, in 2000, the government proposed to remove religious affiliation, together with other information, from identity cards so as to bring Greek practice into line with that of her European partners, Archbishop of Athens and all Greece, Khristodoulos, and the Holy Synod organised massive protest demonstrations in Thessaloniki and Athens. The protestors claimed that the measure struck at the heart of Greek identity, which, according to the archbishop, was shaped largely by the East, whereas the West was seeking to undermine traditional Greek values. The European Union's emphasis on minority rights might, he protested, lead to the 'de-Christianisation' of Europe. In contrast to many of his predecessors, Khristodoulos adopted a high profile on political issues and his enthusiastic championing of nationalist causes was something of an embarrassment to the government of Costas Simitis, which was anxious to demonstrate Greece's western, European credentials.

In the year 2000 it remained to be seen whether the much improved climate in relations between Greece and Turkey that had emerged in the second half of 1999 would lead to a lasting break-through in the hitherto troubled relationship between the two countries. Serious though the problems, domestic and external, facing Greece were, they paled into insignificance when contrasted with those confronting her northern neighbours, who shared with Greece a common heritage of Byzantine and Ottoman rule and of Orthodox Christianity. Greece had paid a high price in terms of bloodshed, delayed economic development and bitterness in the turmoil of the 1940s. Yet in the 1990s, unlike her Balkan neighbours, she was spared the problem of having to recreate civil society from scratch and of having to rebuild the economy from a very low base. Moreover, her membership of the European Union had proved to be an ever more valuable asset, both economically and politically. The country's material progress since the end of the civil war in 1949 had been truly remarkable. Living standards for the Greek people had improved immeasurably over the past half century. On the threshold of the new millennium it remained to be seen whether Greece's institutional and political infrastructure could demonstrate the same ability to adapt and modernise.

8

Greece in the new Millennium: from affluence to austerity

Greece is rich but the Greeks are poor.

Andreas Papandreou

During the 1990s Greece had one of the fastest growth rates within the European Union, and its status as a fully fledged member of the Union was sealed by acceptance into the eurozone in 2001, with the euro replacing the drachma in 2002. It soon became clear, however, that EU rules relating to the permitted size of the budget deficit had been contravened. Complaints began to be heard about the inflationary effects of the adoption of the new currency, and aggrieved citizens sought to organise an unsuccessful consumer boycott in protest.

There were other indications during the early years of the new millennium of a country on an upward trajectory. After almost thirty years, the incubus of the '17 November' terrorist group was brought to an end. During this time it had carried out with impunity assassinations (twenty-three in all) of US military personnel and spies, Turkish and British diplomats, Greek politicians, policemen, newspaper editors, and members of what the group termed the 'lumpen big bourgeoisie', ship-owners and industrialists. The British military attaché, Brigadier Stephen Saunders, was the last victim of '17 November' when, in June 2000, he was shot while his car was stuck in Athens' notorious traffic. His killing prompted British police to assist the Greek authorities in tracking down those responsible. It was not police intelligence, however, but a blunder on the part of one of the members of the group that was to lead to its dismantling two years later. In June 2002, Savvas

Xiros was seriously injured by the premature detonation of an explosive device that he was intending to plant in Piraeus. Two safe houses, and much weaponry, were quickly uncovered. Two of Xiros' brothers were found to be implicated in what proved to be virtually a family (and money-making) enterprise. Unusually, Xiros combined planting bombs with painting religious icons, but it was clear that the principal source of the group's funding was bank robbery. After several weeks on the run, Dimitris Koufodinas, a bee-keeper-cum-assassin responsible for many of the killings, turned himself in to the police. The leader of the group, and the author of its turgid, jargon-laden manifestos, proved to be the Sorbonne-educated 58-year-old Alexandros Giotopoulos, who was arrested on the remote island of Lipsi in the eastern Aegean as he was about to flee to Turkey. In December 2003, following the longest trial ever to be held in Greece, fifteen members of the group were found guilty. Giotopoulos received twenty-one life terms, an unprecedentedly heavy sentence, and Koufodinas fifteen.

Although there were subsequent sporadic attacks by small, shadowy left-wing groups, they were on nothing like the scale of those of '17 November'. One such, Revolutionary Struggle, fired a rocket-propelled grenade at the US embassy in January 2007. There had been little enthusiasm for President George W. Bush's 'war on terror' following the 9/11 attack on the World Trade Center in 2001, and the subsequent invasion of Iraq gave rise to huge protest demonstrations. The April 2006 visit of US Secretary of State Condoleezza Rice, likewise prompted massive protests.

An important step in the modernisation of the country's infrastructure was the opening in 2001 of a modern airport in place of the existing Ellinikon airport, whose only advantage had been proximity to the centre of Athens. Ellinikon had for long proved inadequate for a country so dependent for its prosperity on tourism, while the new Eleftherios Venizelos airport, although situated much further from the city centre, has good road and public transport connections. In 2004, the Athens metro, the construction of which had started in 1991 and which began operation in 2000, was extended to the new airport. This excellent system, which continues to expand, made a marked contribution to improving the city's chronic transport (and pollution) problems. A number of stations have remarkable displays of antiquities unearthed in the course of their construction.

57 Archbishop Khristodoulos with Pope John Paul II beside an icon of the Apostle Paul on the Areopagos in Athens, where Paul is reputed to have preached. The visit of Pope John Paul II to Greece in May 2001, against the background of extraordinary security measures, was an event of considerable symbolic significance, coming as it did nearly 1,000 years after the 'Great Schism' of 1054, which is conventionally held to mark the split between the Roman Catholic and Eastern Orthodox Churches. Archbishop Khristodoulos of Athens had the reputation of being a doughty defender of Orthodoxy, despite, or perhaps because of, his education at a school run by the Catholic Marist Fathers. The archbishop, in the presence of the pope, read out a list of thirteen ways in which the Catholic Church had offended against the Orthodox. The most important of these had occurred in 1204 when the Fourth Crusade was diverted from the Holy Land to the sack of Constantinople. In reply, the pope asked for forgiveness for acts and omissions by Catholics against their Orthodox brothers and sisters. The status of the Uniates, who follow the liturgical and other practices of the Eastern Churches but are in full communion with Rome, is a long-standing cause of friction between the Papacy and the Orthodox Churches. Staunch in defence of Orthodoxy, Archbishop Khristodoulos was a fierce opponent of proposals to build a mosque in Athens for the city's growing Muslim population, consisting mainly of immigrants (not all of them legal) from Afghanistan, Pakistan, Bangladesh,

Improved communications helped secure the 2004 Olympic Games. Greece had made a chaotic and unsuccessful bid for the 1996 Olympics, the centenary of the first modern games that had been held in Athens in 1896, an amateurish event in every sense of the word and a world away from the over-commercialised machine into which the Olympic movement has metamorphosed. When prime minister in the 1970s, after the fall of the junta, Konstantinos Karamanlis had suggested that the modern Olympics should have a permanent home near ancient Olympia, but this idea was not taken up. Many observers questioned whether a small country such as Greece could organise games capable of competing with the grandiose, and expensive, manifestations of national pride characteristic of the modern games. Doubts were expressed as to whether the new facilities would be completed in time. They were, if only just. Moreover, they were very costly. Elaborate security measures helped make the games the most expensive held up until then, with the cost of security alone for each competing athlete amounting to £90,000. Overall, the cost of the Athens games reached 9 billion euros, nearly double the original budget. Some 4 billion viewers worldwide tuned in at various times to watch the events on television, more than at any previous games. The spectacular closing ceremony, focusing on Greek history down the ages, attracted a particularly large audience. Overall, the 2004 Olympics were a triumphant success in promoting a positive image of the country, but they left a legacy of underused and rapidly decaying facilities, the cost of which contributed significantly to the debt mountain that finally caught up with Greece at the end of the decade.

The momentum of a significant improvement in the climate of relations with Turkey, which had been poor for much of the previous half-century, was maintained. In May 2004, Recep Tayyip Erdoğan paid the first visit to Greece by a Turkish prime minister for sixteen

---

Caption for Plate 57 (*cont.*).

Egypt and West Africa. It was not until 2011, during the tenure of Khristodoulos' successor as archbishop of Athens, Ieronymos II, that parliament voted funds for a mosque to be built in what was the only EU capital without one.

years. In part, this was prompted by recognition that Greece was a strong supporter of the accession of Turkey to the European Union. But the rapprochement between the two countries continued to be more at the level of rhetoric than of substance. Dangerous manoeuvres involving Greek and Turkish fighters continued in disputed air space in the eastern Aegean. In 2006, these led to a mid-air collision, which resulted in the death of a Greek pilot.

Greek foreign policy received a setback when, in 2004, the Greek Cypriots decisively rejected a United Nations plan for ending the long-lasting division of the island. Athens had supported the plan as part of a policy of helping to pave the way for Turkey's entry into the European Union, a development which, it was hoped, would put the improved Greek–Turkish relationship on a permanently firmer footing. Five versions, the last one totalling 9,000 pages, of the highly complex Annan plan, as it was known, were produced. This provided for the evolution of the common, although divided, state into two devolved federal constituent states, one Greek-controlled and the other Turkish-controlled. The common state would determine issues such as external relations, citizenship, immigration and the functioning of the central bank. Other matters would be the responsibility of the two constituent states. Limits would be placed on the numbers of Greek Cypriots who would be entitled to live within the bounds of the Turkish component state and of Turkish Cypriots in the Greek component state. Some 85,000 of the 185,000 Greek Cypriot refugees from the north would have the right of return. Greek and Turkish military contingents were to remain on the island, in smaller numbers but with rights of intervention anywhere in the island. This right of Turkish military intervention throughout the island was a major factor in the rejection of the plan by the Greek Cypriots. Local Greek and Turkish Cypriot forces would be disbanded.

There would also be adjustments in the size of the territories of the two component states. Since the Turkish invasion of 1974, the Greeks had controlled almost 60% of the island's territory, the Turks 37%, with the United Nations buffer zone and the British sovereign base areas extending to rather over 3%. Under the Annan plan, the Greek Cypriot entity would have extended to almost 70% of the island, reducing the Turkish Cypriot entity to almost 28%. The status of the two British sovereign base areas, Akrotiri and Dhekelia, which had been ceded in perpetuity in the 1960 settlement that resulted in an independent Cyprus, would be unchanged, although an offer would be made to cede almost half of the base areas to the Republic of Cyprus. In April 2004, the final version of the plan was put to a referendum. The turn-out in both communities was very high. Over 75% of the Greek Cypriots rejected the plan, while 65% of the Turkish Cypriot community, which included a large number of settlers from the Turkish mainland, accepted it.

In the following month, May 2004, as had already been agreed, the internationally recognised, Greek-controlled Republic of Cyprus, but not the Turkish-controlled north of the island, became a member of the European Union, along with eight central and east European countries and Malta. A positive development was that in 2003 the Turkish Cypriot administration had partially lifted restrictions on movement between the northern and southern sectors of the island. Members of both communities (as well as non-Cypriots) were now able to cross the hitherto largely impermeable buffer zone and to visit their old homes (except for those in Varosha, the abandoned quarter of Famagusta which had remained unoccupied since 1974) and religious and other sites. All those crossing the UN-controlled 'Green Line' were, however, required to present identity documents.

Greek foreign policy suffered a further reversal when, in November 2005, the US administration accepted the name of the country's northern neighbour as the Republic of Macedonia, rather than that promoted by Greece, i.e. the Former Yugoslav Republic of Macedonia (FYROM). It was under this latter designation that the new state had become a member of the United Nations in 1993. Many Greeks saw the name 'Macedonia' as implying territorial designs on Greek Macedonia. It would seem that the US decision was a reward for Macedonia's participation in President Bush's 'war on terror'. The Macedonian contribution was modest, but Greece's was even more so: unlike Macedonia, Greece had contributed no frontline troops to the wars in Iraq and Afghanistan. Greece warned that recognition would have 'multiple negative repercussions', but it was clear that the battle over the naming of Macedonia had been lost, although Greece in 2008 did manage to veto the entry of Macedonia into the NATO alliance. Despite the continuing stalemate over the name, Greek firms became major investors in Macedonia, as they were in other formerly communist countries in the region, such as Bulgaria, Serbia and Romania. Macedonia was not the only country in the region with which Greece had differences: Greece was one of five EU states that did not recognise Kosovo's declaration of independence in 2008.

In early 2004, Kostas Simitis, then aged sixty-seven, resigned as leader of PASOK to make way, as he maintained, for a younger generation, although advanced age has never been an obstacle to holding high office in Greece. He represented the modernising, as opposed to populist, wing of PASOK, but had had limited success in challenging the vested interests that stood in the way of reform. These ranged from farmers and taxi-drivers to doctors and lawyers. Giorgos Papandreou, the sole candidate, was elected as the new leader of PASOK. Papandreou was the son and grandson of prime ministers, and was a member of an inbred political elite that was to come under much criticism during the financial and political crisis in the years after 2009.

The March 2004 election signalled the end of the long period of PASOK's domination of the political scene following its foundation after the downfall of the Colonels' junta in 1974, the party having been in power for twenty of the previous twenty-three years. With 45 per cent of the popular vote, ND, under the leadership of Kostas Karamanlis, won 165 out of 300 seats. PASOK, with 41 per cent of the vote, won 117 seats. Karamanlis subsequently proposed Karolos Papoulias, a prominent PASOK politician, for the presidency of the Republic when Kostis Stephanopoulos' second term came to an end in March 2005. This made it certain that he would receive the necessary three-fifths majority in parliament prescribed by the constitution. One of the reasons for PASOK's 2004 defeat was growing disquiet over the level of corruption. But corruption continued under the new government. Senior judges were found to be in receipt of bribes, while one minister was forced to resign after urging customs officials to solicit smaller bribes. By the end of the decade, Greece was ranked by Transparency International as the most corrupt state in the EU. New Democracy's efforts to introduce necessary reforms met with scant success, in part because its ministers had little previous government experience. It was unable to bring about changes in the

58 'Like father, like son, like grandson'. Juxtaposed photographs of Georgios, Andreas and Giorgos Papandreou (l–r). Greece is a society without distinctions of rank, and still less hereditary titles. Nonetheless, it has to a significant degree been governed by a quasi-hereditary political caste. In a 1965 newspaper interview, a prominent politician, Konstantinos Mitsotakis, had declared that 'leadership ... is neither bestowed, nor is it inherited'. But his father and an uncle had been members of parliament and he himself was related to Eleftherios Venizelos. A member of parliament for over fifty years, Mitsotakis held a number of ministerial posts and was prime minister between 1990 and 1993. His daughter, Dora Bakoyanni, between 2006 and 2009, was foreign minister in Kostas Karamanlis' government, the highest political office ever held by a woman in Greece. She had previously been the first woman mayor of Athens between 2002 and 2006. Her brother, Kyriakos, is a member of parliament. Giorgos Papandreou is the prime exemplar of this hereditary tendency. In 2009, he became prime minister, a post that had been held by his father, Andreas (1981–9, 1993–6), in whose governments Giorgos had served, and by his grandfather Georgios (1944–5, 1963–5), in whose last government Andreas Papandreou had likewise been a minister. In 1981, Andreas Papandreou had succeeded Georgios Rallis of New Democracy as prime minister. Rallis' paternal (Dimitrios Rallis) and maternal (Georgios Theotokis) grandfathers had both been prime ministers. Giorgos Papandreou, on becoming prime minister in 2009, succeeded Kostas Karamanlis, the nephew of Konstantinos Karamanlis, who had been prime minister in the 1950s, 1960s and 1970s and president in the 1980s and 1990s.

59 A fire raging at Pikermi in Attica, not far from Athens, in August 2008. Visible behind the trees is a fire-fighting plane. A particularly devastating series of forest fires in 2007 left sixty-seven dead and resulted in the destruction of many thousands of acres of forest. The growing green movement in Greece questioned whether the environment could ever fully recover from this conflagration. There were fears that heat waves, and the forest fires often accompanying them, which recurred almost every summer, could result in the gradual desertification of the country. This would clearly have dire

complex social security system, while, in 2007, protests against reforms in higher education forced it to abandon a proposed constitutional amendment that would have permitted the establishment of private universities. In the same year, the weather was a cause for concern. The highest temperatures for over 100 years were recorded – reaching 46 degrees Celsius – and resulted in a number of deaths from heat exhaustion.

In the election of 2007, ND's share of the vote fell from 45% to 42%, its seats from 165 to 152. PASOK's vote fell from 41% to 38%, its seats from 117 to 102. There were small increases in the seats received by the parties of the left. A new entrant in the political spectrum was the Laikos Orthodoxos Synagermos (Popular Orthodox Rally). This had been founded by Giorgos Karatzaferis, a defector from ND. Its acronym, appropriately for a right-wing populist party, was LAOS, the word for 'people'. Its 4% share of the vote resulted in 10 seats.

That corruption continued was demonstrated as an extraordinary story of malfeasance in high places unravelled. This was truly 'byzantine' in both senses of the word. Its origins lay in the Byzantine milieu of the monastic republic of Mount Athos, while it was, in the current English usage of the word, a tale of devious complexity. The revelations held many Greeks gripped with fascinated horror. The scandal involved mysterious but highly profitable land deals carried out by financially astute, jet-setting monks, with friends in high places and equipped with high-tech means of communication in the medieval surroundings of the Holy Mountain. The scam emanated from Vatopaidi, one of the country's wealthiest monastic foundations, and the host in recent years to both Prince Charles and Vladimir Putin.

Caption for Plate 59 (*cont.*).

consequences for a country so dependent on tourism for economic survival. The inadequacy of the government response to ecological disaster was much criticised, as was its inability to curb instances of arson aimed at making way for illegal house building. After the crisis of 2009, illegal loggers, exploiting huge rises in the cost of heating oil, began to slash their way through forests already devastated by years of summer wildfires. Air pollution, as wood replaced oil smoke, became a problem in the country's main cities.

Although the Athonite monasteries had been stripped of their extensive land holdings outside the peninsula, the monks of Vatopaidi, invoking title bestowed on the monastery in the fourteenth century by the Byzantine Emperor John V Palaiologos, laid claim to a lake and the surrounding land in northern Greece. This was somehow exchanged for seventy-three state-owned properties, worth several hundreds of millions of euros. When the scandal came to light, in 2008, two ministers were forced to resign. Public outrage at the astonishing revelations and at (subsequently proven) allegations of bribery by the German firm Siemens was one of the factors contributing to the downfall of the New Democracy government in 2009.

In the same year, a striking new museum housing antiquities from the Athenian Acropolis was opened. Much attention was focused on the third-floor gallery, which enjoyed a spectacular view of the Parthenon. This contained the surviving metopes, the carved marble panels which had been removed from the temple, alongside plaster casts of the missing 'Elgin' marbles housed in the British Museum. The message was clear: many Greeks wanted the metopes removed by the Earl of Elgin to London at the beginning of the nineteenth century to be returned to Athens. But there has been no response to repeated requests for their return.

In December 2008, Athens was convulsed by days of rioting and arson following the shooting by police of a fifteen-year-old schoolboy. The police claim, that this followed an attack on a police car by a stone-throwing crowd, proved to be false. This was an early indication of the trouble that lay ahead as the world financial crisis began to affect Greece. The election of October 2009, which took place two years early, resulted in a crushing defeat for ND. The party lost 61 seats: its 33% share of the vote, almost 10 percentage points less than it had received in 2004, resulted in 91 seats. PASOK, with a 44% share of the vote, won 160 seats, a gain of 58. The Communist Party, with 21 seats and an 8% share of the vote, lost one seat. LAOS made significant gains, 6% of the vote resulting in 15 seats, and the Coalition of the Radical Left (SYRIZA), a grouping of twelve radical leftist groups, including former communists, Maoists, feminists and environmentalists, with 5%, won 13 seats. This was ND's worst result since its foundation in the aftermath of the collapse of the Colonels' dictatorship in 1974, and Kostas Karamanlis, the party leader, had little option but to step down. He was succeeded by Antonis Samaras, who had been foreign minister between 1990 and 1993, when he had resigned in protest at what he regarded as the government's failure to pursue sufficiently vigorously the Greek case over Macedonia. He had then set up his own breakaway party, as a consequence of which the Mitsotakis government lost its majority in parliament, but subsequently he had rejoined New Democracy.

During the election campaign, Giorgos Papandreou had promised measures to stimulate the economy, including pay rises for the bloated public sector. But almost immediately it became clear that Greece faced a financial crisis of potentially catastrophic proportions. Eurozone membership had given access to the cheap funding that was one of the factors leading to a massive build-up of indebtedness. This became apparent when Greece was caught up in the turmoil of the global financial crisis of 2008. Moreover, eurozone membership meant that Greece could not respond to the crisis by devaluing its currency. 'Internal devaluation' and harsh measures of austerity appeared to be the only remedy. With the country sinking into recession and with a debt mountain of 112 per cent of gross domestic product, it was clear that without a massive injection of outside funding the country faced the prospect of defaulting on its loans.

There had been such defaults earlier in its history. In 1893, for instance, a declaration of national bankruptcy by the prime minister, Kharilaos Trikoupis, followed by crushing defeat in the thirty-day war of 1897 with Turkey, had led to the establishment of an International Financial Commission, which, until the Second World War, oversaw the payment to foreign bondholders of certain government revenues. There was thus a precedent for the degree of external oversight over the economy that was to develop after 2009. Another financial crisis in 1932 had forced the suspension of debt service charges and amortisation payments on Greece's debts.

Although Greece's gross domestic product amounted to a little over 2 per cent of that of the eurozone as a whole, the country's economic and financial problems were to be the focus of much of the EU's attention in the years after 2009. As eurozone politicians dithered over how to deal with the country's problems, it became clear that its sovereign debt crisis had the capacity to impact in a seriously negative fashion on the wider world economy. Greece's economic plight continued to worsen. Billions of euros began to be withdrawn from the banks. In 2010, government revenues amounted to some 50 billion euros, while expenditures were of the order of 75 billion.

This highlighted the deficiencies of a taxation system that was ineffective, under-resourced and at times corrupt, and which has given rise to a huge backlog of unresolved tax cases. Revenue from personal income tax was, proportionately, significantly less than in most eurozone countries. A sizeable number of the self-employed, who comprised a high proportion of the workforce, looked on the payment of taxes as optional, while some tax inspectors, in return for bribes, had turned a blind eye to tax evasion. As few as a third of doctors declared incomes of more than 12,000 euros and the bribes frequently paid by patients to doctors necessarily fell outside the tax system. It has been estimated that underpayment of tax may have amounted to as much as 30 billion euros a year. Naming and, hopefully, shaming tax-dodging celebrities and the rich in the press was one weapon that began to be used in the effort to ensure that people paid their fair share. Attention was also focused on such anomalies as a 21.5 per cent levy on media advertising (in addition to VAT) that was paid not to the state but to the pension and health fund of journalists and publishers. Other favoured professions, among them lawyers and engineers, enjoyed similar breaks.

There was hesitation on the part of the EU to come to the rescue. This was partly caused by the unwillingness of Germany, the paymaster of the seventeen-member eurozone, to bail out what were caricatured in its tabloid press as lazy Greeks, whose principal aim in life was held to be to retire early on a fat pension. This revived memories of the devastation wrought by the wartime German occupation and – alongside the burning of German flags and the cartoons lampooning Angela Merkel, the German chancellor, as a Nazi – there were calls for the further payment of Second World War reparations, which, according to one estimate, amounted to 162 billion euros.

As the country's financial situation continued to worsen, with the credit rating agencies downgrading government bonds as junk, Germany and the EU came to accept the idea of a bailout in cooperation with the International Monetary Fund. This first bailout in 2010 amounted to 110 billion euros. It was accompanied by an unprecedented memorandum of understanding which specified, in great detail and with target dates for completion, some 200 measures aimed at making the economy more competitive. Adherence to the memorandum was a condition of the assistance from what came to be known as the 'troika' of the EU, the International Monetary Fund and the European Central Bank. Provision was made for monitoring the stipulated measures by a technical assistance task force, the first members of which began work in Athens in the spring of 2012. Over the previous thirty years, attempts at reform had been torpedoed by resistance on the part of the trades unions or by other vested interests, including the media barons and their allies in the business community. If the measures mandated by the memorandum were to be implemented, so it was hoped, then Greece might be transformed from a near-bankrupt, clientelistic, overly bureaucratic, poorly governed and at times corrupt polity.

These measures built on a stability and growth programme that had earlier been introduced by PASOK itself. Value added tax was increased from 19 to 23 per cent, and additional property taxes, which were more difficult to evade than income tax or VAT, were imposed, as were higher duties on alcohol, tobacco, fuel and luxury goods. Steep reductions in public-sector salaries, cuts in pensions and increases in the retirement age (professions deemed 'arduous', among them hairdressing, had particularly low retirement ages) were coupled with demands for huge reductions in the number and job security of those employed in the public sector. Measures to increase competitiveness included the deregulation of the domestic freight sector, the removal of impediments to entrepreneurship and the curtailing of the privileges of the professions. An important reform was the establishment of an independent statistical service so as to lessen the risk of official figures being manipulated.

The imposition of this unprecedented programme of austerity resulted in increased homelessness, which had not been a problem since the civil war, and in begging in the streets. Business bankruptcies were widespread. Wages in some cases went unpaid. Food banks, soup kitchens, and, in some areas, a resort to bartering made their appearance. Hospitals and pharmacies ran out of life-saving medicines and foreign pharmaceutical companies were reluctant to despatch supplies for fear that they would not be paid. The National Health Service came under great strain. Tourism, which was such an important contributor to the balance of payments, declined, although it was calculated that as many as a million Russian tourists would visit Greece in 2012. This would help to compensate for any fall in the number of German tourists, given the ill will that had developed between Greece and Germany during the crisis.

In May 2010, agreement to the conditions of the first bailout was passed in parliament by 172 out of 300 votes, with ND and the parties of the left voting against. Throughout this and subsequent years, there were strikes, some of them general, and continual demonstrations. These were noisy but generally peaceful, although some ended with 'anarchists' – groups of unemployed young men with grievances against the police – confronting the riot squads, which showed little hesitation in meeting violence with violence. It was these clashes rather than the peaceful demonstrations that appeared on television screens outside Greece. In May of 2010 a branch of Marfin Bank was fire-bombed, resulting in the death of three employees, one of whom was pregnant. Another casualty of the crisis was an elderly retired pharmacist, who had in the summer of 2011 been one of the *aganaktismenoi*, the 'outraged' ones, camped in Constitution Square in the centre of Athens. In April 2012, he shot himself near the parliament building, leaving a note to say that he did not want to be reduced to foraging for food in rubbish bins. The site of his suicide rapidly became an improvised memorial. Suicide rates, hitherto among the lowest in Europe, rose. One of the saddest sights in Athens was that of destitute Greeks and migrant workers searching for food in rubbish bins.

Those observers who argued that the first bailout in 2010 was unlikely to prove adequate were shown to be right. Throughout much of the following year, 2011, Greece was in a state of political and economic turmoil, while government indebtedness grew inexorably. Many outsiders were puzzled as to how Greece had managed to amass such a huge mountain of debt. One obvious contributory factor was wholly disproportionate expenditure on defence. Another was the cost of government subsidies to social insurance funds, of which, by the end of the 1990s, there were well over 300. As Greece entered the fourth year of recession, overall unemployment rose to 21 per cent and unemployment among the under twenty-fives was over 50 per cent. In 2012 these figures became even higher. The

60 'Greece is not for sale.' Following the onset in 2008 of the economic and fiscal crisis, the worst during the postwar period, demonstrations and strikes in protest against the harsh austerity measures imposed by the troika have been a regular occurrence. This photograph depicts a protest organised in 2012 outside the parliament building in Athens jointly by GSEE – the umbrella trade union organisation for private-sector workers, founded in 1918 and with a membership of 450,000 – and ADEDY, its counterpart for those in the public sector, with a membership of 300,000. The slogan *I Ellada den poleitai* (Greece is not for sale) refers to the troika's demand that state assets, including the former royal estate of Tatoi, to the value of 50 billion euros, be sold to reduce the country's deficit. Port facilities in Piraeus, the harbour for Athens, have been sold to Chinese interests, while early in 2013 the Emir of Qatar purchased a number of small islands in the Ionian Sea. In 2013 the home of the Greek consul-general in London was sold for £23 million. But such sales have often encountered bureaucratic obstacles and have not proved easy to achieve in practice. A serious difficulty in such asset sales is the absence of a land register. One tract of government-owned coastal land in the north-western Peloponnese that might have been sold to foreign investors was found to have been colonised by 7,000 illegally built houses. Most of the numerous anti-austerity demonstrations have been orderly, if noisy, although some have ended in stone-throwing and petrol-bombing by anarchists, whose violence provoked violence by the police. Much of central Athens has been disfigured by politically inspired graffiti.

61 'Cutting out the middleman'. As Greece's economic situation worsened after 2009, food banks became commonplace, bartering occurred, and some communities introduced their own form of currency. Farmers sought to cut out the middlemen, as in this 2012 picture, by selling their produce, in this case potatoes, directly to the consumer.

62 Tanks preparing for the *Ochi* (No) Day parade, commemorating Greece's refusal to accept a humiliating Italian ultimatum in October 1940, in Thessaloniki in 2006. In the early 1980s Greece's defence spending was almost double the average expenditure of other eurozone countries. It has been estimated that the savings that Greece would have made had its defence expenditures been at the average of those of its EU partners would have amounted to 150 billion euros, more than it received under the terms of the troika's second bailout in 2012. Between 2002 and 2006 Greece, a small country with a population of some 11 million, was the fourth-largest importer of weaponry in the world. The only conceivable use for this sophisticated equipment would have been in a war with Turkey, its ally in the NATO alliance. The armament inventory of the Greek armed forces is huge in relation to the size of the country and includes 900 German Tiger tanks, French Mirage and American F-16 jets, 11 submarines, and 14 frigates armed with Exocet missiles. Many of the allegations of corruption on the part of politicians and others were linked to these very expensive arms purchases. In the often fraught negotiations between Greece and its eurozone partners after the beginning of the financial crisis, Germany and France, while demanding ever harsher measures of austerity, insisted at the same time that Greece honour existing arms contracts.

troika demanded, *inter alia*, a 22 per cent cut in the minimum wage and the elimination of 150,000 public-sector jobs. The politicians responsible for implementing this harsh programme of retrenchment increasingly became targets of abuse. The annual ceremonies to commemorate the 28 October 1940 *Ochi* (No) Day, when Greece had resisted Italian bullying, were disrupted in 2011, with the main parade in Thessaloniki being cancelled after the president was branded a traitor. Although the political elite came in for bitter criticism, few of its members accused of corruption were brought to justice, and fewer still were convicted. Corrupt politicians proved adept at sheltering behind the statute of limitations and parliamentary immunity. In March 2013, however, Akis Tsokhatzopoulos, a prominent PASOK politician who, in the 1990s, almost became prime minister, received an eight-year sentence for corruption, and faced further trials. A few days earlier, a former New Democracy mayor of Thessaloniki, Vasilis Papageorgopoulos, was, with two aides, sentenced to life imprisonment for embezzling 18 million euros.

In June 2011, Papandreou secured a narrow vote for a new programme of austerity: the medium-term programme of retrenchment. With tax receipts proving to be inadequate, a one-off property tax – which, to prevent evasion, was added to electricity bills – was introduced. But despite these additional measures, European politicians and bankers began to talk openly of the possibility of a Greek default and of a return to the drachma. Moreover, the PASOK government began to contemplate trying to renegotiate the troika's demands and, at the end of October, Papandreou, apparently without consulting cabinet colleagues, declared that he would put the conditions attaching to the second (130 billion euro) bailout to a referendum. This provoked a further political crisis, and Papandreou, whose standing in the opinion polls had slumped drastically, was forced by EU pressure to withdraw the proposal. Soon afterwards, he stood down as prime minister. Following several days of intense bargaining, a coalition government was formed. This consisted of deputies drawn from PASOK, ND and the populist LAOS, which entered government for the first time, although it later withdrew. The unelected prime minister, Loukas Papademos, was an academic economist who had been governor of the Bank of Greece and vice-president of the European Central Bank. Papademos was charged with negotiating the second bailout with the troika, and with preparing the way for new elections.

There were intensive, and, at times, cliff-hanging negotiations over the second bailout, as the deadline, March 2012, approached when a large loan repayment was scheduled. The bailout aimed to reduce the debt to 120 per cent of gross domestic product by 2020. Agreement was finally reached, with banks and private-sector bondholders accepting, without enthusiasm, a 53.5% 'haircut', or loss, on the value of their government bonds. This wiped some 107 billion euros off the country's debts. Greek banks had not indulged in the risky financial practices of many foreign banks that had precipitated the near-collapse of the world financial system in 2008, but they had been substantial purchasers of government bonds. The damage they had suffered from the terms of the second bailout was demonstrated in April 2012, when the combined losses of two of the country's largest banks were revealed as 9.3 billion euros. In 2012, the debt contagion spread from Greece to Cyprus, whose banks were likewise heavily invested in Greek bonds. As a result, Cyprus was also forced to appeal to the troika for help. This was only grudgingly forth-coming in March 2013, when such assistance took the form not of a bailout but a bail-in. Initially all those with holdings in Cypriot banks were expected to take a substantial loss on their savings. This was subsequently amended to include a larger 'haircut' for those with holdings over 100,000 euros. At the same time, the Cypriot Laiki Bank was wound up.

In the 2009 elections, PASOK and New Democracy between them had secured 77% of the popular vote. In the run-up to the May 2012 elections, however, it soon became apparent that their dominance of the political scene over the past thirty-five years was under threat. A breakdown in party discipline resulted in many defections and expulsions from the ruling parties, together with a precipitous collapse in support registered in opinion polls. Of the thirty-two parties (one, calling itself Tyrannicides, had been disqualified) contesting the elections, it was thought that as many as ten might be represented in the new parliament. In the event there were seven, two more than in 2009. The results for PASOK and ND were even worse than the polls had predicted. ND's share of the vote was 19% (with 58 plus 50 seats as the highest-scoring party), down from 33% in 2009. PASOK's decline was even more marked: from 44%, its share fell to 13% (41 seats, barely a quarter of those it received in the 2009 election). It was pushed into third place by SYRIZA, the Coalition of the Radical Left, with 17% (up from 5% in 2009) and 52 seats. Headed by an energetic and telegenic 38-year-old, Alexis Tsipras, SYRIZA rejected the bailout outright, while nonetheless seeking to remain in the eurozone. Its utopian policies included large-scale re-nationalisation of former state enterprises, heavy taxation of the rich, unemployment benefits for illegal immigrants, no redundancies in the public sector and pensions of 100% of final salary. The fourth party was Independent Greeks, a right-wing anti-austerity party headed by a defecting ND deputy, with 11% (33 seats). In fifth place, at 8% (26 seats), the Communist Party, which advocated leaving not only the eurozone but the EU itself, marginally increased its vote.

In sixth place was the ultra-right-wing Chrysi Avgi (Golden Dawn) whose share of the vote at 7% (21 seats) was almost 25 times higher than the 0.29% it had received in 2009. It is virulently, and at times violently, anti-leftist and anti-immigrant, and calls for the planting of landmines along Greece's land border with Turkey to deter clandestine immigrants. Soon after the elections, it attracted much adverse publicity when one of its spokesmen physically lashed out at a woman communist deputy during the course of a televised political discussion. The party has links with neo-Nazi groups elsewhere in Europe. Its symbol is the ancient Greek meander, which was also employed by the quasi-fascist pre-war dictator General Metaxas. The seventh party was Dimokratiki Aristera (Democratic Left), a party of the left accepting the values of European social democracy, with a 6% (19 seats) share of the vote. A surprise was the failure of the right-wing populist party, LAOS, to reach the 3% threshold for entry into parliament.

Although voting is notionally compulsory, the turn-out was low by Greek standards: 65%, as opposed to 71% in 2009. The current version of the electoral law rewards the party receiving the largest share of the vote with fifty additional seats. Thus, although ND received only 2% more votes than SYRIZA, it had more than double the number of seats in parliament. The leaders of the three largest parties, Antonis Samaras, Alexis Tsipras and Evangelos Venizelos, Giorgos Papandreou's successor as leader of PASOK, were charged in turn by President Papoulias with forming a government. Predictably, they failed, and new elections were called for 17 June in the hope of producing a stable government. Meanwhile, the continued political uncertainty led to substantial falls in the Athens stock market, while German politicians began to talk openly of Greece having to leave the eurozone.

The failure of a government to emerge from the May elections focused the attention of much of the world on the possible outcome of the 17 June elections, which were widely regarded as the most critical in the country's postwar history. Root-and-branch opponents of the harsh terms imposed by the troika looked to SYRIZA, with its policy of outright rejection, coupled with insistence that it wished to remain in the eurozone. During a tense election campaign, Angela Merkel insisted that there could be no relaxation of the troika's demands. Another representative of the troika, Christine Lagarde, the head of the International Monetary Fund, made an ill-judged intervention when she publicly criticised the Greeks for their reluctance to pay taxes. The validity of this point was undermined by the revelation that her own very large salary was tax-free.

For a time it looked as though SYRIZA might emerge as the largest party. In the event, it was New Democracy, one of the traditional parties, that narrowly emerged as the largest party after an election in which the turn-out was 62% – despite the fact that, with its rival PASOK, it bore a heavy responsibility for the crisis. ND's share of the vote increased from 19% in May to 30% in June. It is clear that at least some of those voting for ND heeded the warning of the country's eurozone partners, particularly Germany, that the party was the only one with a chance of securing a European future for Greece. SYRIZA's votes also increased by a substantial margin, from 19 to 27%. ND's share of the vote was only 2.8% greater than that of SYRIZA but, thanks to the idiosyncrasies of the electoral system, it received 129 seats to SYRIZA's 71. PASOK's vote fell even further to 12% (33 seats). Independent Greeks, with an 8 per cent share of the vote, received 20 seats, 2 more than Chrysi Avgi, whose share of the vote fell slightly. The Democratic Left, with 6% of the vote, received 17 seats, while the Communist Party, with a 5% share of the vote, secured 12 seats. The process of forming a coalition government, with a workable majority, soon got under way.

Within days, a coalition government consisting of New Democracy, PASOK and the Democratic Left emerged with a clear majority in parliament. PASOK and the Democratic Left did not, however, accept seats in cabinet for fear of the opprobrium they might suffer if a relaxation of the troika's terms were not secured. The new government quickly declared that its objectives included a two-year extension to the time allowed for a substantial reduction in the fiscal deficit. Angela Merkel, whose visit to Greece in October met with large-scale protests, continued to insist on adherence to the harsh conditions imposed by the troika.

In November, the prime minister, Antonis Samaras, who, ironically, had initially opposed Giorgos Papandreou's austerity measures, managed to secure a parliamentary majority for further retrenchment amounting to 13.5 billion euros. These included further cuts in pensions and public-sector wages, and the raising of the retirement age from 65 to 67. These additional measures were aimed at securing a further release of bailout funding from the troika. This was forthcoming, although Chancellor Merkel experienced considerable difficulty in securing support in the German parliament. Following a marathon negotiating session, the troika accepted Greece's aim to reduce the country's debt to 124 per cent of gross domestic product by 2020 and made other concessions.

The revelation of mysterious delays in examining the tax affairs of some 2,000 Greek holders of Swiss bank accounts, details of which were contained in a memory stick made available by the French government, gave rise to anger and ridicule. In December 2012 a bill was introduced in parliament designed to reform the tax system and, in particular, to ensure that the self-employed paid a fair share of tax. This met with predictable opposition. A disturbing development in early 2013 was the firing of shots at the offices of the ruling New Democracy party and the detonation of a bomb in a shopping mall.

Despite internal friction within the coalition, Samaras met most of the demands of the troika. The problems involved in shrinking the size of the bloated public sector, however, were strikingly demonstrated in June 2013 when the abrupt closure of ERT, the public broadcasting service, on the ground that it was chronically overmanned, gave rise to a serious political crisis. The Democratic Left withdrew from the ruling coalition, with the result that the Samaras government now had a perilously small majority in parliament. Whether, in the end, the sacrifices imposed on the Greek people – austerity which posed a serious threat to the social order – would be enough to ensure continued membership of the eurozone, as almost all political parties, SYRIZA included, wished, remained to be seen. But it became apparent that Greece's eurozone partners, following earlier prevarication, were now determined that the country should retain the euro, while in March 2013 the country's finance minister, Yannis Stournaras, opined that Greece was largely 'out of the woods'. But there was still the possibility that, in the end, the country's enormous debts, expected to reach 185 per cent of GDP by the end of 2013, would prove to be unsustainable, and Greece would have to return to the drachma, a move which would have incalculable consequences.

What was clear beyond doubt was that it would be a long time before Greece returned to the prosperity of the early years of the new millennium. Few observers of the Greek scene in the year 2000 could have predicted the dire situation in which the country would find itself within less than a decade. Greece in the sixty years since the end of the civil war, a conflict described by one contemporary observer as a war of the poor against the very poor, had transformed itself from an impoverished, battle-scarred backwater, heavily dependent on US Marshall aid for its very survival, into one of the twenty-eight most developed countries in the world. In 2005, a year after the triumph of the Athens Olympics, the ministry of foreign affairs declared that Greece had now become 'a global humanitarian power', in a position to contribute to the alleviation of poverty and distress in almost fifty countries. But, within five years, Greece found itself facing years of austerity, barely capable of fielding a representative Olympic team let alone of contributing to a global crusade against poverty.

Until the last decades of the twentieth century, Greece had traditionally been an exporter of manpower which had led to the emergence of a worldwide diaspora. From the 1980s, however, it became a country of immigration. Some members of the diaspora settled back in Greece, together with many immigrants of Greek descent from the former Soviet Union. To these were added substantial communities of Albanians (including members of the Greek minority), Poles, Romanians, Bulgarians, Ukrainians, Russians, Georgians and economic migrants from the Middle East, South Asia and Africa, many of whom had illegally entered via the country's porous land and sea borders with Turkey. These incomers constituted some 10 per cent of the population. By 2013, however, emigration was once again the aim of many Greeks, particularly on the part of the best educated of the country's young people, who could see little future in the land of their birth.

Much-increased productivity was seen as the answer to the country's difficulties, but it was not easy to see how this would be achieved for Greece with an economy highly dependent on tourism – amounting to 18 per cent of gross domestic product – and with relatively little to export. Exports of manufactured goods accounted for only some 10 per cent of gross domestic product, much lower than the eurozone average. Greece was an exporter of agricultural products and a major producer of high-quality olive oil, but only a small proportion was exported directly; most was shipped in bulk to Italy and was then bottled as of Italian origin.

In addition to low productivity, the problems resulting from clientelism, cronyism, nepotism and outright corruption were deeply entrenched in society, and these would not be readily overcome. There are, nonetheless, instances in the country's modern history of horrendous disasters that have been successfully overcome and these constitute a hopeful precedent. The Asia Minor catastrophe and the ensuing massive influx of hundreds of thousands of destitute refugees in the 1920s was one such disaster. The devastation caused by the German, Italian and Bulgarian occupation during the Second World War and the ensuing civil war was another. But Greece had in time rebounded from such crippling setbacks. The road to recovery from the economic, financial and political crisis that convulsed the country in 2009, and the following years of economic recession, would clearly be long, arduous and painful. But it was one that, on past precedent, could be achieved, perhaps by 2021 when Greece would celebrate the 200th anniversary of the outbreak of the war for independence from the Ottoman Empire, when in the course of a decade, and following a protracted struggle against much superior odds, it emerged as an independent state.

BIOGRAPHIES

CONSTANTINE I, KING OF THE HELLENES (1868–1922)

King of Greece 1913–17: 1920–2. Eldest son of King George I (q.v.) and Queen Olga. Trained as a soldier in Athens and Germany. Married Sophia, the sister of Kaiser Wilhelm II. During 1897 Greek–Turkish war commanded Greek army in Thessaly. Made a scapegoat for defeat. Appointed to high rank in the army in 1900, he and the other royal princes were required to resign after the Goudi military coup of 1909. Appointed commander-in-chief by Prime Minister Eleftherios Venizelos in 1911, his command of Greek forces during the Balkan wars of 1912–13 meant that, by the time of his accession to the throne in 1913 on the death of his father George I, he enjoyed considerable popularity. On the outbreak of the First World War he quarrelled with Venizelos over Greece's alignment, Venizelos favouring the *Entente*, Constantine neutrality. These disagreements resulted in the 'National Schism' and the establishment by Venizelos in 1916 of a rival provisional government in Salonica. Constantine was forced to leave Greece as a result of British and French pressure in June 1917. He did not formally abdicate and was replaced by his second son, Alexander. Following Alexander's death in October 1920 and Venizelos' surprise defeat in elections the following month, Constantine, following a dubious plebiscite, returned to the throne in December 1920. In 1922, after the defeat of the Greek armies in Asia Minor, he was overthrown in a coup led by Colonel Nikolaos Plastiras (q.v.). He was succeeded by his eldest son, George, who ruled as George II (q.v.). Three months later Constantine died in exile in Palermo.

DELIYANNIS, THEODOROS (1826–1905)

Prominent politician during later nineteenth century. An orphan, he had to struggle to complete his studies in the Law Faculty of the University of

Athens. First entered parliament as a deputy for Gortynia in the National Assembly of 1862–4, which drafted the 1864 constitution. Leader of the Greek delegation to the Congress of Berlin (1878). A populist and demagogue, and a master in the art of *rouspheti*, the reciprocal dispensation of favours, he was much more attuned to popular sentiment than his rival, the westerniser, Kharilaos Trikoupis (q.v.). For much of the last twenty years of the nineteenth century he alternated in power with Trikoupis, of whom Deliyannis declared, with commendable frankness, 'I am against everything that Trikoupis is for.' Prime minister 1885–6; 1890–2; 1895–7; 1902–3; 1904–5. During the eastern Rumelian crisis of 1885 Deliyannis responded to nationalist enthusiasm by ordering an expensive general mobilisation, which inflicted severe damage on the economy and provoked a Great Power blockade in 1886, which in turn resulted in his resignation. He again caught the popular mood by dispatching, in January 1897, an expeditionary force to Crete in support of demands by the Cretans for the *enosis*, or union, of the 'Great Island' with the kingdom. On this occasion the Powers could not prevent outright war between Greece and the Ottoman Empire and the 'Thirty Day War' (April/May 1897) resulted in humiliating defeat for Greece and Deliyannis' resignation. Deliyannis remained a popular politician and his party won elections in 1902 and 1905. In 1905, after a period of over forty years in parliament, he was assassinated by a gambler infuriated by his drive against gambling dens.

GEORGE I (1845–1913)

King of Greece 1863–1913. Second son of Christian IX of Denmark, of the house of Schleswig-Holstein-Sonderburg-Glücksburg. Succeeded Otto of Wittelsbach. Following Otto's deposition in 1862 a successor had to be found, no easy task in view of Otto's fate. The favoured candidate in Greece was Prince Alfred, the second son of Queen Victoria. He received 230,016 out of 244,202 votes in an unofficial referendum. (The future King George I received a mere six votes.) Alfred, however, was ruled out as he was a member of the ruling dynasty of one of the Protecting Powers. After some difficulty, the Powers agreed to King George's accession as 'George I, King of the Greeks'. (Otto had been merely king of Greece.) In 1867 he married Olga Konstantinovna, niece of Tsar Alexander II, with whom he had seven children. A frequent traveller, he sought to use his extensive connections with the ruling families of Europe to further Greece's diplomatic objectives. Following a dispute with Kharilaos Trikoupis, who blamed continuing political instability on George's practice of forming minority governments, George in 1875 accepted the principle of the *dedilomeni*. Henceforth he would entrust the formation of governments only to politicians enjoying the 'declared' support of a majority of deputies. This had the desired effect of introducing greater stability to political life. George surmounted the anti-dynastic feeling that surfaced at the time of Greece's defeat in the 1897 war with Turkey and responded sensitively to the demands made at the time of the Goudi coup of 1909 for the removal of the royal princes from their command positions in the army. In March 1913, while on a visit to Salonica, which had been newly incorporated into the Greek state, he was assassinated by a madman. (Further reading: Walter Christmas, *King George of Greece* (London 1914))

GEORGE II (1890–1947)

The eldest son of King Constantine and Queen Sophia, George succeeded to the throne in September 1922, following his father's abdication in the wake of Colonel Plastiras' coup of 1922. Before his departure from Greece on 'leave' in December 1923, three months before the abolition of the monarchy and the establishment of the first Greek Republic (25 March 1924), his position had been anomalous and his powers restricted. In exile, he lived for a time in Bucharest, the home of Princess Elisabeth of Romania, whom he had married in 1921. The childless marriage soon broke down and, from 1931 onwards, following divorce, he settled in London, where he established a permanent liaison with an Englishwoman. He returned to Greece in November 1935, following a rigged plebiscite (98 per cent for restoration of the monarchy, 2 per cent against), genuinely concerned to do what he could to heal the divisions caused by the 'National Schism'. Within less than a year, however, he had sanctioned the establishment by General Metaxas of his dictatorial 'Regime of the Fourth of August 1936'. Much of the unpopularity of the Metaxas regime rubbed off on the king, who, on the dictator's death in January 1941, missed the opportunity of signalling a clean break with Metaxas' dictatorial practices. On the fall of Crete in May 1941, he went into exile with his government, first of all in London and, from March 1943, in Cairo. The British government regarded George as the symbol of constitutional continuity and legitimacy and Winston Churchill felt a strong sense of personal obligation towards him on account of his steadfast stand during the winter of 1940–1. Within occupied Greece, however, there was a great groundswell of republican sentiment and George was only with difficulty prevailed upon not to return on liberation in October 1944 and, in December, to appoint Archbishop Damaskinos as regent, pending a plebiscite on the constitutional question. Such a plebiscite was held, in anomalous circumstances, in September 1946 and resulted in a 68 per cent vote in favour of his restoration. Six months after his return, George died in April 1947, to be succeeded by his brother, Paul.

GRIGORIOS V (1746–1821)

Patriarch of Constantinople (1797–8; 1806–8; 1818–21) and 'national martyr'. Born in Dimitsana in the Peloponnese, studied in Athens and possibly at the Monastery of St John the Divine on Patmos. Became metropolitan of Smyrna in 1785 and demonstrated a marked interest in educational matters, translating some of the works of St John Chrysostom into modern Greek. During his three periods on the patriarchal throne showed himself a determined critic of the ideas of the Enlightenment. In an encyclical of 1819, issued with the Holy Synod of the Orthodox Church in Constantinople, he asked what benefit young Greeks derived from a knowledge of science and mathematics if their speech were barbarous, if they were ignorant in matters of religion, if their morals were degenerate. Allied himself with the Ottoman authorities in seeking to counter the influence of western ideas and of the French Revolution and in calling on his flock to be obedient to the Ottoman powers that be. Gave considerable encouragement to the press of the Patriarchate in publishing religious literature designed to protect the Orthodox faith from contamination by western heresies. Once the war for Greek independence had broken out in 1821 in the Danubian principalities, Grigorios and the Holy Synod issued encyclicals anathematising Alexandros Ypsilantis and Mikhail Soutsos and their followers. These appear to have contributed to avoiding a general slaughter of Greeks in Constantinople but did not save Grigorios from being hanged at the entrance to the Patriarchate on 10 April 1821. In Ottoman eyes he had failed in his duty of ensuring the loyalty of the Orthodox populations to the sultan, which was the expected *quid pro quo* for the considerable degree of religious freedom enjoyed by the Orthodox Church. His body was recovered from the Golden Horn and taken to Odessa, where he was buried in June 1821. In 1921, on the centenary of his execution, he was formally proclaimed a saint.

KAPODISTRIAS, COUNT IOANNIS (1776–1831)

First president of Greece (1828–31). Born in Corfu. Studied medicine in Padua. Secretary of State of the Septinsular [Ionian] Republic during the Russian protectorate over the Ionian islands between 1800 and 1807. Subsequently joined Russian diplomatic service. Member of Russian delegation at Congress of Vienna. In 1816, at the age of thirty-nine, became joint foreign minister, with Count Nesselrode, to Tsar Alexander I, charged principally with matters relating to the Near East. In 1817 he received the first of two approaches (the second was in 1820) to assume the leadership of the *Philiki Etairia*, the secret revolutionary society founded in Odessa in 1814 to prepare the ground for the Greek revolt. Kapodistrias, believing the conspirators' plans to be wildly unrealistic, declined the offer, counselling his fellow countrymen to bide their time in the hope that some kind of autonomous status would be granted in the aftermath of the Russo–Turkish war that he believed to be sooner or later inevitable. In 1822, after the outbreak of the struggle for independence, he resigned from the Tsar's service and, from

Geneva, did what he could to promote the Greek cause. His acknowledged diplomatic skills, allied to the fact that he had stood apart from the complex politics of the liberation struggle, made him an obvious choice as the first president (*kyvernitis*) of Greece, a post which he took up in January 1828 at a time when neither Greece's independent existence was formally recognised nor her frontiers established. His energies and diplomatic talents were devoted to securing as favourable frontiers as possible and to creating the essential infrastructure of a new state in lands that had been devastated by years of bitter fighting. Although his paternalist ways were popular with the peasantry, the leaders of the struggle for independence were offended by his abrogation of the democratic constitution of Troezene and his replacement of the national assembly by a small council, the *Panhellenion*, under his direct control. He soon aroused the opposition of the traditional elites in Greek society, who were hoping to regain the influence that they had enjoyed during the pre-independence period and there were a number of uprisings against his authoritarian rule. In October 1831 he was assassinated as he was about to enter church by the brother and son of one of the powerful figures whom he had crossed, Petrobey Mavromikhalis of the Mani. (Further reading: C. M. Woodhouse, *Capodistria: the founder of Greek independence* (Oxford 1973))

KARAMANLIS, KONSTANTINOS (1907–1998)

As prime minister (1955–63; 1974–80) and president (1980–5; 1990–5), Karamanlis, with Andreas Papandreou, dominated the politics of Greece in the later twentieth century. Born in Küpköy, Macedonia, when it was still part of the Ottoman Empire, the son of a schoolmaster turned tobacco merchant. Unusually for a Greek politician he had no family ties to the political world, although he married a niece of Panayiotis Kanellopoulos, a prominent conservative politician. First entered politics as a People's Party (conservative) deputy in 1935–6 but political career temporarily cut short by Metaxas dictatorship and wartime occupation. Re-entered politics, again with the People's Party, in elections of March 1946. Held minor ministerial office but first impinged on national scene as an autocratic and publicity-conscious, but efficient, minister of public works in Marshal Papagos' Greek Rally government between 1952 and 1955. On Papagos' death in 1955 chosen by King Paul as a 'dark horse' successor. Reconstituted Greek Rally as National Radical Union. His eight-year premiership between 1955 and 1963 equalled only by Andreas Papandreou (1981–9). The palace's initial support for Karamanlis degenerated into hostility, particularly on the part of the strong-willed Queen Frederica. Disputes with the palace and a general feeling of disillusionment with politics led him into a self-imposed eleven-year exile in France, following defeat in the election of 1963. From Paris he made his distaste for the Colonels' dictatorship (1967–74) clear, while standing aloof from attempts to accelerate the regime's downfall. When the dictatorship collapsed in shambles after the Cyprus débâcle of July 1974 Karamanlis was summoned back to clear up the mess. Presided over return to civilian rule and punishment of the ringleaders of the junta with much skill and without bloodshed. Espoused markedly more liberal policies than during pre-coup period, legalised the communist party(ies) outlawed since 1947, and responded to widespread anti-American and anti-NATO sentiment by withdrawing Greece from the military arm of the alliance. He sought, in accelerated accession to the EC, an alternative to the traditional reliance on US patronage. Less successful in his attempts to modernise the right, now labelled New Democracy, and in countering the enticing rhetoric of Andreas Papandreou's (q.v.) PASOK. Having secured Greece's accession to the EC, he engineered his election to the presidency, in which office he oversaw the handover of power by the right to a left-wing government for the first time in Greece. Resigned from presidency in March 1985, at very end of five-year term, when it became clear that, contrary to almost universal expectation, he was not going to be nominated for a second five-year term. Re-elected president, at the age of 83, for a five-year term in May 1990. Died in 1998 at the age of 91. (Further reading: C. M. Woodhouse, *Karamanlis: the restorer of Greek democracy* (Oxford 1982))

KOLETTIS, IOANNIS (1774–1847)

Influential politician during the early years of the independent state. A Vlach by origin, born in Syrrakos in the Pindos mountains of north-western Greece. Studied medicine in Pisa. Became personal physician to Moukhtar Pasha, the son of Ali Pasha, the satrap of Ioannina, a Muslim Albanian who controlled huge areas of Greek-inhabited territory in the years before 1821. Initiated into the *Philiki Etairia* in 1819. Played leading role in political and military affairs of the war of independence. After holding office during the period of the Bavarian regency, Kolettis was removed from the political scene by being appointed ambassador to Paris, where he caused a stir by his insistence on wearing the *foustanella* or kilt, a practice which he continued until the end of his life. In France he developed close links with the politician François-Pierre Guizot and was always linked with the French interest in Greece. Returned to Greece following the coup of 3 September 1843 and took influential part in the deliberations of the constituent assembly charged with drafting the constitution that had been imposed on King Otto. Himself from Epirus, he espoused the cause of the *heterochthons*, the Greeks from outside the frontiers, who had come under fire from the *autochthons*, the natives of the regions that comprised the first independent state. In defending their claims to be treated equally with the natives he articulated the classic definition of the *Megali Idea*, the 'Great Idea'. As prime minister between

1844 and 1847, with the connivance of King Otto, he made a mockery of the liberal provisions of the 1844 constitution by establishing what was in effect a 'parliamentary dictatorship', ruthlessly deploying brigandage, the dispensation of favours, bribery and electoral manipulation to consolidate his grip on power. His anti-Turkish policies, however, gave him a strong popular base.

KOLOKOTRONIS, THEODOROS (1770–1843)

Pre-eminent military leader during the war of independence. During the pre-independence period alternately a *kleft* (a bandit warrior), an *armatolos* (a Christian irregular in the Ottoman service) and a *kapos* (an armed militia-man in the employ of the Greek notables of the Peloponnese). Acquired wealth through sheep-stealing and marriage to daughter of wealthy Peloponnesian notable. The great Ottoman drive against the *klefts* of 1805–6 forced him to flee to Zakynthos (Zante) and, like many *klefts*, he frequently crossed over from the Peloponnese to the Ionian islands to lie up for the winter or escape Ottoman persecution. Following the British occupation of Zakynthos he gained useful military experience in the Duke of York's Greek Light Infantry, being promoted major in 1810. This was commanded by Richard Church, a philhellene volunteer who became commander-in-chief of the Greek forces in 1827. His experience of irregular warfare and training under Church stood him in good stead during the war of independence when he emerged as one of the leaders of the 'military' or 'democratic' party, which frequently found itself in opposition to, and sometimes in conflict with, the 'civilian' or 'aristocratic' party, led by the Peloponnesian primates, the notables of the 'Nautical Islands' and the Phanariot politicians. During the civil strife that accompanied the war for independence Kolokotronis was briefly imprisoned and in danger of his life. A supporter of President Kapodistrias, he clashed with the regency under King Otto and was sentenced to death, but was reprieved and eventually given the rank of general. In his old age dictated his richly interesting memoirs to Georgios Tertsetis, declaring that, in his judgement, 'the French Revolution and the doings of Napoleon opened the eyes of the world. The nations knew nothing before, and the people thought that kings were gods upon the earth, and that they were bound to say that whatever they did was well done.' (Further reading: E. M. Edmonds, *Kolokotrones, the klepht and the warrior* . . . (London 1893))

KORAIS, ADAMANTIOS (1748–1833)

The leading figure in the pre-independence intellectual revival. Born in Smyrna, the son of a merchant from Chios, Korais obsessively identified with Chios, although it is not certain that he ever visited the island.

Introduced to Latin and the riches of western classical scholarship by Bernhard Keun, a Dutch Protestant pastor in Smyrna. Between 1771 and 1778 spent an unhappy period as a merchant in Amsterdam, where the experience of freedom fuelled his hatred for the Turks, whom he considered to be synonymous with wild beasts. Between 1782 and 1786 studied medicine at the University of Montpellier, but his main interests lay in classical philology and he soon developed into one of the foremost classical scholars of the day. From 1788 until 1833 he lived in Paris, experiencing at first hand the turbulent events of the French Revolution and the revolutionary and Napoleonic wars. Ever the proponent of the 'middle way', he was alarmed by manifestations of mob rule and came to regard Napoleon as a 'despot of despots'. A desiccated and hypochondriacal bachelor, his concerns in Paris lay in pursuing classical scholarship and in raising the educational level of his fellow countrymen and in instilling in them an awareness of a glorious past that was universally admired in civilised Europe. To this end he conceived the idea of publishing an 'Hellenic Library', consisting of editions of the ancient Greek authors, aimed specifically at a Greek audience and prefaced with improving introductions. A vigorous participant in the debates of the nascent intelligentsia as to the form of the language appropriate to a regenerated Greece, Korais advocated a middle course, adopting the spoken (or 'demotic') language as the norm but 'purifying' it of foreign words and constructions. Repelled by Greece's medieval, Byzantine past Korais was a fierce critic of the ignorance of the clergy and of their subservience to the Ottoman powers that be, although he was careful to steer between 'the Scylla of superstition and the Charybdis of unbelief'. He thought the outbreak of the war of independence to be premature by a generation, believing that the Greeks had not yet reached the required educational level. Nonetheless he redoubled his efforts to publish uplifting texts aimed at ensuring that his compatriots did not merely substitute native tyrants for their Ottoman overlords. In the same vein, he was highly critical of Ioannis Kapodistrias (q.v.), the first president of Greece, whom he regarded as a tyrant and for whose overthrow he insistently called. (Further reading: Korais' autobiography in Richard Clogg, ed. and trans., *The movement for Greek independence 1770–1821: a collection of documents* (London 1976) 119–31)

MAKARIOS III (1913–77)

Archbishop of Cyprus 1950–77: president of Cyprus 1960–77. Born Mikhail Mouskos in Panaghia, Paphos in 1913, Makarios became a novice monk in the Kykkos monastery. Following theological studies at the universities of Athens and Boston he was elected metropolitan of Kitium in 1948. In this office he organised in 1950 a plebiscite among Greek Cypriots which resulted in an overwhelming vote in favour of the *enosis* or union of Cyprus with Greece. Shortly afterwards he was elected archbishop of

Cyprus, an office which, in the Ottoman tradition, combined the spiritual with the civil leadership of the Greek Cypriots who totalled some 80 per cent of the population of the island. He was a committed champion of the *enosist* cause, pressing the somewhat reluctant Greek government to raise the Cyprus question at the United Nations. When recourse to the United Nations failed to produce results, Makarios authorised General Georgios Grivas, the leader of the EOKA underground movement, to launch the armed struggle against British rule in April 1955. In March 1956, the British authorities on the island exiled him to the Seychelles. On his release in April 1957 he moved to Athens, from where he continued to direct the struggle for *enosis*. After having rejected various constitutional proposals that fell short of self-determination, Makarios suggested in a 1958 newspaper interview that he would be prepared to accept an independent sovereign status for the island and would not insist on *enosis*. This significant shift in attitude prepared the way for the Zurich and London agreements of 1959 by which the British government, following agreement with Greece and Turkey but without serious consultation with the Greek and Turkish communities on the island itself, formally granted independence to Cyprus in 1960, while retaining two sovereign base areas in perpetuity. When, in November 1963, Makarios demanded amendments to the essentially unworkable constitution with which the new state had been lumbered, fighting broke out between the two communities, an invasion by Turkey was narrowly averted and a United Nations peace-keeping force preserved an uneasy peace in an increasingly polarised atmosphere. During the seventeen years of his presidency, Makarios marshalled his considerable diplomatic skills in steering a course between *enosis*, still the goal of those grouped in EOKA-B under the leadership of General Grivas, and partition of the island between Greece and Turkey. During these years the sense of a distinct Cypriot identity came into being. Makarios made no secret of his distaste for the military dictatorship that seized power in Greece in 1967 and the Athens regime was behind several attempts to overthrow him. These culminated in his deposition in July 1974 and shortlived replacement as president by Nikos Sampson, a prominent EOKA member much feared in the Turkish community. The coup prompted the Turkish occupation of nearly 40 per cent of the island. Makarios survived the coup and returned to Cyprus as president in December 1974. But no solution to the problems of the divided island was in sight by the time of his death in 1977. (Further reading: Stanley Mayes, *Makarios: a biography* (London 1981))

METAXAS, IOANNIS (1871–1941)

Dictator of Greece 1936–41. Studied at the Prussian Military Academy in Berlin. Life-long admirer of German order and seriousness, which he contrasted with what he saw as the ill-disciplined individualism of his fellow countrymen. Resigned in 1915 as acting chief of the general staff in protest against Prime Minister Venizelos' (q.v.) plans to commit Greek troops to Gallipoli campaign. Resigned from army in 1920. Strong critic on military grounds of Greece's Anatolian entanglement. Minor politician on the far right during inter-war period. King George II appointed Metaxas minister of war in March 1936 in 'caretaker' government of Konstantinos Demertzis and, on latter's sudden death, prime minister. Exploited the inability of two main parliamentary blocs, Venizelists and anti-Venizelists, to compose differences and form a government to establish, with King George's backing, dictatorship on 4 August 1936. Abrogated key articles in the constitution on spurious ground that country threatened by communist take-over. Dictatorial powers enabled him to crush the 'political world' which he much detested, reserving particular animosity for the communists. His quasi-fascist regime adopted many of the trappings of contemporary fascist systems but had more in common, in its authoritarian paternalism, with the 'royal' dictatorships established elsewhere in the Balkans in the 1930s. He expounded the notion of the 'Third Hellenic Civilisation', an attempt to meld the values of the ancient, pagan with those of the medieval, Christian Greek worlds. Set great store by his National Youth Organisation (EON) as the putative standard bearer of his ideals after his death. Despite imitation of fascist models he held firm to Greece's traditional orientation towards Britain in matters of foreign policy. On outbreak of Second World War in September 1939 strove for a neutrality benevolently disposed towards Great Britain. When faced with humiliating Italian ultimatum on 28 October 1940 caught popular mood in rejecting it with courage and dignity. His concern with country's defences reflected in successful Greek resistance to Italian invasion and counter-attack across border into Italian-occupied Albania. Died January 1941, two months before the German invasion. (Further reading: P.J. Vatikiotis, *Popular autocracy in Greece 1936–41: a political biography of General Ioannis Metaxas* (London 1998))

OTTO OF WITTELSBACH (1815–67)

King of Greece 1832–62. Born in Salzburg in 1815, the second son of King Ludwig I of Bavaria. At the age of seventeen chosen as king by the Protecting Powers (Britain, France and Russia). He arrived in Greece, aboard a British frigate, in January 1833, accompanied by some 4,000 Bavarian troops. As he was a minor, the new kingdom was ruled between 1833 and 1835 by a regency council made up of Bavarians. Between 1835 and 1843 he ruled as an absolute monarch. Following a bloodless coup on 3 September 1843 was forced to concede a constitution. The liberal provisions of the 1844 constitution were, however, subverted by Ioannis Kolettis (q.v.) who, with the king, ruled through a form of parliamentary dictatorship. Otto's enthusiastic espousal of the 'Great Idea' earned him considerable popularity.

This was enhanced by Great Power interference in Greece's affairs, as in the Don Pacifico incident of 1850 and the Anglo-French occupation of Piraeus between 1854 and 1857. His inability to accommodate the aspirations of a rising generation of politicians and continuing manipulation of the political system; his failure to convert to Orthodoxy and produce an heir to the throne; and his espousal of the unpopular cause of Austria against Garibaldi and the Italian nationalists in 1859/60 all contributed to the growth of anti-dynastic sentiment. Student unrest was followed in September 1861 by an unsuccessful attempt on the life of Queen Amalia of Oldenburg, whom he had married in 1836. Scattered uprisings in 1862 led to his overthrow, with the king leaving his adopted country, as he had arrived, on a British warship. In exile in Bamberg he manifested his devotion to Greece by wearing the traditional *foustanella* or kilt. (Further reading: Leonard Bower and Gordon Bolitho, *Otho I, king of Greece: a biography* (London 1939))

PAPADIAMANTIS, ALEXANDROS (1851–1911)

Short story writer. Born in Skiathos, the son of a poor priest, Papadiamantis studied briefly at the University of Athens. He subsequently earned a modest living as a translator and prolific writer of novels and short stories (none of his writings appeared in book form during his lifetime). Abandoning his youthful intention of becoming a monk, he became a *kosmokalogeros*, a 'monk of the world'. Never marrying, he led an ascetic life, dominated by the religious cycle of the Orthodox Church, for whose traditions his writings are suffused with nostalgia. His religious conservatism was paralleled by linguistic conservatism, for he wrote in the purified *katharevousa*, rejecting the demotic or spoken form of the language that increasingly became the literary fashion in the later nineteenth century. His short stories and novels centre on historical and ethnographic themes. His best known work, *I phonissa* (The murderess), was published in 1903. (Further reading: *The murderess*, trans. Peter Levi (London 1983) and *Tales from a Greek island*, trans. Elizabeth Constantinides (Baltimore 1987))

PAPAGOS, ALEXANDROS (1883–1955)

Soldier and politician. Following military studies in Belgium served in the Balkan wars of 1912–13. Purged and exiled in 1917 as anti-Venizelist. Reinstated in 1920 following restoration of King Constantine. Served on Asia Minor front and purged again in 1923. Returned to army in 1926. One of the three high-ranking officers who forced the resignation of Prime Minister Panayis Tsaldaris in October 1935. Became minister of war and subsequently appointed chief of the general staff during the dictatorship of General Ioannis Metaxas (q.v.). Commander-in-chief of the army during the Italian and German invasions of 1940–1. Between 1943 and 1945 in German prison camps. In January 1949, during later stages of the civil war, once again appointed commander-in-chief with wide-ranging powers. Following defeat of the communist Democratic Army in the summer of 1949, promoted to the rank of marshal, the only Greek officer to have held this rank. Following his retirement from the army in controversial circumstances in May 1951, in August of the same year founded his own political party, the Greek Rally, modelled on General de Gaulle's *Rassemblement du peuple français*. This attracted the support of the bulk of the right-wing People's Party. The Rally's 49 per cent of the popular vote in the 1952 elections, held as a result of American pressure under the majority system, gave him control of 247 out of 300 seats in parliament. During Papagos' premiership (1952–5) a delayed start made on the process of postwar reconstruction.

PAPANDREOU, ANDREAS (1919–1996)

Politician who, with Konstantinos Karamanlis (q.v.), dominated the political scene in the later twentieth century. Prime minister 1981–9; 1993–6. Born in Chios in 1919, the son, by his first marriage, of Georgios Papandreou, politician (q.v.). Left Greece for the United States in 1938 after being arrested for alleged Trotskyist activity while a student. Became a US citizen and followed a distinguished career as an academic economist, latterly at the University of California, Berkeley. Returned to Greece, at request of prime minister Konstantinos Karamanlis, in 1961 to head Centre of Economic Research and Planning. Entered parliament for first time in 1964 as deputy for Achaia, his father's birthplace, and became minister in father's Centre Union government. Arrested in 1967 under Colonels' dictatorship, allowed to leave country after intense US pressure. In exile founded Panhellenic Liberation Movement (PAK), espoused far more radical positions than he had in Greece, called for armed uprising against the dictatorship and was bitterly critical of US, NATO and EC policies towards the junta. Returned to Greece on downfall of dictatorship in 1974 and founded Panhellenic Socialist Movement (PASOK), calling for an end to dependence on the US and for radical domestic reform. Despite promises of democratic structures for PASOK, his authority over the party, in keeping with Greek political tradition, was absolute and dissenters received short shrift. 'Short march to power' culminated in election of first 'socialist' (more accurately populist) government in country's history in 1981, after virtually doubling share of vote in successive elections (14 per cent in 1974; 25 per cent in 1977; 48 per cent in 1981). Changes in government were more in style than in substance and, despite earlier harsh criticisms, the US bases remained and Greece continued to be a member of both NATO and the EC. Won a second term in 1985 with 46 per cent of popular vote. Second term overshadowed by mounting economic problems and latterly by a series of major scandals touching his government at the highest level, as well as by a highly publicised affair with a former air hostess. Despite this sea of troubles he still managed to achieve a very respectable 39 per cent share of the popular vote in the first 1989 election, increasing this to a remarkable 41 per cent in the second. In the third election in the cycle, in April 1990, his share of the vote fell to 39 per cent, enabling the opposition New Democracy party to secure the narrowest of majorities in parliament. Following his fall from power a parliamentary committee resolved that he be tried over allegations of corruption and phone tapping. He was subsequently acquitted. Re-elected prime minister in 1993, he resigned due to ill-health early in 1996 and died a few months later. (Further reading: Andreas Papandreou, *Democracy at gunpoint: the Greek front* (London 1971); Michalis Spourdalakis, *The rise of the Greek socialist party* (London 1988))

PAPANDREOU, GEORGIOS (1888–1968)

Prime minister 1944–5 and 1963–5. Born in Kaletzi, Achaia, Papandreou followed studies at the Law Faculty of University of Athens with postgraduate work in Germany. A protégé of the Liberal politician Eleftherios Venizelos (q.v.), between 1917 and 1920 served as governor of the newly acquired Aegean islands. Entered parliament in 1923 as a deputy for Mytilini. As Venizelos' minister of education between 1930 and 1932 he initiated a large school building programme. Disenchanted by the resort to extra-parliamentary methods by some of Venizelos' supporters in the 1930s he founded his own small Democratic Socialist Party. Exiled under the Metaxas dictatorship, he was briefly imprisoned during the Axis occupation. On escaping to the Middle East in 1944 he became prime minister of the government of national unity which returned on the liberation of the country in October 1944. A staunch anti-communist, his government was the target of the communist insurgency of December 1944. Although British intervention ensured the government's survival, Papandreou himelf was replaced as prime minister by General Nikolaos Plastiras (q.v.). In 1950 founded the Georgios Papandreou Party and served in the short-lived centre governments of 1950–1. Fought the 1952 election on the ticket of Marshal Papagos, subsequently becoming an independent. After a period in the late 1950s as joint leader of the Liberal Party, Papandreou masterminded the regrouping of the forces of the centre in the Centre Union in 1961. Disputing the legitimacy of the right's victory in the elections of the same year, Papandreou launched the 'unyielding struggle' to overturn the results. A master of political rhetoric and more comfortable in opposition than in government, Papandreou contributed powerfully to undermining the self-confidence of the right. His persistence was rewarded by a narrow victory over Konstantinos Karamanlis' National Radical Union in November 1963. This was followed by a convincing victory in February 1964 when Papandreou secured an unprecedented (for the postwar period) 53 per cent of the popular vote. His Centre Union government achieved some important reforms, notably in the field of education, in which Papandreou had always had a particular interest. But its achievements were overshadowed by strife in Cyprus and the government was brought down in July 1965 following a bitter clash between Papandreou and the young King Constantine II over control of the ministry of defence. During the ensuing period of political instability Papandreou repeatedly demanded new elections. These were eventually scheduled for May 1967 and Papandreou was widely expected to win them. The military coup of 21 April 1967, however, supervened and Papandreou spent much of the period until his death in November 1968 under house arrest. His funeral, attended by a fifth of the population of Athens, was the first manifestation of popular resistance to the dictatorship.

PAPANIKOLAOU, GEORGIOS (1883–1962)

Medical researcher and discoverer of the 'Pap smear' test for cervical cancer. Born in Kymi, Euboea in 1883, his medical studies in Athens were followed by postgraduate studies in Germany. From there he went to the United States, where he followed a distinguished career for almost fifty years at Cornell University. In the 1920s he developed the smear test, which is credited with saving the lives of many hundreds of thousands of women throughout the world. He resisted attempts by Eleftherios Venizelos (q.v.) to lure him back to Greece and became a US citizen in 1928. The author of numerous scientific publications, he was nominated for the Nobel Prize in medicine although he did not receive it. He became the first honorary member of the Academy of Athens in 1932. (Further reading: D. E. Carmichael, *The Pap smear: the life of G. N. Papanicolaou* (Springfield, Ill. 1973))

PLASTIRAS, NIKOLAOS (1883–1953)

Soldier and politician. Involved in Goudi military coup of 1909. Following distinguished service in the Balkan wars, which earned him the nickname the 'Black Cavalier', in 1916 he enlisted in pro-Venizelist 'National Defence'. Fought on Macedonian front and took part in Greek expedition to the Ukraine to fight against the Bolsheviks. Further added to his already formidable military reputation during the Asia Minor campaign. The force behind the military coup that overthrew the government and King Constantine I in the chaos of defeat in 1922. Played critical role in defeat of attempted royalist counter-coup in 1923. Masterminded attempted coup of March 1933 in reaction to defeat of his hero Venizelos (q.v.) at the polls. Obliged to flee abroad, where he adopted an uncompromising stand towards the Metaxas (q.v.) dictatorship of 1936–41. During occupation was nominal head of non-communist resistance movement EDES (National Republican Greek League) but remained in France. As a result of British pressure briefly became prime minister in early 1945 in the immediate aftermath of the suppression of the communist insurgency of December 1944. He was regarded as being more acceptable to the left than his predecessor, Georgios Papandreou (q.v.), but was forced out of office following the publication of a defeatist letter that he had written at the beginning of the war. Returned to political life following the end of the civil war as leader of National Progressive Centre Union, which advocated a measure of leniency towards the defeated communists. In 1950–2 headed centrist coalition governments but was not re-elected to parliament in the November 1952 election and died shortly afterwards.

THEOTOKAS, GEORGIOS (1905–66)

Novelist, essayist and critic. A leading member of the 'Generation of the Thirties'. Born to a family of Chiot origin and raised in Constantinople, he left the city in 1922, in the wake of the Asia Minor disaster. He returned only once in 1962, a few years before his death. Nostalgia for the Greek presence in the Ottoman capital suffuses his best known novel *Argo*, a chronicle of the turbulent experience of the Greek people in the inter-war period; *Leonis*, a novel about growing up as a Greek in Constantinople; and *Euripides Pendozalis and other stories*. He studied in Athens, Paris and London and acquired a wide knowledge of European culture. A progressive intellectual, he rejected the extremes of political life in Greece, whose troubled history in the twentieth century forms the backdrop to much of his writing. A playwright as well as novelist, he was for a time director of the National Theatre. (Further reading: English translations of *Argo* (London 1951) and *Leonis* (Minneapolis 1985) and Thomas Doulis, *George Theotokas* (Boston 1975))

TRIKOUPIS, KHARILAOS (1832–96)

Seven times prime minister (1875; 1878; 1880; 1882–5; 1886–90; 1892–3; 1893–5) and the foremost modernising politician in the nineteenth century. Born Nafplion 1832, the son of Spyridon Trikoupis, the historian of the war of independence and Greek minister in London. Trikoupis served in his father's embassy and his phlegmatic character was sometimes attributed to his fourteen years in England. Represented the substantial Greek community of London at the constitutional convention that gave rise to the 1864 constitution. Formally entered politics as the deputy for Mesolonghi and soon became foreign minister in Alexandros Koumoundouros' third administration. In this capacity he was responsible for the negotiation of the 1867 treaty of alliance with Prince Michael of Serbia, which was Greece's first treaty with one of its Balkan neighbours and which marked the first stage in a long history of Greek-Serb/Yugoslav co-operation. But Trikoupis' principal achievements were to lie in the domestic sphere. In a famous anonymous article entitled 'Who is to blame?', published in the newspaper *Kairoi* in July

1874, Trikoupis articulated the frustrations of younger politicians and laid the blame for recurrent political crises squarely on the shoulders of King George I (q.v.) for giving power to minority governments. In the ensuing uproar he was briefly imprisoned. But the king accepted his demand that power should be entrusted only to those with the 'declared' support of a majority in parliament. It was not until 1882, however, that Trikoupis himself secured a clear majority in parliament and was able to embark on his modernising programme. His economic policies enhanced Greece's creditworthiness in international money markets; he sought investment capital from foreign and diaspora sources; railway construction developed apace; the ambitious scheme for draining Lake Copais for agricultural purposes was initiated and the Corinth canal was opened in 1893. To lessen the impact of jobbery he reduced the number of constituencies and sought to diminish the dependence of the large state bureaucracy on political patronage. He also sought to modernise the country's armed forces and to curb the brigandage that was rife in the country. Many of his policies were undermined, however, by his arch-rival, the populist Theodoros Deliyannis (q.v.), with whom he alternated in power between 1882 and 1895. In 1893 Trikoupis was forced to default on the servicing of external loans and the ensuing austerity measures ensured his defeat in 1895. Trikoupis' modernising efforts met with only limited success and he died the following year in self-imposed exile in Cannes.

VELESTINLIS (PHERAIOS), RIGAS (1757–98)

Proto-martyr of Greek independence. Born Velestino, Thessaly. A Hellenised Vlach, he was forced, in obscure circumstances, to emigrate. Popular mythology has it that it was because he had killed a Turk. After acting as secretary to Alexandros Ypsilantis, principal interpreter (*dragoman*) to the Ottoman Porte (government) in Constantinople, he subsequently entered the service of Phanariot *hospodars* (princes) of Wallachia. It has been suggested that during a visit (his second) to Vienna in 1796 he founded a secret revolutionary society. This is uncertain but from this period dates his revolutionary proclamation; his *Declaration of the Rights of Man*; his *Thourios* (war hymn); and, most important, his *New Political Constitution of the Inhabitants of Rumeli* [European Turkey], *Asia Minor, the Archipelago, Moldavia and Wallachia*. This document, which was clearly influenced by the French revolutionary constitutions of 1793 and 1795, was his blueprint for the state that he wished to succeed the Ottoman Empire. Essentially what he envisaged was a kind of restored Byzantine Empire with republican (on the French model), in the place of monarchical, institutions. Although Rigas preached the equality, without distinction of religion and language, of all of the peoples of the Empire, the Turks included, it is clear that the Greeks were to enjoy a privileged position in the new state, of which Greek was to be the official language. Rigas had 3,000 copies of his revolutionary pamphlet secretly printed in Vienna and shipped to Trieste, whence he intended to travel the Balkans preaching the gospel of revolution, seeing in the French occupation of the Ionian islands in 1797, conducted with all the trappings of revolutionary 'liberation', a portent of wider French interest in the emancipation of the subject peoples of the Ottoman Empire. Soon after his arrival in Trieste in December 1797, however, he was betrayed by a fellow Greek to the Austrian authorities, who handed over Rigas, and those of his fellow conspirators who were Ottoman citizens, to the Turks at the fortress of Belgrade. Here they were strangled before being cast into the river Sava in June 1798. Although his efforts to revolutionise the Balkans met with little practical success, Rigas' martyrdom proved a potent symbol to future generations of Greek nationalists. (Further reading: C.M. Woodhouse, *Rhigas Velestinlis: the proto-martyr of the Greek revolution* (Limni 1995))

VELOUKHIOTIS, ARES (ALIAS OF KLARAS, THANASIS) (1905–45)

Kapetanios (politico-military leader) of ELAS, the communist-controlled resistance army in occupied Greece during the Second World War. Born Thanasis Klaras, in Lamia in 1905, he qualified as an agriculturalist. Joined the communist party (KKE) at the age of nineteen. Arrested under the Metaxas dictatorship he signed, to secure his release, a declaration whereby he publicly renounced his communist ideals. Thereafter, he, and those of his comrades who had signed similar declarations, were regarded with suspicion by the party leadership. After fighting on the Albanian front during the winter of 1940/1, formed, early in 1942, the first guerrilla band raised by ELAS, the military arm of the National Liberation Front (EAM). Took as his *nom de guerre* the name of Ares (after the god of war) Veloukhiotis (after Mount Veloukhi). Led the ELAS band which, with a contingent of Napoleon Zervas' (q.v.) EDES and a group of British saboteurs, destroyed the Gorgopotamos railway viaduct on the night of 25/26 November 1942, one of the most spectacular acts of resistance in occupied Europe. Subsequently became *kapetanios* of ELAS, with Georgios Siantos, the acting secretary-general of the KKE as political commissar and General Stephanos Sarafis as the military commander. With a fearsome reputation as a hardliner and strict disciplinarian (his opponents denounced him as a sadist) Ares was the most charismatic figure in the resistance. In the spring of 1944 was dispatched to the Peloponnese where the anti-communist security battalions, armed by the Germans and under the control of the quisling Greek government, were particularly strong. As liberation approached in the autumn of 1944 Veloukhiotis engaged in bloody reprisals against these collaborationist forces. Increasingly out of tune with the KKE leadership, Veloukhiotis regarded the Varkiza agreement of February 1945, which brought an end to the communist insurgency of December 1944, as a needless capitulation to the British. Critical of the divided counsels in the leadership of the KKE, believed confrontation and armed struggle to be inevitable if the communists were to achieve power. At a time when party policy advocated competition for power through constitutional means, Veloukhiotis and a small group of supporters took to the hills to continue the struggle. Cornered by the National Guard, he appears to have committed suicide on 18 June 1945 near the village of Mesounda. His severed head and those of some of his followers were subsequently displayed in Larisa. The day before his death the KKE politburo had publicly accused him of betraying the party for a second time.

VENIZELOS, ELEFTHERIOS (1864–1936)

The leading statesman of the first half of the twentieth century. Prime minister for a total of twelve years. Born in Crete, like so many Greek politicians he trained as a lawyer. First attracted attention in the politics of his native island when it still formed part of the Ottoman Empire. Was particularly active during the Cretan revolt of 1897 in favour of the *enosis*, or union, of the island with the kingdom. When Crete became autonomous as a result of the Greek–Turkish war of 1897, helped to draft the constitution, became member of the island's assembly. Active in promoting the unionist cause, he fell foul of the high commissioner, Prince George. Following the Goudi military coup of 1909 became the choice of the Military League for prime minister, assuming office in October 1910. During the following two years he presided over a vigorous programme of constitutional, military and social reform. Led Greece into alliance with Balkan neighbours, Serbia, Bulgaria and Montenegro. As a result of successes in Balkan wars Greece expanded greatly in size. On the outbreak of the First World War his enthusiastic support of the *Entente* (Britain, France and Russia) cause brought him into conflict with King Constantine I (q.v.), who favoured neutrality. Clashes over foreign policy twice resulted in his forced resignation in 1915. In 1916 the 'National Schism' became irreversible with establishment by Venizelos in Salonica in September of a rival provisional government. In 1917, as a result of pressure from Britain and France, King Constantine left Greece and Venizelos became prime minister of a unified, but not united, Greece. Brought Greece into war on side of the *Entente* and represented Greece at the Paris Peace Conference. Secured allied consent to occupation in May 1919 of Smyrna and its hinterland, an occupation ratified in the Treaty of Sèvres of August 1920. The architect of a short-lived 'Greece of the Two Continents and the Five Seas', suffered a humiliating defeat in elections of November 1920, following which went into self-imposed exile. After the 1922 defeat in Asia Minor acted as his country's representative at the Lausanne conference where he sought to salvage what he could from the wreckage of the 'Great Idea'. Returned to politics in 1928, but in 1933, his government knocked off course by the international economic crisis, he fell from power. An abortive pro-Venizelos coup in March 1933 was followed by an attempt, one of several, on his life. His involvement in a further attempted coup, in March 1935, resulted in his having to flee to France, where he died the following year, 1936. Shortly before his death he urged his followers to co-operate with King George II (q.v.), who had recently returned to Greece. (Further reading: Doros Alastos, *Venizelos: patriot, statesman, revolutionary* (London 1942))

ZAKHARIADIS, NIKOS (1903–73)

Secretary-general of the Communist Party of Greece (KKE) 1935–56 (in prison 1935–45). Born in Adrianople in 1903, the son of an employee of the Ottoman tobacco monopoly. Worked as seaman on the Black Sea, where he came under the influence of the Bolshevik revolution. Studied at the Communist University of the Peoples of the East (KUTV) in Moscow. Sent to Greece in 1923 to organise youth wing of the fledgeling KKE. Imprisoned and subsequently fled to Soviet Union. In 1931 sent back to Greece by the Comintern to restore order to a highly factionalised party, of which he became secretary-general in 1935. Imprisoned under Metaxas dictatorship. From prison issued a letter urging all Greeks to rally behind Metaxas in resisting the Italian invasion of October 1940. This was given much publicity although in two subsequent letters he denounced the war between Britain and Germany as 'imperialist'. After the German invasion he was sent to Dachau concentration camp during which period Giorgos Siantos served as acting secretary-general of the KKE. Returned to Greece in 1945, resuming leadership of party during the transition to civil war. In November 1948 he purged his arch-rival Markos Vafiadis and assumed command of the communist Democratic Army. After the defeat of the communist forces in 1949 Zakhariadis denounced Siantos as a 'British agent'. His insistence on keeping the remnants of Democratic Army in eastern Europe and the Soviet Union on a war footing and his harsh treatment of dissenters provoked serious rioting in Tashkent in 1955. In response to Nikita Khruschev's calls for de-Stalinisation, Zakhariadis, following the intervention of other communist parties, was deposed as secretary-general in 1956. In 1957 he was expelled from the party and exiled to Siberia, where he died in 1973.

ZERVAS, NAPOLEON (1891–1957)

Soldier and politician. After service in the Balkan wars, enlisted in 1916 in the pro-Venizelist 'National Defence' and served on the Macedonian front. Following Venizelos' defeat in the 1920 elections active in pro-Venizelist committee in Constantinople. Returned to army following the coup of 1922.

Garrison commander of Athens during Pangalos dictatorship (1925–6) but turned against his former patron by joining coup that resulted in Pangalos' overthrow in 1926, following which was appointed commander of the Republican Guard. His resistance to the dissolution of the Guard resulted in bloody clashes and a life sentence for rebellion. Pardoned by Venizelos in 1928. In 1941 founded the resistance organisation, the National Republican Greek League (EDES). Under the nominal leadership of the exiled General Nikolaos Plastiras (q.v.), this, as its title suggests, was of Venizelist (and, on paper, socialist) inspiration although Zervas later, at British behest, expressed support for the return of the exiled King George II (q.v.). EDES forces, under the command of Zervas, played important role in destruction of the Gorgopotamos viaduct on the night of 25/26 November 1942. Attacked by forces of EAM/ELAS in October 1943, Zervas and EDES survived in its power base of Epirus, Zervas' birthplace, only as result of British support. During the December 1944 communist insurgency, EDES was attacked and dispersed by ELAS. In 1945 Zervas resigned from the army in which he had been appointed general to found the right-wing National Party. Elected deputy for Ioannina, briefly served as minister of public order in 1947, in which office he was noted for his harsh measures against the communists. In 1950 joined the Liberal Party and served as minister of public works in 1950–1.

The royal houses of Greece

House of Wittelsbach (Bavaria)

Otto (second son of King Ludwig I of Bavaria) = Amalia of Oldenburg
(1816–67: reigned 1833–62)   (1818–75)

House of Schleswig-Holstein-Sonderburg-Glücksburg [usually known as Glücksburg] (Denmark)

George I (William: second son of King Christian IX of Denmark) = Olga of Russia (1851–1926)
(1845–1913: reigned 1863–1913)

Constantine I
(1868–1922: reigned 1913–17, 1920–2)
= Sophia of Prussia
(1870–1932)

George
(1869–1957)
(High Commissioner
of Crete 1898–1906)

Alexandra
(1870–92)

Nicholas
(1872–1938)

Maria
(1876–1940)

Andrew = Alice of Battenberg
(1882–1944)   (1885–1969)

Christopher
(1888–1940)

George II
(1890–1947: reigned 1922–3, 1935–47;
outside Greece 1941–7; regency 1945–6)
= Elsabeth of Romania
(1894–1956: divorced 1935)

Alexander
(1893–1920: reigned
1917–20)
= Aspasia Manos
(1896–1972)

Helen
(1896–1982)
= King Carol II
of Romania
(1893–1953)

Paul
(1901–64: reigned 1947–64)
= Frederica of Brunswick
(1917–81)

4 daughters

Philip, Duke of Edinburgh
(1921–)
= Queen Elizabeth II
(1926–)

Katherine
(1913–2007)

Irene
(1904–74)

Sophia
(1938–)
= King Juan Carlos of Spain
(1938–)

Constantine II
(1940– : reigned 1964–73; regency 1967–73)
= Anne Marie of Denmark
(1946–)

Irene
(1942–)

Alexia
(1965–)

Paul
(1967–)

Nicholas
(1969–)

Theodora
(1983–)

Philip
(1986–)

PRESIDENTS

1828–31	Ioannis Kapodistrias
1924–6	Admiral Pavlos Koundouriotis
1926	[General Theodoros Pangalos]
1926–9	Admiral Pavlos Koundouriotis
1929–35	Alexandros Zaimis
1973	[Colonel Georgios Papadopoulos]
1973–4	[General Phaidon Gizikis]
1974–5	Mikhail Stasinopoulos
1975–80	Konstantinos Tsatsos
1980–5	Konstantinos Karamanlis
1985–90	Khristos Sartzetakis
1990–5	Konstantinos Karamanlis
1995–2005	Kostis Stephanopoulos
2005–	Karolos Papoulias

(Those in square brackets held office by virtue of usurped power.)

TABLES

Table 1 *Population of the Greek State*[1]

1838	752,007
1856	1,062,627
1870	1,457,894
1896	2,433,806
1907	2,631,952
1920	5,531,474
1928	6,204,684
1940	7,344,860
1951	7,632,801
1961	8,388,553
1971	8,768,641
1981	9,740,417
1991	10,259,899
2001	10,964,020
2011	10,815,197

Note: [1] The figures for the nineteenth century are approximate.

Table 2 *Distribution of population*

	Urban	%	Semi-urban	%	Rural	%	Total
1940	2,411,647	33	1,086,079	15	3,847,134	52	7,344,860
1951	2,879,994	38	1,130,188	15	3,622,619	47	7,632,801
1961	3,628,105	43	1,085,856	13	3,674,592	44	8,388,553
1971	4,667,489	53	1,019,421	12	3,081,731	35	8,768,641
1981	5,659,528	58	1,125,547	12	2,955,342	30	9,740,417
1991	6,036,659	59	1,312,774	13	2,910,466	28	10,259,899

Table 3 *Population movements since the Second World War*

	1961	% change	1971	% change	1981	% change	1991	% change
Greater Athens	1,852,709	+37.1	2,540,241	+19	3,027,331	+19	3,072,921	+1
Central Greece and Euboea	970,949	+2.2	992,077	+11	1,099,841	+11	1,240,945	+16
Peloponnese	1,096,390	-10.0	986,912	+3	1,012,528	+3	1,046,935	+7
Ionian islands	212,573	-13.2	184,443	-1	182,651	-1	193,734	+6
Epirus	352,604	-12.0	310,334	+5	324,541	+5	339,728	+5
Thessaly	689,927	-4.4	659,913	+5	695,654	+5	734,846	+4
Macedonia	1,896,112	-0.3	1,890,684	+12	2,121,953	+12	2,236,089	+5
Thrace	356,555	-7.6	329,582	+5	345,220	+5	338,065	-2
Aegean islands	477,476	-12.5	417,813	+3	428,533	+3	456,712	+7
Crete	483,258	-5.5	456,642	+10	502,165	+10	540,054	+8
Greece, *total*	8,388,553	+4.5	8,768,641	+11	9,740,417	+11	10,259,899	+5

Table 4 *Population growth of the ten major urban centres*

	1951	1961	1971	1981	1991
Athens	1,378,586	1,852,709	2,540,241	3,027,331	3,072,921
Salonica	302,124	380,654	557,360	706,180	749,048
Patras	86,267	103,941	120,847	154,596	170,452
Iraklion	54,758	69,983	84,710	110,958	126,907
Volos	73,817	80,846	88,096	107,407	116,031
Larissa	41,016	55,391	72,336	102,048	113,090
Chania	37,788	49,058	53,026	61,976	72,092
Kavala	42,102	44,517	46,234	56,375	56,571
Agrinion	26,582	33,281	41,794	45,087	52,896
Serres	37,207	41,133	41,091	45,213	49,380

Table 5a *Religious affiliation*[1]

Total population	7,632,801	%
Orthodox	7,472,559	97.9
Catholic	28,430	0.4
Protestant and other Christian	12,677	0.2
Muslim	112,665	1.4
Jewish	6,325	0.1
None	121	

Table 5b *Mother-tongue*[1]

Total population	7,632,801	%
Greek	7,297,878	95.6
Turkish[2]	179,895	2.4
Slavic	41,017	0.5
Vlach[3]	39,855	0.5
Albanian	22,736	0.3
Others	51,420	0.7

Note: [1] Figures based on the 1951 census, the latest to give details of religious affiliation and mother-tongue.

[2] Half as many again gave their mother-tongue as Turkish as gave their religious affiliation as Muslim. The apparent discrepancy is explained by the fact that many of the incoming refugees in the 1920s were mother-tongue Turkish-speakers.

[3] A form of Romanian.

Table 6 *Election results 1952–2000*

	% of votes	Seats (out of 300)	Prime minister
1952			
Greek Rally (right)	49	247	Marshal Alexandros Papagos
Union of the Parties (centre coalition)	34	51	
United Democratic Left (far left)	10	0	
1956			
National Radical Union (right)	47	165	Konstantinos Karamanlis
Democratic Union (centre/far left coalition)	48	132	
1958			
National Radical Union (right)	41	171	Konstantinos Karamanlis
United Democratic Left (far left)	24	79	
Liberal Party (centre)	21	36	
1961			
National Radical Union (right)	51	176	Konstantinos Karamanlis
Centre Union (centre)	34	100	
United Democratic Left (far left)	15	24	
1963			
Centre Union (centre)	42	138	Georgios Papandreou
National Radical Union (right)	39	132	
United Democratic Left (far left)	14	28	
1964			
Centre Union (centre)	53	171	Georgios Papandreou
National Radical Union (right)	35	107	
United Democratic Left (far left)	12	22	
(1967–74 Military dictatorship)			

Table 6 (*cont.*)

	% of votes	Seats (out of 300)	Prime minister
1974			
New Democracy (right)	54	220	Konstantinos Karamanlis
Centre Union (centre)	20	60	
Panhellenic Socialist Movement (centre/left)	14	12	
United Left (far left)	10	8	
1977			
New Democracy (right)	42	171	Konstantinos Karamanlis
Panhellenic Socialist Movement (centre/left)	25	93	
Union of the Democratic Centre (centre)	12	16	
Communist Party of Greece	9	11	
National Camp (far right)	7	5	
Alliance of Progressive and Left-Wing Forces (far left)	3	2	
1981			
Panhellenic Socialist Movement (centre/left)	48	172	Andreas Papandreou
New Democracy (right)	36	115	
Communist Party of Greece	11	13	
1985			
Panhellenic Socialist Movement (centre/left)	46	161	Andreas Papandreou
New Democracy (right)	41	126	
Communist Party of Greece	10	12	
Communist Party of Greece (Interior)	2	1	

	%	Seats	
1989			
June			
New Democracy (right)	44	144	Tzannis Tzannetakis (conservative/communist coalition)
Panhellenic Socialist Movement (centre/left)	39	125	
Alliance of the Left and of Progress (far left)	13	28	
November			
New Democracy (right)	46	148	Xenophon Zolotas (all-party 'ecumenical' government)
Panhellenic Socialist Movement (centre/left)	41	128	
Alliance of the Left and of Progress (far left)	11	21	
1990			
New Democracy (right)	47	150	Konstantinos Mitsotakis
Panhellenic Socialist Movement (centre/left)	39	123	
Alliance of the Left and of Progress (far left)	10	19	
Alternative Ecologists	0.8	1	
Democratic Renewal (right)	0.6	1	
Independent Muslim (Rodopi)	0.5	1	
Independent Muslim (Xanthi)	0.3	1	
Independents	1	4	
1993			
Panhellenic Socialist Movement (centre/left)	47	170	Andreas Papandreou
New Democracy (right)	39	111	
Political Spring (right)	5	10	
Communist Party of Greece	5	9	

Table 6 (*cont.*)

	% of votes	Seats (out of 300)	Prime minister
1996			
Panhellenic Socialist Movement (centre/left)	42	162	Kostas Simitis
New Democracy (right)	38	108	
Communist Party of Greece	6	11	
Alliance of the Left and of Progress (far left)	5	10	
Democratic Social Movement (left)	4	9	
2000			
Panhellenic Socialist Movement (centre/left)	44	158	Kostas Simitis
New Democracy (right)	43	125	
Communist Party of Greece	5	11	
Coalition of the Left	3	6	
2004			
New Democracy (right)	45	165	Kostas Karamanlis
Panhellenic Socialist Movement (centre/left)	41	117	
Communist Party of Greece	6	12	
Coalition of the Radical Left	3	6	
2007			
New Democracy (right)	42	152	Kostas Karamanlis
Panhellenic Socialist Movement (centre/left)	38	102	
Communist Party of Greece	8	22	
Coalition of the Radical Left	5	14	
Popular Orthodox Rally (right)	4	10	

2009

Party			
Panhellenic Socialist Movement (centre/left)	44	160	Giorgos Papandreou
New Democracy (right)	33	91	
Communist Party of Greece	8	21	
Popular Orthodox Rally (right)	6	15	
Coalition of the Radical Left	5	13	

2012
May

Party			
New Democracy (right)	19	108	Antonis Samaras
Coalition of the Radical Left	17	52	
Panhellenic Socialist Movement (centre/left)	13	41	
Independent Greeks (right)	11	33	
Communist Party of Greece	8	26	
Golden Dawn (far right)	7	21	
Democratic Left	6	19	

June

Party			
New Democracy (right)	30	129	Antonis Samaras
Coalition of the Radical Left	27	71	
Panhellenic Socialist Movement (centre/left)	12	33	
Independent Greeks (right)	8	20	
Golden Dawn (far right)	7	18	
Democratic Left	6	17	
Communist Party of Greece	5	12	

Table 7 *Political families*

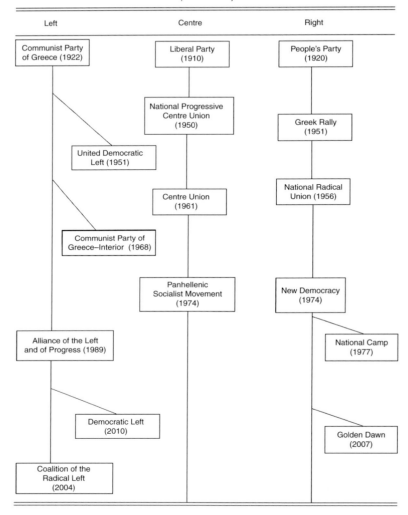

KEY DATES

1453	May 29: fall of Constantinople to the Ottoman Turks.
1461	Capture of the pocket Empire of Trebizond, the last area of sovereign Byzantine territory to fall to the Ottoman Turks.
1571	Venetian-ruled Cyprus captured by the Ottoman Turks.
1669	Venetian-ruled Crete falls to the Ottoman Turks following a twenty-year siege.
1709	Nikolaos Mavrokordatos appointed first Phanariot *hospodar* of Moldavia.
1748	Adamantios Korais, the intellectual mentor of the national revival, born in Smyrna.
1774	Treaty of Küçük Kaynarca ends Russo–Turkish war of 1768–74. Russia claims protectorate over the Orthodox Christians of the Ottoman Empire.
1783	Russo–Turkish commercial convention permits Greek ships to trade in the Black Sea under the Russian flag.
1797	Ionian islands ceded to revolutionary France by the Treaty of Campo Formio.
1798	Execution of Rigas Velestinlis (Pheraios) in Belgrade following his abortive attempt to inspire a revolt against the Ottoman Turks.
1806	Publication of the *Elliniki Nomarkhia* (Hellenic Nomarchy), one of the most important polemical texts of the Greek national movement.
1814	*Philiki Etairia* (Friendly Society), the secret society which laid the groundwork for the war of independence, founded in Odessa by Emmanouil Xanthos, Nikolaos Skouphas and Athanasios Tsakaloff.
1815	Septinsular Republic of the Ionian islands established under British protection.

1821   February: invasion of Moldavia by Greek army commanded by General Alexandros Ypsilantis.

March (by tradition 25 March): outbreak of revolt in the Peloponnese.

April: execution of the Ecumenical Patriarch Grigorios V in Constantinople.

1822   Proclamation of the first constitution of independent Greece.

1823   British foreign secretary, George Canning, recognises the Greek insurgents as belligerents.

1825   Canning rejects Act of Submission which sought to place insurgent Greece under British protection.

1827   April/May: assembly of Troezene elects Count Ioannis Kapodistrias as president of Greece and enacts third constitution of independence period.

July: by Treaty of London, Britain, Russia and France initiate policy of 'peaceful interference' to secure Greek autonomy.

October: combined British, Russian and French fleet destroys Turco-Egyptian fleet at Navarino.

1831   Assassination of President Kapodistrias.

1832   Convention of London confirms offer of 'hereditary sovereignty' of Greece to Otto, 17-year-old second son of Ludwig I of Bavaria and places 'monarchical and independent' state of Greece under British, Russian and French guarantee.

1833   King Otto arrives in Nafplion, provisional capital of Greece.

1834   Athens replaces Nafplion as capital.

1835   End of Bavarian regency.

1843   Army-backed coup forces King Otto to concede a constitution.

1844   Promulgation of constitution.

1854–7 Anglo-French occupation of Piraeus, the port of Athens, to enforce neutrality during the Crimean war.

1862   King Otto forced from throne in army-backed revolt.

1863   Prince Christian William Ferdinand Adolphus George of the Danish Holstein-Sonderburg-Glücksburg dynasty ascends the throne as George I, King of the Hellenes.

1864   March: Ionian islands ceded to Greece by Great Britain.

October: enactment of new constitution.

1866   Outbreak of revolt in Crete.

1875   King George accepts principle of the *dedilomeni*, the obligation of the sovereign to call upon the party leader with the 'declared' support of a majority in parliament to form a government.

1878   At Congress of Berlin the Great Powers 'invite' the Ottoman Porte to modify her frontiers in favour of Greece. Great Britain acquires administration of Cyprus.

1881   Thessaly and the Arta region of Epirus ceded to Greece by Ottoman Empire.

1885/6 Theodoros Deliyannis mobilises armed forces to take advantage of Serb–Bulgarian hostilities, leading the Powers to impose a naval blockade of Greece.

1893   Greece defaults on external loans.

1897   Thirty-day Greek–Turkish war arising from revolt in Crete results in defeat for Greece. Establishment of International Financial Commission to oversee state finances.

1909   Military coup at Goudi on outskirts of Athens leads to downfall of government.

1910   Eleftherios Venizelos, founder of Liberal Party, becomes prime minister.

1911   Revised constitution comes into force.

1912   October: outbreak of first Balkan war. Greece, Serbia, Bulgaria and Montenegro combine to attack the Ottoman Empire.
        November: capture of Salonica, Greece's second city.

1913   March: King George I assassinated by madman in Salonica. Succeeded by King Constantine I.
        June/July: second Balkan war: Greece and Serbia repulse Bulgarian attack and, by Treaty of Bucharest (August), share most of Macedonia.

1914   November: annexation of Cyprus by Great Britain.

1915   March: Venizelos resigns following clash with King Constantine over entry into First World War.
        June: election in which Venizelos wins 184 out of 317 seats.
        August: Venizelos returns to power.
        October: second forced resignation of Venizelos.
        December: election from which supporters of Venizelos abstain.

1916   September: Venizelos establishes provisional government in Salonica, principal city of 'New' Greece.
        December: royalist government repels Anglo–French landings in Piraeus and Athens. Britain and France establish blockade of 'Old' Greece.

1917   June: King Constantine I leaves Greece without abdicating the throne. Succeeded by second son, Alexander. Recall of parliament elected in June 1915, the so-called 'Lazarus chamber'.

1919   May: landing of Greek troops in Smyrna (Izmir).

1920   August: Treaty of Sèvres creates the Greece of the 'two continents and the five seas'.
        October: King Alexander dies from monkey bite.
        November: elections in which anti-Venizelists secure 260 out of 370 seats. Venizelos leaves Greece.
        December: rigged plebiscite votes for return of King Constantine I.

1921   August: Greek advance on Ankara, Turkish nationalist strong-
        hold, checked at battle of Sakarya river.
1922   August/September: Greek armies driven from Asia Minor.
        Burning of Smyrna.
        September: Colonel Nikolaos Plastiras launches coup. King
        Constantine I driven into exile, succeeded by eldest son King
        George II.
        November: execution of 'The Six' for high treason.
1923   January: convention on compulsory exchange of populations
        between Greece and Turkey.
        July: Treaty of Lausanne reverses Greece's gains by the Treaty of
        Sèvres.
        December: King George II departs Greece on 'extended leave'.
1924   March: proclamation of republic.
        April: plebiscite ratifies establishment of republic.
1925   March: Cyprus becomes a British crown colony.
        June: establishment of dictatorship by General Theodoros
        Pangalos.
1926   August: overthrow of Pangalos dictatorship.
        November: adoption of proportional representation and forma-
        tion of 'ecumenical' (all-party) government.
1927   June: promulgation of republican constitution.
1928   July: beginning of Venizelos' last administration.
1930   June: Ankara Convention inaugurates period of reconciliation
        with Turkey.
1933   March: unsuccessful Venizelist coup launched by Colonel
        Nikolaos Plastiras.
        June: attempt on Venizelos' life.
1935   March: attempted Venizelist coup; Venizelos leaves Greece.
        October: downfall of Tsaldaris government as result of putsch.
        November: rigged plebiscite votes for return of King George II.
1936   January: elections result in parliamentary deadlock with commu-
        nists holding balance of power.
        March: death of Venizelos in exile in France.
        August: establishment by General Metaxas of dictatorship of 4
        August 1936.
1940   October: Italian invasion of Greece followed by Greek counter-
        attack into Albania.
1941   April: German invasion of Greece.
        September: foundation of National Liberation Front (EAM).
1942   November: destruction of Gorgopotamos viaduct by Greek
        resistance forces and British saboteurs.
1943   September: outbreak of civil war within the resistance.

1944   April: outbreak of mutinies in Greek armed forces in Middle East.
        October: liberation of Greece. Moscow 'percentages' agreement
        between Churchill and Stalin assigns Greece to British sphere of
        influence.
        December: police shooting of demonstrators in Athens catalyst
        for communist insurgency. Churchill's abortive peace-making
        mission to Athens results in appointment of Archbishop
        Damaskinos of Athens as regent.
1945   February: Varkiza agreement ends communist insurgency.
1946   March: first postwar election gives victory to royalists.
        September: plebiscite votes for restoration of king. King George II
        returns to Greece.
        October: establishment of (communist) Democratic Army of
        Greece. Beginning of civil war.
1947   March: proclamation of Truman Doctrine results in massive US
        military and economic assistance to national government.
        April: King Paul succeeds to throne on death of brother George II.
1949   August: remnants of Democratic Army, defeated in battles of
        Grammos and Vitsi, flee into Albania.
        October: Communist Party of Greece announces 'temporary ces-
        sation' of hostilities, bringing civil war to close.
1952   January: promulgation of new constitution.
        November: electoral victory of Marshal Papagos' Greek Rally.
1955   April: beginning of armed EOKA struggle in Cyprus for *enosis*
        (union) with Greece.
1958   May: far-left United Democratic Left becomes official opposition
        with 24 per cent of vote.
1960   August: Cyprus becomes independent republic within the British
        Commonwealth.
1961   October: Georgios Papandreou launches 'unyielding struggle' to
        overturn Konstantinos Karamanlis' election victory.
1963   November: Papandreou's Centre Union secures narrow victory in
        elections.
        December: breakdown of 1960 constitutional settlement in
        Cyprus.
1964   February: Centre Union secures decisive parliamentary majority.
        March: death of King Paul. Accession to throne of King
        Constantine II.
1965   July: constitutional clash with King Constantine results in resig-
        nation of prime minister Papandreou.
        September: formation of 'apostate' Centre Union government,
        with support of conservative National Radical Union.
1967   April: military coup forestalls elections scheduled for May.

	December: King Constantine launches abortive counter-coup, flees into exile. Regency established.
1968	September: authoritarian constitution ratified in plebiscite held under martial law.
1973	March: student occupation of Law Faculty of Athens University.
	May: abortive naval mutiny.
	June: proclamation of a 'presidential parliamentary republic'.
	July: election of Colonel Georgios Papadopoulos, the only candidate, as president in a plebiscite held under martial law.
	November: student occupation of Athens Polytechnic suppressed by the army. Papadopoulos replaced as president by General Phaidon Gizikis.
1974	July: Archbishop Makarios deposed as president of Cyprus in coup backed by military junta in Athens. Turkish invasion and occupation of northern Cyprus. Collapse of military regime and replacement by civilian government headed by Konstantinos Karamanlis.
	November: Karamanlis' New Democracy secures 220 out of 300 seats in parliament.
	December: plebiscite records 70 per cent vote for abolition of monarchy.
1975	June: promulgation of new constitution, reinforcing the powers of the president.
1977	November: Andreas Papandreou's Panhellenic Socialist Movement (PASOK) becomes main opposition party.
1980	May: Karamanlis elected president.
1981	January: Greece enters European Community as tenth member.
	October: Papandreou's PASOK forms Greece's first 'socialist' government.
1985	March: constitutional crisis leads to resignation of Karamanlis as president and election of Khristos Sartzetakis.
	June: PASOK re-elected for a second term.
1987	March: Aegean incident brings Greece and Turkey to the brink of armed conflict.
1988	January: Davos agreement holds out promise of Greek–Turkish *rapprochement*.
1989	June: election in which no party wins overall majority leads to temporary conservative/communist coalition.
	November: inconclusive election leads to formation of all-party 'ecumenical' government.
1990	April: Konstantinos Mitsotakis' New Democracy secures 150 out of 300 seats in parliament and forms government.
	May: Konstantinos Karamanlis elected president.
1993	October: Andreas Papandreou's PASOK returns to power.

1996   January: Andreas Papandreou forced to resign due to ill-health, succeeded as prime minister by Kostas Simitis.

Greece and Turkey come close to war over sovereignty over islet of Imia/Kardak.

1999   August/September: Earthquakes in Turkey and Greece promote *rapprochement* between the two countries.

2000   April: Kostas Simitis returned to power at head of PASOK government.

2002   April: Liquidation of '17 November' terrorist group.

2004   March: New Democracy, under leadership of Kostas Karamanlis, wins election.

August: Olympic Games held in Athens.

2007   September: New Democracy returns to power with reduced majority.

2009   October: PASOK wins election under the leadership of Giorgos Papandreou.

2010   May: 'Troika' (European Union, European Central Bank and International Monetary Fund) agree 110 billion euro bailout.

2011   October: 'Troika' agrees further 130 billion euro bailout subject to conditions.

November: Giorgos Papandreou replaced as prime minister by technocrat Loukas Papademos.

2012   May: Inconclusive election. No party secures clear majority.

June: New Democracy, headed by Antonis Samaras, committed to austerity measures, emerges as largest party in new elections. Three-party coalition formed.

GUIDE TO FURTHER READING

This selective guide to further reading lists titles in English only, many of which contain detailed bibliographies.

BIBLIOGRAPHY

Mary Jo Clogg and Richard Clogg, *Greece*, World Bibliographical Series, vol. XVII (Oxford/Santa Barbara: Clio Press, 1980)

Thanos Veremis and Mark Dragoumis, *Greece*, World Bibliographical Series, vol. xvii (Oxford/Santa Barbara, 1998), revised and amplified edition.

Paschalis M. Kitromilides and Marios Evriviades, *Cyprus*, World Bibliographical Series, vol. xxviii (Oxford/Santa Barbara: Clio Press, 1982; revised and amplified edition 1995)

GENERAL

Greece, 3 vols. (London: Admiralty, Naval Intelligence Division, 1944–5) (Geographical Handbook Series)

Dodecanese (London: Admiralty, Naval Intelligence Division, 1943) (Geographical Handbook Series)

John Campbell and Philip Sherrard, *Modern Greece* (London: Ernest Benn, 1968)

Richard Clogg, *A short history of modern Greece*, 2nd edition (Cambridge: Cambridge University Press, 1986)

Douglas Dakin, *The unification of Greece 1770–1923* (London: Ernest Benn, 1972)

Yorgos A. Kourvetaris and Betty A. Dobratz, *A profile of modern Greece in search of identity* (Oxford: Clarendon Press, 1987)

Thomas Gallant, *Modern Greece* (London: Arnold, 2001)

John Koliopoulos and Thanos Veremis, *Modern Greece: a history since 1821* (Chichester: Wiley-Blackwell, 2009)

Nicholas Doumanis, *A history of Greece* (Basingstoke: Palgrave Macmillan, 2010)

Timothy Boatswain and Colin Nicolson, *A traveller's history of Greece* (London: The bookHaus, 2011)

Yannis Hamilakis, *The nation and its ruins: antiquity, archaeology, and national imagination in Greece* (Oxford: Oxford University Press, 2007)

William Miller, *Greek life in town and country* (London: George Newnes, 1905)

C. M. Woodhouse, *Modern Greece. A short history* (London: Faber and Faber, 1999)

OTTOMAN RULE AND THE STRUGGLE FOR INDEPENDENCE

Apostolos E. Vacalopoulos, *The Greek nation, 1453–1669: the cultural and economic background of modern Greek society* (New Brunswick: Rutgers University Press, 1976)

D. A. Zakythinos, *The making of modern Greece: from Byzantium to independence* (Oxford: Basil Blackwell, 1976)

Steven Runciman, *The Great Church in captivity: a study of the Patriarchate of Constantinople from the eve of the Turkish conquest to the Greek war of independence* (Cambridge: Cambridge University Press, 1968)

Richard Clogg, ed. and trans., *The movement for Greek independence 1770–1821: a collection of documents* (London: Macmillan, 1976)

G. P. Henderson, *The revival of Greek thought 1620–1830* (Edinburgh: Scottish Academic Press, 1971)

Constanze Guthenke, *Placing modern Greece: the dynamics of romantic Hellenism 1770–1840* (Oxford: Oxford University Press, 2008)

Paschalis M. Kitromilides, *The Enlightenment as social criticism: Iosipos Moisiodax and Greek culture in the eighteenth century* (Princeton: Princeton University Press, 1992)

David Brewer, *Greece, the hidden centuries: Turkish rule from the fall of Constantinople to Greek independence* (London: I. B. Tauris, 2012)

Helen Angelomatis-Tsougarakis, *The eve of the Greek revival. British travellers' perceptions of early nineteenth-century Greece* (London: Routledge, 1990)

Douglas Dakin, *The Greek struggle for independence, 1821–1833* (London: Batsford, 1973)

C. M. Woodhouse, *The Greek war of independence: its historical setting* (London: Hutchinson, 1952)

C. W. Crawley, *The question of Greek independence: a study of British policy in the Near East, 1821–1833* (Cambridge: Cambridge University Press, 1930)

E. M. Edmonds, trans., *Kolokotrones: the klepht and the warrior: sixty years of peril and daring: an autobiography* (London: T. Fisher Unwin, 1893)

H. A. Lidderdale, trans., *Makriyannis: the memoirs of General Makriyannis 1797–1864* (London: Oxford University Press, 1966)

William St Clair, *That Greece might still be free: the philhellenes in the war of independence* (London: Oxford University Press, 1972)

C. M. Woodhouse, *The battle of Navarino* (London: Hodder and Stoughton, 1965)

C. M. Woodhouse, *Capodistria: the founder of Greek independence* (London: Oxford University Press, 1973)

INDEPENDENT GREECE 1830–1923

Leonard Bower and Gordon Bolitho, *Otho I, king of Greece: a biography* (London: Selwyn and Blount, 1939)

John Anthony Petropulos, *Politics and statecraft in the kingdom of Greece, 1833–43* (Princeton: Princeton University Press, 1968)

Charles A. Frazee, *The Orthodox Church and independent Greece, 1821–52* (Cambridge: Cambridge University Press, 1969)

Marietta Economopoulou, *Parties and politics in Greece 1844–55* (Athens: 1984)

Robert Holland and Diana Markides, *The British and the Hellenes: struggles for mastery in the Eastern Mediterranean 1850–1960* (Oxford: Oxford University Press, 2006)

Domna N. Dontas, *Greece and the great powers 1863–75* (Thessaloniki: Institute for Balkan Studies, 1966)

Roderick Beaton and David Ricks, eds., *The making of modern Greece: nationalism, romanticism and the uses of the past (1797–1896)* (Aldershot: Ashgate, 2009)

Romilly Jenkins, *The Dilessi murders* (London: Longman, 1961)

John S. Koliopoulos, *Brigands with a cause. Brigandage and irredentism in modern Greece 1821–1912* (Oxford: Clarendon Press, 1987)

R. A. H. Bickford-Smith, *Greece under King George* (London: Richard Bentley, 1893)

Philip Carabott, ed., *Greek society in the making, 1863–1913: realities, symbols and visions* (Aldershot: Ashgate, 1997)

Evangelos Kofos, *Greece and the eastern crisis, 1875–78* (Thessaloniki: Institute for Balkan Studies, 1975)

Theodore George Tatsios, *The Megali Idea and the Greek–Turkish war of 1897: the impact of the Cretan problem on Greek irredentism, 1866–97* (New York: Columbia University Press, 1984)

Charles K. Tuckerman, *The Greeks of today* (New York: Putnam, 1878)

John A. Levandis, *The Greek foreign debt and the Great Powers 1821–98* (New York: Columbia University Press, 1944)

Pinar Senisik, *The transformation of Ottoman Crete: revolts, politics and identity in the late nineteenth century* (London: I. B. Tauris, 2011)

Gerasimos Augustinos, *Consciousness and history: nationalist critics of Greek society, 1897–1914* (New York: Columbia University Press, 1977)

Douglas Dakin, *The Greek struggle in Macedonia 1897–1913* (Thessaloniki: Institute for Balkan Studies, 1966)

S. Victor Papacosma, *The military in Greek politics: the 1909 coup d'état* (Kent: Kent State University Press, 1977)

Doros Alastos [Evdoros Joannides], *Venizelos: patriot, statesman, revolutionary* (London: Lund Humphries, 1942)

George B. Leon, *Greece and the great powers, 1914–17* (Thessaloniki: Institute for Balkan Studies, 1974)

George B. Leon, *The Greek socialist movement and the First World War: the road to unity* (New York: Columbia University Press, 1976)

N. Petsalis-Diomidis, *Greece at the Paris Peace Conference 1919* (Thessaloniki: Institute for Balkan Studies, 1978)

Gerasimos Augustinos, *The Greeks of Asia Minor: confession, community and ethnicity in the nineteenth century* (Kent, Ohio: Kent State University Press, 1992)

Nicholas Doumanis, *Before the nation: Muslim–Christian coexistence and its destruction in late Ottoman Anatolia* (Oxford: Oxford University Press, 2013)

Michael Llewellyn Smith, *Ionian vision: Greece in Asia Minor, 1919–22* (London: Allen Lane,1973, 1998)

Arnold J. Toynbee, *The western question in Greece and Turkey: a study in the contact of civilisations* (London: Constable, 1922)

Marjorie Housepian, *Smyrna 1922: the destruction of a city* (London: Faber and Faber, 1972)

Harry J. Psomiades, *The eastern question, the last phase: a study in Greek–Turkish diplomacy* (Thessaloniki: Institute for Balkan Studies, 1968)

GREECE 1924–49

George Mavrogordatos, *Stillborn republic: social coalitions and party strategies in Greece 1922–36* (Berkeley: University of California Press, 1983)

Dimitri Pentzopoulos, *The Balkan exchange of minorities and its impact upon Greece* (The Hague: Mouton, 1962)

Bruce Clark, *Twice a stranger: how mass expulsion forged modern Greece and Turkey* (London: Granta Books, 2006)

Charles B. Eddy, *Greece and the Greek refugees* (London: George Allen and Unwin, 1931)

William Miller, *Greece* (London: Ernest Benn, 1928)

Elliot Grinnell Mears, *Greece today: the aftermath of the refugee impact* (Stanford: Stanford University Press, 1929)

Elisabeth Kontogiorgi, *Population exchange in Greek Macedonia: the rural settlement of refugees 1922–1933* (Oxford: Clarendon Press, 2006)

Mark Mazower, *Greece and the inter-war economic crisis* (Oxford: Clarendon Press, 1991)

John S. Koliopoulos, *Greece and the British connection 1935–41* (Oxford: Clarendon Press, 1977)

Mario Cervi, *The hollow legions: Mussolini's blunder in Greece 1940–1* (London: Chatto and Windus, 1972)

Matthew Willingham, *Perilous commitments: the battle for Greece and Crete 1940–41* (Staplehurst, Kent: Spellmount, 2005)

Robin Higham, *Diary of a disaster. British aid to Greece, 1940–1* (Lexington: The University Press of Kentucky, 1986)

Bickham Sweet-Escott, *Greece: a political and economic survey 1939–53* (London: Royal Institute of International Affairs, 1954)

C. M. Woodhouse, *The struggle for Greece 1941–9* (London: Hart-Davis, MacGibbon, 1976)

Violetta Hionidou, *Famine and death in occupied Greece, 1941–1944* (Cambridge: Cambridge University Press, 2006)

Mark Mazower, *Inside Hitler's Greece: the experience of occupation, 1941–44* (New Haven: Yale University Press, 1993)

Sheila Lecoeur, *Mussolini's Greek island: fascism and the Italian occupation of Syros in World War II* (London: I. B. Tauris, 2009)

John Hondros, *Occupation and resistance. The Greek agony 1941–4* (New York: Pella, 1983)

Anthony Rogers, *Churchill's folly: Leros and the Aegean. The last great defeat of the Second World War* (London: Cassell, 2003)

Richard Clogg, ed., *Bearing gifts to Greeks: humanitarian aid to Greece in the 1940s* (Basingstoke: Palgrave Macmillan / St Antony's College, 2008)

Alan Ogden, *Sons of Odysseus: SOE heroes in Greece* (London: Bene Factum Publishing, 2012)

John O. Iatrides, *Revolt in Athens: the Greek communist 'second round' 1944–5* (Princeton: Princeton University Press, 1972)

George Alexander, *The prelude to the Truman doctrine. British policy in Greece 1944–7* (Oxford: Clarendon Press, 1982)

William Hardy McNeill, *The Greek dilemma: war and aftermath* (London: Gollancz, 1947)

Heinz Richter, *British intervention in Greece. From Varkiza to civil war, February 1945 to August 1946* (London: Merlin Press, 1986)

David Close, *The origins of the Greek civil war* (London: Longman, 1995)

Peter J. Stavrakis, *Moscow and Greek communism 1944–9* (Ithaca: Cornell University Press, 1989)

Mark Mazower, ed., *After the war was over: reconstructing the family, nation, and state in Greece, 1943–1960* (Princeton: Princeton University Press, 2000)

Philip Carabott and Thanasis D. Sfikas, *The Greek civil war: essays on a conflict of exceptionalism and silences* (Aldershot: Ashgate, 2004)

Loring M. Danforth and Riki van Boeschoten, *Children of the Greek civil war: refugees and the politics of memory* (Chicago: University of Chicago Press, 2012)

Polymeris Voglis, *Becoming a subject: political prisoners during the Greek civil war* (Oxford: Berghahn, 2002)

Howard Jones, 'A new kind of war': America's global strategy and the *Truman Doctrine in Greece* (Oxford: Oxford University Press, 1989)

John S. Koliopoulos, *Plundered loyalties: Axis occupation and civil strife in Greek West Macedonia, 1941–1949* (London: Hurst and Company, 1999)

Lawrence S. Wittner, *American intervention in Greece, 1943–9* (New York: Columbia University Press, 1982)

John O. Iatrides and Linda Wrigley, eds., *Greece at the crossroads: the civil war and its legacy* (University Park, PA: Pennsylvania State University Press, 1995)

GREECE SINCE 1950

William H. McNeill, *The metamorphosis of Greece since World War II* (Chicago: University of Chicago Press, 1978)

David Close, *Greece since 1945: politics, economy and society* (Harlow: Pearson Education, 2002)

Ioannis Stefanidis, *Stirring the Greek nation: political culture, irredentism and anti-Americanism in post-war Greece, 1945–1967* (Aldershot: Ashgate, 2007)

Evanthis Hatzivassiliou, *Greece and the Cold War: frontline state, 1952–1967* (London: Routledge, 2006)

Speros Vryonis, Jr, *The mechanism of catastrophe: the Turkish pogrom of September 6–7, 1955, and the destruction of the Greek community of Istanbul* (New York: Greekworks.com, 2005)

Keith R. Legg, *Politics in modern Greece* (Stanford: Stanford University Press, 1969)

Richard Clogg, *Parties and elections in Greece: the search for legitimacy* (London: C. Hurst, 1987)

Stan Draenos, *Andreas Papandreou: the making of a Greek democrat and political maverick* (London: I. B. Tauris, 2012)

Alexandros Nafpliotis, *Britain and the Greek Colonels: accommodating the Junta in the Cold War* (London: I. B. Tauris, 2013)

James E. Miller, *The United States and the making of modern Greece. History and power: 1950–1974* (Chapel Hill, NC: The University of North Carolina Press, 2009)

C. M. Woodhouse, *The rise and fall of the Greek Colonels* (London: Grafton, 1985)

Christos Kassimeris, *Greece and the American embrace: Greek foreign policy towards Turkey, the US and the western alliance* (London: I. B. Tauris, 2009)

Nicos Mouzelis, *Modern Greece: facets of underdevelopment* (London: Macmillan, 1978)

Theodore A. Couloumbis, *The United States, Greece and Turkey: the troubled triangle* (New York: Praeger, 1983)

Michalis Spourdalakis, *The rise of the Greek socialist party* (London: Routledge, 1988)

George Kassimeris, *Europe's last red terrorists: the revolutionary organization 17 November* (London: Hurst and Company, 2001)

Vicky Pryce, *Greekonomics: the euro crisis and why politicians don't get it* (London: Biteback Publishing, 2012)

CYPRUS

H. D. Purcell, *Cyprus* (London: Ernest Benn, 1969)

George Hill, *A history of Cyprus*, vol. IV, The Ottoman province, the British colony 1571–1928 (Cambridge: Cambridge University Press, 1952)

Anastasia Yiangou, *Cyprus in World War II: politics and conflict in the eastern Mediterranean* (London: I. B. Tauris, 2010)

Stephen Xydis, *Cyprus: conflict and conciliation 1954–8* (Columbus: Ohio State University, 1967)

Stephen Xydis, *Cyprus: reluctant republic* (The Hague: Mouton, 1973)

Nancy Crawshaw, *The Cyprus revolt: an account of the struggle for union with Greece* (London: George Allen and Unwin, 1978)

Robert Holland, *Britain and the revolt in Cyprus 1954–1959* (Oxford: Clarendon Press, 1998)

Stanley Kyriakides, *Cyprus: constitutionalism and crisis government* (Philadelphia: University of Pennsylvania Press, 1968)

Kyriacos C. Markides, *The rise and fall of the Cyprus republic* (New Haven: Yale University Press, 1977)

Rebecca Bryant, *Imagining the modern: the cultures of nationalism in Cyprus* (London: I. B. Tauris, 2004)

GREEKS ABROAD

Richard Clogg, ed., *The Greek diaspora in the twentieth century* (Basingstoke: Macmillan, 1999)

Theodore Saloutos, *The Greeks in the United States* (Cambridge: Harvard University Press, 1964)

Charles C. Moskos, *Greek Americans: struggle and success* (New Brunswick: Transaction Publishers, 1989)

Anastasios M. Tamis, *The immigration and settlement of Macedonian Greeks in Australia* (Melbourne: La Trobe University Press, 1994)

Peter D. Chimbos, ed., *The Canadian Odyssey: the Greek experience in Canada* (Toronto: McClelland and Stewart, 1980)

Alexander Kitroeff, *The Greeks in Egypt, 1919–1937: ethnicity and class* (London: Ithaca Press, 1989)

Dimitris Tziovas, ed., *Greek diaspora and migration since 1700: society, politics and culture* (Aldershot: Ashgate, 2009)

RELIGION

K. E. Fleming, *Greece: a Jewish history* (Princeton: Princeton University Press, 2008)

Bea Lewkowicz, *The Jewish community of Salonika: history, memory, identity* (London: Vallentine Mitchell, 2006)

Richard Clogg, ed., *Minorities in Greece: aspects of a plural society* (London: Hurst and Company, 2002)

Victor Roudometof and Vasilios N. Makrides, eds., *Orthodox Christianity in 21st-century Greece: the role of religion in culture, ethnicity and politics* (Aldershot: Ashgate, 2010)

INDEX

CAMBRIDGE CONCISE HISTORIES